THE
REPUBLICAN PARTY
AND THE
RISE OF CHINA

David Petriello

The Republican Party and the Rise of China

By David Petriello

ISBN-13: 978-988-8422-82-1

Cover design: Jason Wong

This book has been reset in 10pt Book Antiqua. Spellings and punctuations are left as in the original edition.

HISTORY / Asia / China

EB102

Published by Earnshaw Books Ltd. (Hong Kong)

To my Guinevere, who makes this world and this life the best of all possible ones.

CONTENTS

INTRODUCTION

"Thy Godlike crime was to be kind,
To render with thy precepts less
The sum of human wretchedness,
And strengthen Man with his own mind; "
(*Prometheus*, Lord Byron)

FOREIGN POLICY is often seen as a bipartisan issue, as one of the few constants in the otherwise mercurial world of public policy that varies from election cycle to the next. Yet while the various American parties one may from time to time agree on relations with certain regions and countries, policies towards most are often party-dependent. In fact, one of the fundamental differences between Hamilton and his Federalist supporters and Jefferson and his Republican supporters during the administration of Washington was their respective support for England and France. This trend continued with Latin American relations in the nineteenth century, Cold War debates in the twentieth, and re-emerged with regards to Russia in 2017. The idea that politics ends at the nation's shores has always been a myth. Therefore, it is not surprising to see a divergence of opinion when it came to the subject of the path that should be pursued between on China.

The history of Sino-American relations is hardly a new topic. In fact, it has been examined through a variety of lenses over the past century, touching on almost every possible interaction between the two countries. Yet the historiography tends to portray the development of relations between China and the United States as exactly that—developing. Traditional accounts of the various economic, political, and social interactions between Washington and Beijing follow a linear line of development, portraying the connection as one which slowly but systematically evolved into the state which exists today. While the gradualism of this idea may hold true, its path was hardly constant.

The thesis of this book is that the development of relations between the United States and China followed a trend line determined not by economics or international events alone, but by the presence of the Republican Party in American politics. This party and its previous incarnations, the Federalists, National Republicans, and Whigs, represented an ideology that was open towards increased interaction with China. Yet, far from simply being concerned with the East Asian country for economic reasons, the Republicans actively pushed to modernize China as well, serving as a modern day Prometheus to that nation.

China and its promises of riches and resources had long intrigued the West. In fact, the various attempts to reach the nation, especially by sea, had been responsible for the discovery and settlement of the New World. Thus, after the United States achieved its independence it was not surprising that the merchants of New England would strive to actively engage in trade with Canton, then the major port of entry for Western ships. The slowly coalescing Federalist Party saw in the region the potential for both a market as well as a source of materials and resources. While it is not surprising that American merchants would have naturally and eventually gravitated towards trade with China, the level of monetary support and philosophical encouragement by the Federalist Party in this process is.

A half century later, while Europe was busy conquering and dividing up the Qing Empire, the Whig Party, ideological successors to the Federalists, began a process that would eventually open China not just economically but politically and philosophically as well. The birth of this Open Door Policy would be built upon the concept of fair trade and attempts to respect the territorial integrity of the slowly collapsing kingdom.

With the rise of the Republican Party in the 1850s a new element was added to this standard of interaction. Generations of ambassadors and travelers to the nation had become convinced that without outside support, China would not only fail to modernize but would fall before the pressure of European imperialists and slowly awakening Japanese aggression. A process unfolded from the Gilded Age to the onset of the Great Depression that saw American Republicans interested in helping to modernize China. Yet a lack of commitment on the part of the Qing government, when combined with the chaos of the Warlord Era that followed, severely limited the success of the endeavor.

The final era of Republican interaction with China emerged during the administration of Richard Nixon. His opening up of China returned America to the traditions of the initial Open Door Policy. Yet the arrival of Ronald Reagan did not see a mere continuation of this slowly developing trend, but a vast departure. Seizing upon the ideas of Burlingame and others, Reagan combined a truly Open Door approach to China with a desire to modernize the nation. Thanks largely to this, the once-underdeveloped country was able to advance and become a first-rate power by the dawning of the twenty-first century.

The Republican Party in its various forms has stood in sharp contrast to the policies of the Democratic Party, which has historically been opposed to trade with the Pacific nation. This was manifested early on in the American republic due to concerns that capital would drain out of the country. In addition, Southerners were fearful that the acquisition of cheaper Chinese materials would destroy the domestic agricultural economy. Later, with the beginning of Chinese immigration to the west coast of America, both local Democratic groups and the larger national party pushed for decades to stem this flood of Asian laborers. The subsequent Chinese Exclusion Act were not be overturned until the passage of Magnuson Act over sixty years later. The consequent isolation of the People's Republic of China by Truman and his largely Democratic successors was therefore not only in keeping with a George Kennan-inspired strategy to win the Cold War, but also with almost a-century-and-a-half of party policy towards China. While trends within the Democratic Party since the 1990s have moved towards an economic and political engagement of Beijing, it lacked the necessary consequent hardline towards Chinese expansion. Overall, there has been a complete about-face within the party from the old Jeffersonian angle of disinterest bordering upon neglect towards China, to a Clinton-Obama policy of granting comparative advantage to the Chinese. This stands in sharp contrast to a two century-long policy on the part of the Republican Party to economically, socially, and politically engage China, but at all times maintain American power and dominance in the Pacific.

Overall, the Republican Party was largely responsible for the establishment and growth of relations between the United States and China. What began as an earnest effort to expand trade was built upon by successive generations of thinkers and politicians interested in the modernization of the once-powerful empire. With the opening of the "Pacific Century" and the growing dominance of, and threats posed by, China, it remains to be seen whether the party will continue to fully engage Beijing economically, socially, and politically, or whether the disparate components of the party base will cause a rupture in this two-century old foreign policy view.

1

THE SILK ROAD EXTENSION

CHINA AND AMERICA BEFORE THE REVOLUTION

THE HISTORIES OF CHINA and America have been inordinately connected for centuries, before even the establishment of the United States as an independent country. While tales of pre-Colombian exploration of the New World by the Chinese are popular in some circles, the historical possibility of such voyages, as well as their practical impact, relegate them to the level of similar claims about St. Brendan and various other semi-mythical African or European explorers. Yet even without a direct physical link between the two areas prior to the sixteenth century, China did certainly impact America in various other important ways, particularly the founding of the United states of America.

Despite the distances involved, China was from the dawn of history never unknown to the West and is identifiable in ancient Indian as well as Persian texts.[1] From the time of the Hellenistic Age, the names Sin, Thin, and Sinae are to be found in Greek and Latin writings, derivatives it is assumed of the "Qin" kingdom that unified what is today China for the first time in the year 221 BC. Apart from the mention by Publius Annius Florus of a minor diplomatic mission that arrived for the first time in Seres to pay homage to Augustus and several later attempts at exchanging embassies, the vast majority of contact between East and West were purely economic in character.

The amorphous trade routes that ran across Eurasia, first named the Silk Road by a German explorer in the late nineteenth century, helped to move people, ideas, and, most importantly, trade for almost two thousand years. The spices and silk sent west came to be an integral component of the economies of many great empires including that of Rome. Pliny the Elder once wrote that, "By the lowest reckoning, India, Seres, and the Arabian Peninsula take from our empire 100 millions of sesterces every year: that is how much our luxuries and women cost us."[2] Apart from the concern of economists, various moralists also criticized the trade for ethical reasons. In this vein, Seneca the Elder sought to shame the silk wearing women of Rome by writing that, "I can see clothes of silk, if materials that do not hide the body, nor even one's decency, can be called clothes... Wretched flocks of maids labor so that the adulteress may be visible through her thin dress, so that her husband has no more acquaintance than any outsider or foreigner with his wife's body."[3] Nevertheless, the market triumphed over the morals and economic concerns of some Romans. A taste for the exotic goods of the East was sparked, a desire that the fall of both the Roman and Han Empires would only temporarily subdue.

The continued existence of the Eastern Roman Empire meant that interest in Chinese goods did not disappear. Yet political instability in China, the rise of the Sassanid Empire, and the drain on the imperial economy eventually prompted a concentrated effort by Constantinople to found a domestic silk industry. According to tradition, two Nestorian monks stole silk worm eggs and brought them back to Emperor Justinian. Though a rather successful and profitable silk industry was subsequently begun in the Empire, there remained a desire for additional

Chinese goods as well.

Various eastern products, including silk, spices, pepper, porcelain, and lacquer began to be associated with the exotic land of China, regardless of their particular Asian country of origin. The demands for these products only grew during the several centuries of Crusades that characterized European contacts with the Middle East from the eleventh to the fourteenth centuries. The subsequent voyages of Marco Polo, Odoric of Pordenone, John of Montecorvino and others, as well as the legends of Prestor John and John Mandeville, demonstrated the increased interest in reaching China itself directly from Europe. Odoric famously described the city of Lingan as, "the greatest city in the whole world...the finest for merchandise that the whole world containith."[4] While some of this desire to explore the East remained economic in nature, there were also religious and political hopes on the part of the Church and the various Crusading states.

All of these interests were only augmented by the final expulsion of the Crusaders from the Near East and the subsequent consolidation of power in the region by the Ottoman Empire. Renaissance Europe saw an increase in demand for foreign goods, the trade of which was dominated by the Ottoman Empire and Venice. Raising prices by upwards of forty percent by some merchants or states was not unheard of, leading to a draining of gold and silver eastwards.[5] A combination of a demand for cheaper products, growing mercantilist thinking regarding trade and colonization, and a desire on the part of monarchs to strengthen their nations, all led to a push towards finding an alternative route to the trade goods of the East. With land routes either too dangerous or too costly, the discovery of a sea route to the Indies became the focus of western European nations in the fifteenth and sixteenth centuries.

Portugal took the lead in this endeavor, rounding the African continent in 1488 and reaching India by 1498. Yet, Muslim traders in the region resented the arrival of the Portuguese due to the effect it would have on their spice monopoly. A century-long war erupted between Persia, the Ottoman Empire, various Indian states, and Portugal. As the spice trade remained dangerous and expensive, Lisbon sought to bypass the subcontinent as well and began exploring Southeast Asia and the islands of Indonesia. In 1513, only twenty-five years after they had rounded the Cape, the first Portuguese explorer reached China. Jorge Alvares landed on Nei Lingding Island, then an uninhabited rock in the Pearl River estuary. Four years later, Rafael Perestrello arrived in Canton and established the first official relations between a European nation and China. These initial contacts degenerated into conflict due to the actions of some of the Portuguese as well as the spreading of rumors by rival trading partners. A number of naval battles, most notably at Tunmen and Xicaowan in 1521 and 1522, served to limit Portuguese exploration and settlement for almost thirty-five years until the normalization of relations in 1557.

Economics was not the only driving force for European exploration of East Asia in the sixteenth century. A desire to locate fabled Christian monarchs as well as to expand the reach of the religion certainly motivated the Church as well as various monarchs and explorers. Likewise, previous tales of advanced eastern science, technology and medicine intrigued many in the West, enough to convince King Manuel I of Portugal to send Fernao Pires de Andrade as the head of the first official mission to the Ming court in the year 1517. De Andrade was a pharmacist by trade, and it was hoped that he would be able to identify useful Chinese medicines.[6] Writings by him and further works by Gaspar da Cruz and Fernao Mendes Pinto further piqued the interest of Europe as to the possibilities that trade and relations with China could bring.

Due to the Treaty of Tordesillas and the subsequent Treaty of Saragossa, the Spanish largely stayed out of China. Drafted in 1494 and 1529 respectively, the two documents divided up the world between Spain and Portugal. As the majority of spices came from the East Indies, these islands proved to be more of a sticking point in imperial competition than China itself. Magellan's crew, following his death in the Philippines, sailed south to the Moluccas Islands to lay claim to the clove and nutmeg production centers there. Apart from the arrival of two Spanish priests in 1570, Madrid's interest in China was minor and largely confined to religion.

France's contact with China was also originally built more around religion than economics. A desire to align with the powerful, and allegedly Christian, Mongol Empire led the French monarch and the Papacy to send Andre de Longjumeau to the court of Ogedei Khan, and, later Guyuk Khan, to discuss an alliance against the Muslim states in the Middle East. Later French interest in the region tended to be more concerned with goods and trade and led to the search for the then-legendary Northwest Passage. Giovanni de Verrazzano, Jacques Cartier, de la Salle, and others were commissioned by the French government during the sixteenth century to explore the northern coast of America in order to find a sea passage to the Pacific and hence China. In the end the expeditions garnered much land for France, but little access to the Orient. De la Salle's exploration even gave its name to a new village constructed near Montreal named Lachine, derived from the French word for China.

The Dutch, much like the Spanish and Portuguese, tended to focus their energy on the acquisition of goods and the securing of trade routes to the East Indies. The beginnings of this can be dated to the arrival of the first Dutch fleet at Maluku in search of pepper in 1596. Unfortunately, attempts to trade with China were frustrated by mistrust, typhoons, and an alleged slave raid by Dutch sailors. Open warfare between the two erupted in 1622 and the Dutch spent over forty years securing the island of Formosa. Due in part to these troubles, Amsterdam focused its efforts on the East Indies, establishing its main center of trade at Batavia in 1619. Within a generation, the Dutch were shipping 900,000 pieces of kaolin porcelain a year back to the Netherlands, helping to expand the market for Chinese goods to items beyond silk and spices.[7] Dutch efforts to find a Northwest Passage to East Asia in order to augment this trade led directly to the exploration of Henry Hudson in 1609 and the settlement of New Amsterdam.

Much like the Dutch, the English were delayed in their exploration of the Far East. In their case, trading voyages to Asia did not commence until after the defeat of the Spanish Armada. Sporadic attempts to reach the Indies culminated in the chartering of the East India Company in 1600. As the British focused mostly on securing the Indian subcontinent, their efforts to trade with China were largely minor. In a similar vein to the Dutch, they focused their initial energies on Southeast Asia and Taiwan, not acquiring even limited trading rights to China until 1676. Regular yearly trade did not begin until 1715 and the first British factory was established in Canton only thirteen years before the start of the American Revolution.

This delayed interest in trading with the Orient was due more to lack of opportunity than lack of desire. Before the cooling of relations with Spain, the English under Henry VII had in fact dispatched the first major expedition to search for a northwest passage to Asia. While the three voyages of John Cabot around 1497 did not find this fabled route, it did allow the British to lay claim to the North Atlantic seaboard. Subsequent voyages by Sir Martin Frobisher from 1576-1578, while not providing for easier trade with India or China, did further England's colonial holdings. Likewise, when the first permanent colony was established along the James River it was done so under the assumption that this was perhaps a passageway to China.[8]

The various voyages of exploration launched by European states served to create the foundation of America. While the goal of many of those involved may have been quicker access to the markets and materials of China and other nations, the unintended consequences proved to be of greater importance. The very existence of the various American nations is a direct consequence of the desire for trade with China. In fact, the original connection between the two would only be augmented over the next several centuries, specifically through the transfer of animals and goods between the Americas and the Old World of Europe that became known as the Columbian Exchange.

The various European nations quickly discovered that while their own citizens desired any number of exotic, Eastern trade goods, the Chinese in particular only accepted silver in return. The Spanish initially exploited the mines at Potosi in Bolivia in order to provide the bullion that flowed to China. The developing trade imbalance, though, soon worried many Europeans who followed a mercantilist model.

The Americas provided a number of trade items which proved to be of value to partially restoring the East-West trade imbalance. One of these was animal furs. Long used and desired in both Europe and China, both regions had hunted their animals to near extinction. The vast forests of North America in particular yielded immense numbers of furs that were sent both east and west. Apart from this luxury trade, two New World plants would become inexorably linked with East Asia in general and China in particular. The most important for practical reasons was the sweet potato. The sweet potato arrived in China at some point in

7

the sixteenth century, most likely having been brought over from the Spanish colony in the Philippines.

The introduction of the new crop dramatically changed the political, economics and social fabric of the empire. The reduction in drought-related famine brought about a subsequent decline in the number of riots and rebellions across the Ming and Qing eras by almost one-third.[9] A far more important result, though, was the dramatic population increase that accompanied the introduction of the sweet potato. Due to its ability to grow in even the poorest conditions along with its greater nutritional value, the new crop helped alter the demographics of the empire which had remained largely unchanged since the Han Dynasty. China's standard historical population of no more than sixty million people increased seven-fold by the end of the Qing Dynasty. This trend was only furthered by the subsequent development of corn and potato crops as well.

This massive and unprecedented increase in population led to a parallel increase in pestilence that plagued the nation for several centuries. In addition, as the Qing encouraged the spread of these new crops and of excess population to the depopulated northern regions, so too did epidemics travel beyond the Yangtze and Yellow River basins. The subsequent environmental degradation caused by increased farming only worsened the periodic flooding that visited the country, producing more famine and pestilence. At the height of the Ming Dynasty epidemics were being reported almost every other year, a situation that would only worsen as the dynasty waned. The environmental degradation brought about by the introduction of sweet potatoes when combined with the almost yearly outbreaks of disease helped to not only slow the development of China but ensure its conquest by the Manchus as well.[10] The Americas, therefore, proved to be responsible for not only the vast population that

8

was to become associated with China over the next few centuries, but with its subsequent decline and fall as well.

The third product that would impact the development of China was tobacco, which also arrived from the Spanish occupied Philippines around 1620. The rapid spread of the plant led the last Ming emperor Chongzhen, to issue an edict ordering the execution of those who became addicted to the plant.[11] Shortly afterwards, Dutch merchants sailing from Taiwan introduced a product known as madak to the southeastern coastal villages of China. This blend of tobacco and opium proved to be much more addictive than pure tobacco and soon presented an even larger problem for the Ming and Qing dynasties. New World tobacco helped to rapidly expand the preexisting opium problem in China. By the time of the British dominance of the opium trade in the region, a ready consumer base were already present.

Another product found in the Americas which proved to be of economic interest to China was ginseng. A species of the plant was native to eastern Asia and had long been used in traditional Chinese medicine. So popular was it, in fact, that in 1711 Jesuit missionary Father Pierre Jartoux wrote about the plant in a letter to his superiors describing both its popularity and uses: "The most eminent Physicians in China have writ whole Volumes upon the Virtues and Qualities of this Plant and make it an ingredient in almost all Remedies which they give their chief Nobility."[12] Jartoux even recorded his own observations upon using the leaves and root of the plant. The value of the plant is shown by the fact that in 1709, the Kangxi Emperor sent an army of 20,000 soldiers into the wilds of Manchuria to gather up as much as they could, "that the Tartars should have the advantage that is to be made of this Plant rather than the Chinese."[13]

Based on these observations, Father Joseph-François Lafitau found similar specimens growing wild in Canada in 1716. Lafitau had read Jartoux's letter and attempted to discover ginseng growing along the St. Lawrence and use of it by the natives in an attempt to prove the Asiatic origin of these people. Though his subsequent discovery of the plant itself did not necessarily imply a connection between the Native Americans and Mongoloid people, it did excite American, French, and British merchants seeking to gain access to the China Trade. The *Pennsylvania Gazette* reported gleefully in July 1738 when the plant was determined to be present in the colony

"We have the Pleasure of acquainting the World, that the famous Chinese or Tartarian Plant, called *Gin seng*, is now discovered in this Province, near Sasquehannah: From whence several whole Plants with a Quantity of the Root, have been lately sent to Town, and it appears to agree most exactly with the Description given of it in Chambers's Dictionary, and Pere du Halde's Account of China. The Virtues ascrib'd to this Plant are wonderful."[14]

Among some of the more notable families who made their fortunes in part off of ginseng were John Jacob Astor, Daniel Boone, and Davey Crockett. Ginseng would prove to be a fundamental part of the Sino-American trade that would unfold in the eighteenth and nineteenth centuries.

The Columbian Exchange, which saw the sudden and sustained flow of animals, goods, and microbes between the Americas and Eurasia, and subsequent China Trade not only brought economic interchanges between West and East but cultural and artistic ones as well. Chinese fashion, architecture, art, and furniture became the latest crazes for the elites of the West in the seventeenth and eighteenth centuries. When these things proved to be too expensive, Western artists and designers, influenced by Chinese trends, created styles that leaned heavily on East Asian ideas and flavors. Chinoiserie, or the Chinese style, arose in almost all areas of art and culture. Wallpaper, painting, and even architecture took on an Oriental flare. The famed English cabinetmaker Thomas Chippendale helped to popularize Chinese style furniture during the Georgian Period with his designs even influencing part of Thomas Jefferson's Monticello.

With the failure of all involved to find the Northwest Passage, it is not surprising that attention was paid early on to claiming and settling the Pacific Coast of America in order to more effectively trade with China. Spain naturally initiated the process, slowly building off of Balboa's discovery of 1513. Several decades later in 1579, Sir Francis Drake rounded the tip of South America, made his way up the coast, and somewhere near San Francisco Bay claimed the entire region as New Albion for England. In fact, proof of Drake's landing spot has been possibly corroborated by the discovery of Chinese pottery in the area. The *Golden Hind* had pillaged a Spanish ship near Ecuador, carrying off crates of Ming porcelain. Nearly four hundred years later, pieces of the same pottery discovered in the region of West Marin, north of San Francisco, suggest a landing by Drake in the area.

Yet, as the Spanish relied heavily on Acapulco as their Pacific gateway to Asia, development of California and the lands to the north of it was a slow process. It would not be until 1769 that the first Spanish mission was established in California at San Diego. As the Spanish pushed north, Russian explorers pushed south down the coast of Alaska. The latter did not aim at establishing posts to trade with China as they already bordered the Celestial Empire, instead their primary aim was to acquire furs. England and France also expressed interest in the area, as would the fledgling United States a few decades later.

The early history of North America is closely intertwined with Sino-European relations. Efforts by various European states to reach China in order to replace the Silk Road with a maritime exchange led inexorably to the discovery of the New World. Various products located in the Americas proved to be vital to demonetizing the trade between the two regions as well, introducing natural products that would help to alleviate the silver drain that was much feared by the mercantilist European governments. On the other hand, the introduction of American silver and the sweet potato drastically altered the course of Ming history, weakening it and helping to pave the way for the Manchu invasion, and the slow downfall of China two centuries later.

2

THE FEDERALIST PARTY AND CHINA

SINO-AMERICAN RELATIONS TO 1820

THE COMPLAINTS OF the American colonists against Parliament and the King were not limited to issues of taxation. The Navigation Acts and various other pieces of legislation had severely curtailed American opportunities for trade. In the same vein, the Proclamation Act of 1763, which had halted colonial expansion at the Appalachian Mountains, threatened to limit future trade connections with East Asia. Likewise, the furs and ginseng of the region were not only becoming harder to acquire under British regulations but the Navigation Acts were infringing upon the ability of American merchants to ship them directly to China to achieve the most profit and avoid costly delays that favored English merchantmen.

Literature and propaganda from the Revolution is rife with references to foreign trade as a key grievance of the colonists. Amongst the many complaints laid out by Jefferson in the Declaration of Independence was his allegation that the King and Parliament were to blame for "cutting off trade with all parts of the world." He further expanded upon this in *A Summary View of the Rights of British America*: "That the exercise of a free trade with all parts of the world, possessed by the American colonists, as of natural right, and which no law of their own had taken away or abridged, was next the object of unjust encroachment."

Thomas Paine hinged part of his argument on this idea as well, claiming that the new nation would experience a tremendous advantage in the field of international trade.

"Besides, what have we to do with setting the world at defiance? Our plan is commerce, and that, well attended to, will secure us the peace and friendship of all Europe; because it is the interest of all Europe to have America a free port. Her trade will always be a protection, and her barrenness of gold and silver secure her from invaders."

Much like Jefferson, he faults the trade restrictions foisted upon the colonies as harming their standing around the world.

"As Europe is our market for trade, we ought to form no partial connection with any part of it. It is the true interest of America to steer clear of European contentions, which she never can do, while, by her dependence on Britain, she is made the makeweight in the scale of British politics. Europe is too thickly planted with Kingdoms to be long at peace, and whenever a war breaks out between England and any foreign power, the trade of America goes to ruin, BECAUSE OF HER CONNECTION WITH BRITAIN."

John Dickinson argued in a similar way in *Letters from a Pennsylvania Farmer*, speaking in the manner of Prime Minister Pitt:

"'This kingdom, as the supreme governing and legislative power, has always bound the colonies by her regulations and restrictions in trade, in navigation, in manufactures — in everything, *except that of taking their money out of their pockets* without their consent.' Again he says, 'We may bind their trade, confine their manufactures, and exercise every power whatever, *except that of taking their money out of their pockets* without their consent.'"

DAVID PETRIELLO

Though China itself was not specifically mentioned by the Founding Fathers, the concept of worldwide free trade clearly implied being able to deal directly with East Asia. Of all the products available from that region of the world in the eighteenth century, none were more popular in America than tea and porcelain. By the time of the Revolution, Chinese tea had become more of a necessity in the colonies then a luxury. Citizens of Philadelphia were consuming on average over three teacups worth of the product a day, with all of the colonies drinking over 1.5 million pounds annually.[15] Yet British taxation as well as the Navigation Acts meant that around 90% of the trade in tea was illegally smuggled into American ports. Regulations which required all Chinese products to first make port in England meant that tea was often three to four years old before it reached Boston harbor, affecting both quality and desirability. In fact, one of the most notorious occurrences on the path to the Revolution concerned the tea trade with China.

Plummeting profits for the British East India Company due to both over-taxation and smuggling led to the passage of several acts through Parliament in 1773. The Company was granted a monopoly on the ability to import tea into the Americas as well as a reprieve from much of the heavy taxation on the product. Due to these favorable measures, East India Company tea was actually now cheaper than that which was smuggled in by Patrick Henry and others. In response a series of "tea parties" took place up and down the Atlantic Coast aimed at both expressing continued outrage at the taxation policies and methods of Parliament as well as anger on the part of the wealthy smugglers who were now being forced out of business. The most famous of these tea parties, that at Boston in December 1773, destroyed a shipment that had originated in Amoy, China.[16]

Though the American Revolution was largely fought along

the eastern seaboard for demographic and strategic reasons, efforts were made by some to secure the more western lands of the British empire on the continent, those across the Appalachian mountains, as well. While this was undertaken largely to relieve pressure on the western boundaries of the colonies, to prevent Indian incursions, and to secure more favorable borders during treaty negotiations, the long-term effects were much more dramatic. George Rogers Clark's expedition to Vincennes in 1779 would begin the process of Manifest Destiny that would eventually propel the new nation to the Pacific Ocean and allow for direct trade and interaction with China. As Clark himself wrote to Governor Patrick Henry at the time, "Great things have been effected by a few men well conducted."[17]

The China trade itself played a role in the war as well, offering a tempting target for American and allied privateers. The Committee for Foreign Affairs recommended as early as December 1777 that several frigates be sent to the French territory of Mauritius from which they would patrol the Coromandel Coast in order to intercept British merchantmen trading with China.[18] A year later, Benjamin Franklin was in communication with various French officials to construct eight more frigates, which he incidentally proposed could be employed after the war as merchant ships in trading with East Asia.[19]

The new America that emerged after the signing of the Treaty of Paris soon separated into two distinct visions for the future. Perhaps this was only natural considering the vast geographic disparities of the nation as well as its varied economic foci. The southern part of the nation, with its emphasis on slavery, farming and federalism saw the future of the nation as one of agricultural isolationism. On the other hand, the residents of the eastern seaboard stretching from Baltimore to Boston, an area of cities, commerce and trade, argued for an America of industry and global interaction. Despite pleas from President Washington in his Farewell Address not to become a nation of political parties, "they are likely in the course of time and things, to become potent engines, by which cunning, ambitious, and unprincipled men will be enabled to subvert the power of the people and to usurp for themselves the reins of government," the two distinct ideologies naturally coalesced into national groups.[20] It was only natural that the latter group, which became known as the Federalist Party and which was eventually superseded by the Whigs and Republicans, would be the most active in pushing contact, trade and, by extension, interactions with China. Though the majority of the contacts between the various incarnations of the Federalist Party and China would be economic in focus, elements within these parties would also seek philosophical exchanges and social connections as well.

The Founding Fathers and Confucius
Though John Locke and Thomas Hobbes dominate the philosophical history of the revolt of the Thirteen Colonies and the birth of the American republic, the Founding Fathers did have a knowledge of the precepts of Confucius as well. In fact, many of his ideas concerning morality, virtue in government, limited government, and conservativism would help to inspire the Framers as well as set a moral tone for the early years of the republic.

As early as 1766, a devoted follower was already comparing Benjamin Franklin to the great Chinese thinker in terms of his lasting legacy. "Confucius and his Posterity have been honored in China for Twenty Ages – the Electrical Philosopher, the American Inventor of the pointed Rods will live for Ages to come to live with him would please no one more than, my Dear Maecenas Your affectionate Friend."[21] The reference would not have been lost on Franklin, who had begun publishing excerpts from the great philosopher in the *Pennsylvania Gazette* starting in 1737.

David Wang has done much to illuminate the influence that Confucius and other classical Chinese thinkers had on the Founding Fathers and the establishment of the nation. Though in no way a proponent of democracy, the great philosopher's notions of virtue, harmony, education, and rule by merit all appealed to the Founders' notion of an Enlightenment era republic. Franklin, Adams, Madison, and Paine, among others, all spoke highly of Chinese thought and considered its ideas as they worked out their political models. In fact, Jefferson's notion of a right to revolution in the Declaration of Independence can be traced back to the idea of the Mandate of Heaven and Mencius' thought on legitimate rebellion. On his death, James Madison's estate contained both a copy of Confucius' *Great Learning* as well as a portrait of the thinker.

Confucius, as a non-religious moralist, would clearly have appealed to Paine and Jefferson. The former wrote highly of the traditional Golden Rule, and preferred to credit it to Confucius rather than Jesus. "I recommend to them the observance of a commandment that existed before either Christian or Jew existed. Thou shalt make a covenant with thy senses, With thine eye, that it beholds no evil. With thine ear, that it hear no evil. With thy tongue, that it speak no evil. With thy hands that they commit no evils." Jefferson in his First Inaugural Address spoke of the notion of a "benign religion", that should guide the nation. In this, he was favoring the classic Confucian idea of heaven reigning but not ruling, rather than an established church.

The notions of rule by virtue and of an educated elite exercising power would certainly have appealed to the conservative elements of both parties, especially the Federalists. While many of these ideas were also found in Aristotle and Machiavelli, Confucius perhaps carried more weight with the Founders due to the longevity of his philosophy, its success in controlling China for two thousand years, its non-religious basis, and his status as a non-English and non-European thinker, which would have accommodated the desire of those looking for a break with the thought and political systems of the Old World.

Chinese Society and the Founding Fathers

The Far East's association with strange commodities and bizarre inventions, popularized in part by the writings of Marco Polo, was likewise not lost on the Founding Fathers. Perhaps not surprisingly, the man with the single greatest interest in the society, habits, and technology of China was Benjamin Franklin. There exist numerous letters from the famed patriot and scientist discussing his thoughts on various Chinese topics. Writing to John Bartram in 1770, Franklin attempts to make sense of one of the most Chinese of foods. "I think we have Garavances with us; but I know not whether they are the same with these, which actually came from China, and are what the *Tau-fu* is made of."[22] Franklin also seemed to have a knowledge of the Chinese art of paper-making, silk production, and even the Great Wall, discussing them openly with others.[23]

Franklin also seems to have been impressed by the industry, organization, and general social welfare of the Qing Empire. In a letter to Dr. Thomas Percival written in 1773, Franklin discussed the Chinese practice of conducting a yearly census of the people. He argued that this allowed the government to direct resources more efficiently in times of famine or drought.[24] Though the census to be taken in the United States every ten years as mandated by Article I of the Constitution was not necessarily based upon the Chinese model, a forward thinking man such as Franklin would have perceived the opportunities afforded by this tool. The Qing Empire became something of a utopia to the philosopher from Philadelphia, with Franklin writing to Cadwalader Evans in 1769 that, "Hence it is that the most populous of all Countries, China, clothes its Inhabitants with Silk, while it feeds them plentifully and has besides a vast Quantity both of raw and manufactured to spare for Exportation."[25] His Sinophilia became so well-known that he was sent a personal copy of Michel-Ange-Andres Le Roux Des Hautesrayes book on the history of China in 1781, the first such work on the subject to be published in Europe. With Philadelphia controlling the lion's share of North America's trade with China, Franklin would have had many opportunities to gain firsthand knowledge of the nation as well.

The China Trade

Obviously the greatest draw of China after the Revolution to the new nation was the prospect of trade. Though merchants had certainly been suffering under the Navigation Acts as they were restricted from sailing directly to China, the aforementioned fact that almost ninety percent of the colonies' tea was smuggled in meant that direct trade had in fact already been established. Ben Franklin in "The Colonist's Advocate: X" written in 1770 stated that, "What will they say when they find, that Ships are actually fitted out from the Colonies for all Parts of the World; for China, by Cape Horn."[26] His specific mention of East Asia as the destination for some of this trade seems to suggest the importance of the route.

Even before the official end of the war, men such as Franklin and Adams were seeking to encourage more connections with China. The former even discussed the possibility of sailing Austrian ships from Philadelphia to China once the Revolution was over.[27] John Adams reported to Congress in 1783 that while trade with France was possible, the United States needed, "To send ships to China."[28] That same day, John Adams penned a letter to Robert Livingston reiterating that, "There are other ways of serving ourselves, and making Impressions upon the English, to bring them to reason. One is to send Ships immediately to China. This Trade is as open to Us, as to any Nation: And if our natural Advantages are envied Us, we should compensate ourselves in any honest way we can."[29]

Porcelain was equally in high demand among both American colonists and Europeans at the time. Numerous letters exist from Washington, Franklin, and others discussing various purchases of "china" during the eighteenth century. An account of Martha Custis' estate in 1759, the year she married George Washington, includes, "8 dozn & 8 China plates & 15 dishes," as well as assorted cups and saucers.[30] Thomas Jefferson was an even larger collector of Chinese porcelain, acquiring sets from various agents and bring a collection home from his time in France as well. In 1786, as he traveled from England to France, Jefferson wrote to the authorities at Calais to allow in his personal belongings including, "A set of table furniture consisting in China, silver and plated ware, distributed into three or four boxes or canteens for the convenience of removing them."[31] By the time of his presidency he had well over 200 plates at Monticello alone.

Yet not all of the Founding Fathers thought highly of the China Trade or its possibilities. Franklin, though impressed by China itself, opposed an expansion of trade with it along two lines of attack, in terms of it being a luxury and in hopes of boosting the domestic economy. In the former vein, he penned a lengthy critique of the capital wasted on the trade of luxuries, of which tea and silk from China were prime components.

"Look round the World and see the Millions employ'd in doing nothing, or in something that amounts to nothing when the Necessaries and Conveniencies of Life are in Question. What is the Bulk of Commerce, for which we fight and destroy each other but the Toil of Millions for Superfluities to the great Hazard and Loss of many Lives by the constant Dangers of the Sea. How much Labour Spent in Building and Fitting great Ships to go to China and Arabia for Tea and for Coffee, to the West Indies for Sugar, to America for Tobacco! These Things cannot be called the Necessaries of Life, for our Ancestors lived very comfortably without them."[32]

Where goods from China were desired or needed, Franklin favored domestic production over foreign trade. As early as 1772 he wrote to the managers of a silk operation in Philadelphia, advising them that, "The Sample of second Crop Silk was thought as good as any of the others. A great Deal is produced (of the second Crop) in one of the Provinces of China, where the Climate is very like that of North-America. If the Practice of two Crops is not found attended with any great Inconvenience, it might be a great Addition to your annual Quantity."[33] The idea would eventually be pushed by Alexander Hamilton as well and would help to create the first industrial city in the new nation — Paterson, New Jersey.

Yet most of New England and particularly the port cities along the coast quickly became desirous of trading with China once the war was over. John Thaxter, though lamenting the loss of money to the local economy, wrote to John Adams in January 1784 informing him that, "ship building is carried on briskly — Three Vessells are fitting out for China — This discovers an enterprizing Spirit."[34] The merchants of Salem, eager to recoup years of losses during the American Revolution, sought be one of the first ports to dispatch a ship to China:

"A deep interest is felt here at the prospect of extending our foreign trade…We have, at an earlier period than the most sanguine whig could have expected or even hoped, or than the most inveterate tory feared, every pleasing prospect of a very extensive commerce with the most distant parts of the globe."[35]

Similar talk was heard in Connecticut and up and down the seaboard. Even George Washington was caught up in the fervor of the proposed China trade. In the autumn of 1784, the retired general conducted a survey of his extensive land holdings and the areas around it: "I met numbers of Persons & Pack horses going in with Ginsang & for salt & other articles at the Markets below."[36]

Already one of the wealthiest men on the continent, Washington's interest in ginseng was understandable considering the value of the product. Nor was he the only Virginian who hoped to utilize the natural riches of the state. Neil Jamieson wrote to Jefferson in July 1784 that, "As the China Trade is opend to America, if the growing of Ginseng, the curing of it, and getting it under a proper Inspection, this article might be brought to a very, great value, and the State of Virginia alone could supply the whole of the China market with this Article."[37]

Yet all of this interest and prospective wealth would be just pure fantasy and speculation until the first American ship could reach the Far East.

The Empress of China
The interactions between the Federalist Party and China can be said to have begun with Robert Morris. Though he abstained from voting on the Declaration of Independence, Morris served in Congress throughout the war, personally helped to finance it, and became the Superintendent of Finance for the entire nation in 1781. A staunch proponent of free trade, he would go on to champion many of the economic ideas of Hamilton, including a national bank and internal improvements, such as road and

canal construction. Morris himself was also considered by Washington to fill the newly-created Secretary of the Treasury position. He turned it down and recommended Hamilton in his stead. Beyond simply guiding the rebelling colonies financially through the Revolution and establishing the treasury system that would be perfected by Hamilton, Morris also opened up direct trade between the new nation and China. In early 1784, Robert Morris and John Holker, among others, invested in a former privateer renamed the *Empress of China* as part of an attempt to establish trade with the Qing Empire. The cost of the voyage was astronomical for the time—at $120,000 it was around ten times the cost of a normal European trade mission and one hundred times the annual salary of a congressman.

The ship was placed under the command of John Green, a former naval officer, and carried 34 men, a gunner, and several craftsmen. More important were the 242 casks, almost 30 tons, of ginseng that lay in its hold. So valuable was the cargo that most of the ship's crew brought their own supplies of the root to sell on the side once they reached their destination. Accompanying the ginseng was the ship's supercargo, Samuel Shaw. Aide-de-camp to General Henry Knox during the Revolution, Shaw was tasked not only with selling the goods upon arrival but was reminded by Morris that, "you will probably be the first who shall display the American flag in those distant regions...render it respectable by benevolence and integrity in your conduct."[38] Far from simply a trade mission, the success or failure of this voyage was to affect the official opening of relations between the Qing and the new republic.

Morris' interests were also personal as two additional vessels, the *United States* and the *Betsey*, were fitting out in Philadelphia and New York respectively. Success would ensure not only a considerable profit for him, but the promise of future voyages as well. Departing from New York City on February 22, 1784, the *Empress of China* sailed around Africa and through the Sunda Strait where she met up with two French ships that accompanied her to China. In August of that year, it docked in Macao and Captain Green, "had the honour of hoisting the first Continentol Flagg Ever Seen or maid use of in those Seas."

Despite Morris' claims that, "the Chinese are very great rogues," the trade mission was largely a success.[39] The "Flowery Flag Devils", as the Qing termed the Americans, spent four months selling their ginseng and acquiring trade items in return. Upon its return to the nascent United States in May 1785, the *Empress* was filled with tea, nankeen, tableware, silk and spices. The entire voyage returned upwards of 30% profit to its investors, netting Robert Morris and his partners around $30,000. The Federalist had demonstrated the importance of China as an economic opportunity for America, a lesson that the party would continue to follow for the next two centuries.

Others of the party were also quick to acknowledge the success of the *Empress of China*. Richard Henry Lee, as President of Congress, wrote to John Adams in May 1785: "The enterprise of America is well marked by the successful voyage made by a ship from this port, that has returned after a voyage of 14 months from Canton in China with a valuable eastern Cargo. Our people met with great civility from the Chinese. And the Europeans at Canton, altho civil to the Stripes, were not a little surprised to see them there so soon, and at the celerity with which their voyages were effected."[40] Even those who would eventually emerge as opponents of the trade were cautiously praiseworthy of the accomplishment of the *Empress*.

"I imagine you have heard of the arrival of an American vessel at this place in four months from Canton in China laden with the commodities of that country. It seems our Countrymen were treated with as much respect as the Subjects of any other nation: i.e. the whole are looked upon by the Chinese as Barberians: & they have too much Asiactic hauteur to descend to any discrimination. Most of the mercantile people here are of opinion, this commerce can be carried on, on betters from America than Europe: & that we may be able not only to supply our own wants, but to smuggle a very considerable quantity to the West Indies. I could heartily wish to see the merchts. of our State engaged in this business."[41]

The voyage itself would soon be replicated by numerous other ships over the next year. Elias Hasket Derby, perhaps the wealthiest man in Salem, utilized his ship, the *Grand Turk,* in the new China trade. Originally built as a privateer during the war, Derby's vessel became the first from New England to make the trip. By the end of the decade, more than twenty American ships had made the voyage to and from Canton. Some of the more notable included the *Pallas, Astrea, Atlantic, Light Horse, Hope, Betsey, Canton, General Washington, Columbia,* and *Three Sisters.* Derby himself owned several of these vessels and became heavily leveraged in trade with China.

Nor was the trade confined to simply New England. Soon every port up and down the coast was sending ships around the world. Baltimore joined the trend thanks to the efforts of John O'Donnell. His personal success not only enriched himself, but the city as well. A generation later in 1805, Bezaleel Wells christened his newly-formed town in Ohio Territory, Canton due to his admiration for O'Donnell, the China Trade, and O'Donnell's plantation which was also aptly named Canton.

China fever gripped the nation and the possibilities of the Far East seemed endless. John Adams wrote to Lee, then President of Congress, hoping, "soon to hear of a factory there".[42] Numerous American businessmen and politicians at the time

26

including Elias Derby, Daniel Boone, and John Jacob Astor made considerable fortunes from the initial ginseng trade. To many, the trade itself served to signify acceptance of the new country on the world stage. The favor shown by the French merchantmen who escorted the *Empress* to Macao was officially thanked by Congress through a letter sent by Jefferson to the Comte de Vergennes, the chief minister to Louis XVI.

"I have the honour of inclosing to your Excellency a report of the voiage of an American ship, the first which has gone to China. The circumstance which induces Congress to direct this communication is the very friendly conduct of the Consul of his Majesty at Macao, and of the Commanders and other officers of the French vessels in those seas. It has been with singular satisfaction that Congress have seen these added to the many other proofs of the cordiality of this nation towards our citizens."[43]

Adams himself spoke of the Portuguese extending equal docking rights to American ships in the future.[44] The earliest poet of the new nation, Philip Freneau, even penned a poem to the voyage.

"On the First American Ship That Explored the Route to China and the East-Indies, After the Revolution"

She spreads her wings to meet the Sun,
Those golden regions to explore
Where George forbade to sail before.

Thus, grown to strength, the bird of Jove,
Impatient, quits his native grove,
With eyes of fire, and lightning's force
Through the blue aether holds his course.
No foreign tars are here allow'd.

To mingle with her chosen crowd,
Who, when return'd, might, boasting say
They show'd our native oak the way.
To that old track no more confin'd,
By Britain's jealous court assign'd,
She round the stormy cape shall sail
And eastward, catch the odorous gale.

To countries plac'd in burning climes
And islands of remotest times
She now her eager course explores,
And soon shall greet Chinesian shores.
From thence their fragrant teas to bring
Without the leave of Britain's king;
And porcelain ware, enchas'd in gold,
The product of that finer mould.
Thus commerce to our world conveys
All that the varying taste can please;
For us, the Indian looms are free,
And Java strips her spicy tree
Great pile proceed! – and o'er the brine
May every prosperous gale be thine,
'Till, freighted deep with eastern gems,
You reach again your native streams.

Opposition against the trade eventually arose for several reasons. The overzealousness of some of the traders quickly produced a glut of Chinese goods in America. The limited population of the colonies, compared to that of Europe, soon created an imbalance in demand. This was predicted quite early on by Richard Henry Lee, who in a letter to James Madison shortly after the return of the *Empress* stated that, "I fear that our Countrymen will overdo this business. For now there appears every where a Rage for East India Voyages. So that the variety of means may defeat the Attainment of the concurrent end — A regulated & useful commerce with that part of the World."[45] Others feared that along similar lines to what transpired in ancient Rome, the flow of money out of the nation for luxury goods would harm the local economy. Abigail Adams wrote as much in a letter to Cotton Tufts, "tho I fear they will find the publick money making voyages to China."[46] Others, most of whom became adherents to Jeffersonian Republican ideology, saw trade as secondary to the agricultural pursuits of the nation. Finally, some, like Ben Franklin, stood out as the Cato's of their time lamenting the pursuit of foreign luxuries by the citizens of the new republic. "Ships to go to China and Arabia for Tea and for Coffee, to the West Indies for Sugar, to America for Tobacco! These Things cannot be called the Necessaries of Life, for our Ancestors lived very comfortably without them."[47] Despite these concerns, the young Federalist administration that came into power following the drafting of the Constitution only increased contacts between the two nations. Yet for all of its successes, trade with China quickly became a point of contention between the two new, slowly-forming political parties in America.

Washington's Presidency

Though not a member of either emerging party, Washington entrusted the economic future of the young nation to the Federalist Party in the form of Alexander Hamilton. The first president himself had a keen interest in the China trade, having previously surveyed his lands for the growth of ginseng. He also sought to remain abreast of the latest sailings to and from the Orient, writing frequently to his friends and other government officials about the topic.[48]

Yet Washington, much like the Confederation Congress before him, sought to expand beyond simply an economic interest in China. Samuel Shaw, the supercargo aboard the *Empress of China* in 1785, became the first American consul to China upon landing in that nation. President Washington, upon taking office, extended his tenure and Shaw remained in China until 1794, helping to expand trade not only with Canton but various other parts of the East Indies as well.

The vice-counsel, Thomas Randall, wrote a rather extensive letter to Alexander Hamilton in 1791 detailing the current situation and future prospects in East Asia. To Randall, the biggest stumbling block was the feudalistic and non-capitalist power structure that dominated trade in the country. Local merchants answered to the Hongs, who served as trade overseers, who themselves were subject to imperial mandarins. "Private merchants could not ship any goods they might vend, or bring up any they might purchase, or even go to look at goods, without the Chop, or particular permission of one of the Hong merchants."[49] Randall went on to describe that, "frauds and impositions are practiced by the Chinese on every nation trading there."

Chinese trade practices and an overabundance of ginseng being shipped in American hulls led to an early threat to the trade between the two nations. Two solutions seemed to present themselves on this issue — diversifying American trade items or relying upon protective tariffs. In the vein of the former idea, as demonstrated by the voyage of the *Columbia* in 1787, sea otter pelts from the American northwest were found to be of interest in East Asia. Likewise, sandalwood from the Hawaiian Islands or calin from Malaya, as recommended by Randall, were potential sources of trade as well. Finally, some Americans would also enter into the opium trade, beginning with the *Entan* which sailed from Baltimore in 1805.

The idea of protective tariffs would eventually become a cornerstone of Hamilton's economic policy towards both paying off the nation's debt as well as building up domestic industry. Yet various other Federalists, including Adams and Randall, proposed a complimentary system of tariffs that would also help direct trade to other parts of the world, in this case China. Adams expounded his theory in a letter to John Jay late in 1785:

"There is no better Advice to be given to the Merchants of the United States, than to push their Commerce to the East Indies as fast and as far as it will go. If Information from Persons who ought to know may be depended on, the Tobacco and Peltries as well as the Ginseng of the United States, are proper Articles for the China Markett, and have been found to answer very well, and many other of our Commodities may be found in demand there. The states may greatly encourage, these Enterprizes by laying on Duties, upon the Importation of all East India Goods from Europe, and indeed by proceeding in time to Prohibitions. this however may never be necessary. Duties judiciously calculated and made high enough to give a clear Advantage to the direct Importer from India will answer the End as effectually as Prohibitions, and are less odious, and less liable to Exceptions. We should attend to this Intercourse with the East, with the more Ardour, because the Stronger Footing We obtain in those Countries, of more importance will our Friend Ship be, to the Powers of Europe who have large Connections there. —The East Indies will probably be the Object and The Theatre of the next War, and the more familiar We are with every Thing relative to that Country, the more will the contending Parties desire to win Us of their Side, or at least, what We ought to wish for most, to keep Us neutral."[50]

For his part, Randall recommended a more specific tariff to be placed only against tea being imported to America from Europe. Much like Adams, he thought that this would provide an incentive to merchants to make the longer and more costly voyage to China.[51]

Jefferson and the Republicans tended to oppose tariffs for a number of reasons and this soon became a substantial point of contention between them and the Federalists. Only a month after the first sitting of Congress in 1789, Thomas Fitzsimons proposed the laying of a tariff on shipments of tea brought in by foreign ships or from countries other than India or China. James Madison arose in response as the representative of Virginia and expressed the following view as recorded in the Congressional record:

"What, said he, is its object? It is not to add to the revenue, for it will in fact tend to diminish it, in that proportion, which the importation from China lessens that from other parts; it is not to encrease our commerce, for long voyages are unfriendly to it; it is not to encrease the importation of necessary articles, for India goods are mostly articles of luxury; it is not to carry off our superfluities, for these articles are paid for principally, if not altogether, in solid coin... There are no collateral good purposes to claim our attention in this case; it is not in the nature of things that we should derive any other advantage than the one I have mentioned, without it is that of raising our India commerce from its weak and infant state, to strength and vigour; to enable it to continue supplies at a cheaper rate than they could otherwise be obtained at."[52]

Despite Republic opposition, the motion carried as part of the larger Federalist effort at paying off the debt and at promoting industrial protectionism.

Adam's Presidency

The victory of John Adams in the election of 1796 did little to alter the Federalist Party's grasp on power nor its economic interest in China. Adams himself had been notoriously active in his praise for the China trade and for the prospects for America in that part of the world. Only a few months after the return of the *Empress*, Adams wrote to Richard Henry Lee expressing his, "hope soon to hear of an American factory there."[53] In fact Adams was quick to recommend the China trade as a prospective economic opportunity to both family and friends. Writing to Richard Cranch, one of Abigail's brother-in-laws, Adams hoped that,

"Once for all, you may take it from me, that you must Work out your own salvation at home—If you cannot find other Channels of Trade these will remain blocked up—When you have demonstrated to the World that you dont want them, they will be opened but not before—I am informed that the Trade of Boston to the Cape of Good Hope & to Africa succeeds very well, Why has no attempt been made to China, Bengall or Pondichery or other parts of India."[54]

His presidency was largely taken up by the worsening situation in Europe and the continued attacks against American shipping to the Continent. Yet the importance of China in particular and East Asia in general were never lost upon him. Adams even went so far as to predict to John Jay that, "The East Indies will probably be the Object and The Theatre of the next War."[55] Though he would not be proven right until World War II and the subsequent Cold War, his and the Federalist Party's obsession with China would eventually be vindicated. However, this would come too late for Robert Morris. The architect of America's early economic policy as well as the main investor in the *Empress of China* found himself arrested and thrown into debtors' prison in February 1798. Though he was eventually released, the experience broke him and he died several years later in 1806.

Long Republican Decade

For a number of reasons, the Jeffersonian Republican Party, and its later manifestation as the Democratic Party, tended to be opposed to, or at best more neutral towards, interactions with China. This was especially the case with regards to economic cooperation. James Monroe well summed up the general thinking of the party in the following letter to Thomas Jefferson:

"I think the expedience in a great degree of the measure turns on one point (especially to the southern States) whether the obtainment of the carrying trade and the extention of our national resources is an object. And this depends entirely upon the prospect of our connection with other powers; if like the empire of China we were seperated and perfectly independent of them it might perhaps be unnecessary: but even in that event a question arises which may be of consequence, 'whether the giving our own citizens a share in the carrying trade will not otherwise be advantageous to them than as it obtains the particular object which the regulations necessary to effect it have in view; whether it will not in effect increase the value of land, the number of inhabitants, the proportion of circulating medium, and be the foundation upon which all those regulations which are necessary to turn what is call'd 'the balance of trade' in our favor, must be form'd.' A preference to our own citizens is the foundation of the carrying trade and upon it I suspect will depend all these consequences."[56]

To Monroe and others, the question was one of whether aiding the China trade conducted by the North would in any way harm the economy of the South.

The ultimate Jeffersonian dream would be of a self-reliant, largely neutral nation, that devoted itself almost entirely to farming. In fact for the Republicans, traditional China provided the best model of this. "You ask what I think on the expediency of encouraging our states to be commercial? Were I to indulge my own theory, I should wish them to practice neither commerce nor navigation, but to stand with respect to Europe precisely on the footing of China. We should thus avoid wars, and all our citizens would be husbandmen."[57]

Federalist Rufus King of New York, himself an avid supporter of the China Trade, commented on Jefferson's party's adherence to Chinese practices. "The system of passive commerce, like that of China, resting solely on the theory of selling dear and buying cheap, has at all times had its advocates among us."[58]

At the same time, expanded world trade was seen as something that would invite greater possibilities for conflict and potential war. Jefferson highlighted this view to John Jay as, "Indeed I fear that other European Nations do not regard us entirely without Jealousy. There are some little Circumstances which look as if the Dutch regret our having found the Way to China, and that will doubtless be more or less the Case with every Nation with whose commercial Views we may interfere."[59]

The Republicans had to look no further than an incident in 1791, as recorded by Thomas Randall, in which an English gunner accidently killed a Chinese citizen during a cannon salute. In response, the Chinese seized an English diplomat, threatening to torture and kill him. The various European powers present, as well as the few Americans, gathered weapons and supplies and formulated an attack on Canton.[60] A policy of isolationism to avoid such situations, as espoused by Jefferson and his party, necessitated limiting foreign trade as well.

In this, some Federalists shared a similar notion. Many of them were more ardently mercantilist than capitalist and supported domestic manufacturing over the importation of goods. Tench Coxe, who worked closely with Hamilton, wrote in 1794 that silk manufacturing should be promoted in the United States both due to the value of the product and in order to end the reliance upon China. "Silk has long been a profitable production of Georgia, and other parts of the United States; and may be increased, it is presumed, as fast as the demand will rise. This is the strongest of all raw materials, and the great empire of China, though abounding with cotton, finds it the cheapest clothing for her people."[61]

Yet despite these claims, the climate of Georgia combined with the difficulties of the enterprise drove most of the manufacturers towards cotton. This only accelerated after the invention of the cotton gin in the 1790s.

As previously seen, Jefferson himself was an ardent admirer of Chinese culture, philosophy, and arts. For him it was the isolationism of that nation and its focus on agriculture over commerce that made it great and were the aspects to be emulated by America. On a practical level Jefferson incorporated ideas from Chinese landscape design and architecture into his home of Monticello. Likewise, shortly after the ending of the Revolution he became enamored with the idea of bringing dry rice farming to the South. His motive in this had more to do with morality than economics as wet rice farming as carried out by slaves in the Deep South was associated with some of the worst physical and environmental horrors of slavery. After receiving specimens of the rice from Sumatra in 1789 he began to experiment with it on his own property. The success of his endeavors is evidenced by the fact that by 1813 it was being grown from Kentucky to Georgia. Nor was his party in possession of a monopoly on appreciating the culture of China. John Adams frequently wrote of his respect for the philosophy and morality of the nation. He even went so far as to suggest that the Chinese and Japanese should spread their ideologies in America as readily as Europeans did in East Asia.

"I do sincerely wish that the Mandarins of China, the Bramins of Hindostan the Priests of Japan, and of Persia, could be influenced with the same zeal de propaganda fide as the Roman Catholics and Calvanists of this day are for propagating their Creeds, and ceremonies, I wish they would form into societies, open their purses, contribute their diamonds, pearls and precious Stons, as liberally as our people do their treasures, for translating their sacred books into English, French, Italian, Spanish, and German — And send Missionaries to propagate them throughout all Europe and all America North & South. We might then know what the religions really are of the great part of the World. We know as little of them now, as we do of the religion of the Inhabitants of Sirius, the dog Star."[62]

Despite the fact that the Republican Party was now in power, many Federalists continued to proposition the government to support trade and interaction with China. Most notable of these was Tench Coxe, who despite having campaigned for Jefferson in 1800, remained a Federalist in terms of economic policy. Far ahead of his time, Coxe proposed to the president the idea of transforming China into a center of manufacturing. He argued that this would lessen the nation's reliance on Europe in general and England in particular. "The cheapness of living and of labor, and the imitative talents of that Country & people are well understood and ascertained. It has been the interest of the European manufacturing nations to avoid and discourage the importation of China manufactures, because they interfered with their own. But we who do not manufacture piece goods, and shall not for some time, are at present situated differently, for example, from the English."[63]

Coxe urged Jefferson to send a direct communique to the emperor, along with, "A body of useful information upon the nature of our demand & consumption, the numbers of our people and consequent extent of our demand, our increase evidenced by copies of our two Census, our disposition to buy of them for money...Such a communication, to be accompanied by a very copious and nice collection of specimens of the various goods most in demand at all times in our markets, and these to be made up in the most perspicuous & impressive manner and to include the manufactures of all the European nations."[64]

Coxe understood the revolutionary nature of his suggestion, writing in a second letter only a week later that his ideas were both, "visionary and strange".[65] Though Jefferson never dispatched the requested mission, Coxe would eventually see his ideas come to fruition at the end of the twentieth century.

Interestingly, one of Jefferson's crowning achievements as president, the Louisiana Purchase and its subsequent exploration, helped to pave the way for further interaction with China. The President himself gave numerous reasons for the acquisition of this substantial piece of territory including increasing US isolationism, by focusing its interests away from Europe, and the potential discovery of new resources. Meanwhile, Federalists opposed the purchase and expansion for equally plausible reasons, yet a small minority of the latter party was amenable to the project due to the increased interaction with China that it would bring.

As early as 1783, Jefferson had already written to George Rogers Clark, the conqueror of the west and the brother of the future member of the Lewis and Clark Expedition, concerning the future westward push of the new nation. "Some of us have been talking here in a feeble way of making the attempt to search that country. but I doubt whether we have enough of that kind of spirit to raise the money. how would you like to lead such a party?"[66]

He based this idea largely on fears of British expansionism. "I fnd they have subscribed a very large sum of money in England for exploring the country from the Missisipi to California. they pretend it is only to promote knoledge I am afraid they have thoughts of colonising into that quarter."[67] In the end, Jefferson was correct about the lack of interest in the new nation for the funding of such a large expedition. It would take another twenty years, the purchasing of the entire region, and a different Clark before a full exploration of the western regions began.

In the intervening years, a well-known Boston merchant and Federalist, Joseph Barrell, organized a scheme to construct trading posts along the northwest coast. In 1787 a series of investors including Barrell, famed Federalist architect Charles Bulfinch, John Derby of Salem, and others, purchased the ships *Columbia* and *Lady Washington* and dispatched them around South America to present-day Oregon. After picking up furs, they sailed across the Pacific and sold them at Canton. Thus, the famed Old China Trade of Boston was firmly established.

It is doubtful that Jefferson was moved by these events in his decision to acquire Louisiana. Despite this, Merriweather Lewis, writing on the day of the expedition's return to St. Louis, informed Jefferson that, "The furs of all this immence tract of country including such as may be collected on the upper portion of the River St. Peters Red river and the Assenniboin with the immence country watered by the Columbia, may be conveyed to the mouth of the Columbia by the 1st of August in each year and from thence be shiped to, and arrive in Canton earlier than the furs at present shiped from Montreal annually arrive in London."[68] Though the official party line was vehemently opposed to the acquisition of Louisiana, many New England merchants began to dream of a permanent Federalist presence on the West Coast in order to trade with China.

John Jacob Astor, for example, spent much of the time from 1809 to 1812 focused on the region. He had been sending ships to the Oregon region since the sailing of the *Columbia* in 1787. In 1808, he even felt it prudent to write to former president Thomas Jefferson seeking government investment and help in establishing a national fur company to exploit the riches of the area. The latter responded somewhat positively, couching his argument in terms of denying the area, its resources, and the Natives to the British. "You may be assured that in order to get the whole of this business passed into the hands of our own citizens & to oust foreign traders who so much abuse their privilege by endeavoring to excite the Indians to war on us, every reasonable patronage & facility in the power of the Executive will be afforded."[69]

Yet it appears that Astor received little actual support from Washington, as he again wrote to the president, by this time James Madison, in 1813 again repeating many of the same arguments for help. His appeals became more earnest as the British and local Indians were now using force to clear out various trading posts set up by his American Fur Company. Madison appears to have been initially receptive to the idea of sending an armed privateer, the *Siren*, to the northwest coast. But delays, red tape, and differing opinions eventually resulted in the cancellation of the undertaking. Astor's men, fearing attack by the British, sold off their camp to the British North West Company. When America finally did lay claim to the region in 1818, Astor proclaimed he was too old to start again.

Jefferson's professed fear that increased international trade would lead to more instances of conflict were shown to be justified on numerous occasions in the first decade of the nineteenth century. Apart from the more infamous *Chesapeake-Leopard* Affair and numerous other cases of impressment by the British in Atlantic waters, the China trade also produced a number of naval incidents. Secretary of State Madison was confronted with numerous petitions by American captains including some regarding the Spanish seizure of several ships near the Philippines in 1805, the British confiscation of a vessel in Canton the same year, and the English impressment of a man from the *New Jersey*. The Secretary sent a strongly-worded letter to his British counterpart in 1807, warning that due to the large number of pirates off the coast of Guangdong, the province of which Canton was the capital, "it is the determination of the Captains of the American Vessels to repel by force, any attempt in future, to impress their Seamen, when within this Empire."[70]

Clearly Madison and Jefferson were concerned that a minor incident could lead to all-out war in the region. A future naval officer in the War of 1812, Isaac Chauncey, also expressed his frustrations after having his ship stopped by the British near Whampoa, the anchorage off Canton: "I am mortified that I am again under the necessity of complaining to you of the base treatment recieved from a people that we are at peace with and who profess a wish to continue so, yet in the very face of those professions are guilty of the most unwarrantable and insulting conduct towards the Flag and citizens of a nation whom they hypocritically pretend to respect."[71]

Yet despite all of these attacks, the China Trade continued unabated. From 1784 to 1814 around 300 different ships made 618 voyages to Canton and back.[72] Both Secretary of the Navy Robert

Smith and Treasury Secretary Albert Gallatin confronted Jefferson regarding his desire to send a warship to the region, arguing that it, "would excite among the British Cruisers suspicions of war & that the consequent bustle and abrupt departure of the American vessels would be to them confirmations strong. Under these apprehensions it is here feared that speculative captures to a ruinous amount would be made. The merchants of this place are decided in the opinion that no publick vessel ought to be sent."[73]

Unfortunately, Jefferson's philosophical and economical aversion to trade as well as his desire for isolationism pushed him to an unprecedented step in 1807. In December of that year, Congress, with his blessing, passed the Embargo Act, which effectively shut down American trade abroad. The economic consequences of this act were disastrous. The economy of New England largely ground to a halt and numerous petitions were sent to Jefferson to no avail. One of the few exceptions made by the President involved the repatriation of a Chinese mandarin, Punqua Winchung back to his nation:

"I consider it as a case of national amity... the departure of this individual with good dispositions may be the means of making our nation known advantageously at the source of power in China, to which it is otherwise difficult to convey information. it may be of sensible advantage to our merchants in that country. I cannot therefore but consider that a chance of obtaining a permanent national good should over-weigh the effect of a single case taken out of the great field of the embargo. the case too is so singular that it can lead to no embarrasment as a precedent."[74]

In fact, the entire Punqua Winchung episode was merely a clever ploy by John Jacob Astor. The "mandarin" was actually a Chinese shopkeeper who had become stranded in America due to the Embargo Act. Punqua Winchung had arrived in Boston in

1807 aboard the *Favorite* and was on Nantucket with his servant seeking to establish a trade connection with Astor. The latter hoped to not only return him to Canton, but send a shipment of trade goods with him as well. He therefore used his influence to get the merchant in touch with Jefferson. As has been seen, the White House fell for the ploy and quickly granted a passport to the "mandarin" who was able to take a ship of his choosing and return to Canton. Not surprisingly, he chose Astor's *Beaver*, and brought a full cargo of goods to China. Once the Embargo Act was repealed, Astor was able to bring the ship home with over $200,000 worth of Chinese products in its hold. Punqua Winchung actually continued the ruse, sending an official gift to Dolley Madison two years later and a bust of Confucius to the president. Unfortunately, his servant, Quak Te, was left behind on Nantucket with various belongings to await his return. After waiting over a year, the homesick and distraught man hung himself, creating a local sensation.

In the end, the Embargo Act was repealed in the last few weeks of Jefferson's presidency. In its place, Congress authorized the Non-Intercourse Act of 1809. This replacement piece of legislation only outlawed American trade with the United Kingdom and France, the two nations that had been attacking the shipping of the United States and impressing its sailors. Despite his overall philosophical intentions, the act actually benefited both the China Trade as well as industrialization, two Federalist ideals. The downturn in trade with Europe meant that more New England merchants began to sail to Canton. Likewise, the Industrial Revolution took hold in the northeast, with East Asia amongst the willing buyers for the products produced, including finished textiles, furniture and guns.

President James Madison's war against the British, launched in 1812, was highly unpopular with members of the Federalist

Party. This was due in part to geography—their states bordered Canada and would be targeted in an invasion—and in part due to economics, as England was their major trading partner. John Jacob Astor, though, sought to use the conflict to once again push his agenda in the fur-rich northwest. In February 1813, at a time when the War of 1812 had largely ground to a halt for America, Astor wrote to Gallatin and recommended launching a small operation in the area of Oregon. This would allow America to claim the region and draw English troops away from eastern Canada. The Secretary of the Treasury seems to have favored the idea, writing on the letter before sending it to Madison that, "Suppose a frigate to be sent to cruize off Canton or vicinity; to go by way of mouth of Columbia river, & land there a company of marines, so as to embrace this opportunity of taking possession."[75] Though in the end, as previously mentioned, the idea was called off.

The war served to seriously curtail the nation's trade with China, which had only just begun to recover after the repeal of the Embargo Act. A tight British blockade of the coastline reduced the number of ships both leaving from and arriving at American ports. Cargo sat on ships and ginseng rotted in warehouses. Several Chinese merchants even became stranded in the country, unable to leave. One such man, Washing, personally petitioned Madison for an armed American escort in order to return to Canton. "I make this request with the more confidence, from the relations of amity subsisting between the United States & the Emperor of China, which I hope may long be continued."[76]

Despite the best attempts of the Republican Party of Jefferson through the Embargo Act and despite the blockades and destruction of the War of 1812, trade with China continued to flourish following the Treaty of Ghent in 1815. As early as January 1816, a group of American merchants in Canton wrote the

President asking for the appointment of a professional consul, a permanent physician due to the health problems associated with the region, and the purchase of a factory to house both.[77] These were hardly requests relating to a failing endeavor.

The period from the birth of the nation until 1820 is particularly interesting due to the division of power between the two main political parties. The initial natural gravitation of the Federalists towards China had more to do with economics than anything else. Its dominance in power for the first half of this period ensured the opening of communications between the two nations, a trend that would continue despite the counterproductive efforts of the Jeffersonian Republicans from 1800 to 1820. Trade was perhaps the most beneficial method by which to start an interaction between America and China. As was clearly understood by many involved in the China Trade, Peking was hardly open to the normal levels of diplomatic interaction and cultural exchange that predominated in the West and the Middle East. This is well illustrated by an incident that occurred during Monroe's presidency in 1822. In 1812 an American merchant ship, fortuitously named the *President Adams*, became disabled off the coast of China, with its cargo of coins and possibly opium quickly being plundered by pirates or locals.[78] In an attempt to gain compensation for the loss and to support the position of the United States in the region, President Monroe wrote the first official letter between an American head of state and an emperor of China, ten years later in 1822. The delay between the actual incident and Monroe's reply was perhaps due to the slowness of communication at the time, the ensuing War of 1812 and its associated British blockade of American ports, and Madison's own tepid interest in the region and the matter. The terms used in the missive were very Oriental in their level of flattery, with Monroe referring to the emperor as, "the wise, the glory of reason, the great emperor who has received from heaven and revolving natures the government of the Celestial Empire". As for himself, he was content with the more modest, "chief ruler by the will and choice of all the people of this powerful nation of the West". The clear distinction between the mandate of heaven on the one hand and the will of the people on the other was starkly laid out. Interestingly, John Quincy Adams, Monroe's secretary of state and a man of Federalist bent, considered the first draft of the letter to be too weak in terms of the tone that should be taken with China. A second, stronger version ended by referring to the Chinese who plundered the vessel as, "those children of wickedness." Regardless of tone, though, there is no evidence that Monroe ever received a reply from the Jiaqing Emperor or that his letter ever even reached the imperial throne in Peking. Due to situations like the above, economics inevitably became the channel through which the United States would eventually broaden connections with China.

3

NATIONAL REPUBLICANS AND WHIGS

SINO-AMERICAN RELATIONS FROM 1820-1860

THE PERIOD FROM 1820 to the onset of the Civil War saw a marked change in the relationship between China and the United States for a number of reasons. Politically, the White House was controlled by the soon to be re-christened Democratic Party for the vast majority of the period. In fact, the era from 1800 until 1860 saw only twelve years in which non-Democrats held the office of president. Likewise, Democrats held a majority in the Senate for fifty-four out of sixty years and in the House for fifty-two. Thus, there was a long-term trend of focusing on the agrarian expansion and territorial growth of the nation, but not necessarily the augmentation of overseas trade. At the same time, the economics of trade with China was changing as cotton production increased in the United States. Finally, issues with the Qing Empire itself, most notably the British-led forced opening beginning with the Opium War (1839-1842) and the Taiping Rebellion (1850-1854), began to alter the relationship of East Asia with the rest of the world.

Yet this is not to suggest that America abandoned its hope of trading and interacting with China. The National Republican and Whig parties, though not in power for much of this time, still largely held sway at the state level and within Congress itself.

Likewise, the Democratic notion of Manifest Destiny, the widely-held belief that it was the destiny of the Union to occupy all of North America, which had arguably started with the Louisiana Purchase, pushed the fulcrum of the country closer and closer to the Pacific and further from the agrarian dreams of Southern Democrats. Finally, relations with China could still progress at a basic level through individual Americans trading across the Pacific Ocean.

Tea and Opium

The general pattern of trade from 1820 to 1860 witnessed a shift in the products flowing into and out of China. The original China Trade saw tea, cotton, silk and porcelain objects leaving Canton for American harbors. Yet a variety of factors led to a decline in demand for most of these with the exception of tea. Cotton cloth imported from China, though representing only a fraction of what was bought from English mills, was overtaken by domestic production after 1808. The Embargo Act and the subsequent blockade during the War of 1812 led to an explosion of American factory construction and the eventual decline of a market for foreign-made textiles.

At the same time, the market for tea in America continued to expand strongly. The product at the root of so much debate during the road to the Revolution represented 36% of total American imports from China in 1822. By the outbreak of the Civil War it had risen to represent 65% of all products sailing from Canton to the East Coast of the United States. Abraham Lincoln, some say, received his nickname "Honest Abe" while working as a clerk at a store in New Salem. According to the tale, he mistakenly delivered only a quarter of a pound of tea to a customer while charging him for the half-pound ordered. Lincoln woke up early the next day and walked all the way to the customer's home to correct the mistake.[81] True of not, tea had become a mainstay in American homes across the nation.

Yet while there was certainly one Chinese product that America desired, the reverse was becoming less true. Previously popular export products such as furs and ginseng were were with with shrinking demand in Canton. Competition from other foreign suppliers, rising local production and the overall economic decline of China slowly forced American merchants to ship less goods and more silver bullion to the Orient. To offset this, some East Coast merchants turned to a more controversial product.

The obvious solution to many was the growing opium trade that the British had inaugurated several years before. While India produced the most desired strains of the plant, England largely restricted sales to other foreign traders, forcing American merchants to look elsewhere. Beginning in the 1790s, several American ships sailed to the Ottoman Empire to acquire Turkish opium. Though considered inferior to Indian opium, there were no onerous restrictions keeping Yankee traders out. In 1804, Benjamin and James Wilcocks, sailing aboard the *Philadelphia*, purchased 49 chests of the product at Smyrna and shipped it onwards to Canton. The success of the endeavor sparked a trade frenzy not seen since the beginning of the ginseng exchange. Interestingly, Benjamin Wilcocks went on to become the American consul at Canton in 1812, again showing the clear connections between trade and relations.

Other notable traders soon followed, including Stephen Girard who was perhaps the wealthiest American of the era. Girard had been involved in the China trade since the 1780s and in 1807 had sent a ship to Turkey to begin trading opium for tea. As with seal furs and ginseng, the rush by so many merchants to find an alternative to bullion caused a glut in the Canton market, but it was not until the 1830s, when American ships became allowed to buy opium directly from India, that the US became a major supplier of the product. During the 1830s, opium accounted for up to 25% of all American products that flowed into Canton. Yet even at its height, American opium only accounted for 10% of the total amount of the drug that entered China, showing the nation's then still limited trade with China.

With opium basically balancing off tea, American trade with China continued to flourish for the next several decades. From 1815 to 1839 an average of forty American ships a year docked at Canton. Over the fifty-year period starting in 1790, a total of 1,260 vessels would make the voyage, making America second only to the United Kingdom in terms of the number of ships trading with East Asia.[82] It is estimated that overall between 1784 and 1854, $180 million dollars worth of goods departed the United States for Canton. In keeping with some of the voices in the ancient Roman senate, Representative William Lowndes chaired a Democrat-dominated committee in the House in 1819 to investigate the drain on American capital. The report that emerged from this undertaking stated quite harshly that, "the whole amount of our current coin is probably not more than double that which has been exported in a single year to India, including China in the general term."

The China Trade not only benefited the pockets of those directly involved in it, but indirectly helped to develop much of New England as well. Many of the merchants who depended upon the shipment of goods to and from China helped to push and fund many of the railroads and harbor developments that came to characterize the northeastern coast of America. Thomas Handasyd Perkins, a Federalist politician, who spent many years selling opium into Canton, developed one of the first commercial railroads in New England. Dubbed, the Granite Railway, the three-mile stretch of track brought precious granite into Boston which was used to both beautify public buildings as well as construct numerous monuments. In his later years, Perkins used much of his vast fortune to fund schools, orphanages, museums, and hospitals in and around Boston.

John Quincy Adams

With the demise of the Federalist Party by 1820, it seemed as if the nation was destined for one-party rule. In fact, at Monroe's second inauguration, only four Federalists sat among the forty-five senators whom he addressed. Perhaps not surprisingly, almost all of the men were involved in the China Trade in one form or another including Harrison Gray Otis and James Lloyd of Massachusetts and Rufus King of New York. Yet despite the onset of this "Era of Good Feelings", the mercantilist, pro-China thought of many in New England did not collapse along with the Federalist Party. Only four short years later, a particularly vicious election battle between Andrew Jackson and John Quincy Adams once again split the political class of the nation into two groups, with most of the old Federalists drifting into the new National Republican Party.

The victory of John Quincy Adams in that hotly-contested election seemed to offer hope of a return to the pro-China Federalist policies of Washington and Adams. Yet a combination of the viciousness of the campaign, Democratic dominance in Congress, and Adams' own *laissez-faire* style of governance meant that little concrete action was taken. However, Adams four previous years as one of the more active secretaries of state and his subsequent career in Congress, provide several key instances to discern his policy towards the Qing.

During his First Annual Message, which President Adams sent to Congress on December 6, 1825, he mentioned the following concerns that faced America: "An unsettled coast of many degrees of latitude forming a part of our own territory and a flourishing commerce and fishery extending to the islands of the Pacific and to China still require that the protecting power of the Union should be displayed under its flag as well upon the ocean as upon the land."[83]

Adams' interest in securing US control over the Pacific coast had dominated much of his time in Monroe's cabinet as well. Both he and Albert Gallatin had worked to secure several treaties in this area, most notably the Adams-Onis Treaty with Spain and the Treaty of 1818 with the United Kingdom. The former had effectively pushed Spain from the region of Oregon, while the latter proposed that both the United States and United Kingdom should jointly share it.

Congressman John Floyd of Virginia, an opponent of Adams, proposed seeking control of the region almost yearly from 1821 to 1829. In a speech on the House floor, Floyd couched his proposal in various terms that departed from the purely economic ones normally voiced by the Federalists. "Upon the people of Eastern Asia, the establishment of a civilized power on the opposite coast of America could not fail to produce great and wonderful benefits. Science, liberal principles in government, and the true religion, might cast their lights across the intervening sea."[84] Floyd further went on to argue that the Columbia valley could become the, "granary of China and Japan and an outlet to the imprisoned and exuberant population." These two opposite nations, one despotic and one free, could become friends. Floyd's proposals represented the genesis of the interest in the modernization of China that would eventually come to dominate Republican thought towards East Asia even more than trade.

Though Floyd's proposals for the immediate seizure and movement of troops to the region were largely ignored until the

1840s, across the Atlantic the British likewise saw the benefits to be had *vis-à-vis* China with the acquisition of Oregon. George Canning, the British Secretary of State for Foreign Affairs, summarized these feelings in a letter to Prime Minister Robert Jenkinson in 1826. To him, control of Oregon was essential as, "the trade between the Eastern and Western Hemispheres, direct across the Pacific, is the trade of the world most susceptible of rapid augmentation and improvement... I should not like to leave my name affixed to an instrument by which England would have foregone the advantages of an immense direct intercourse between China and what may be."[85]

Henry Clay

Henry Clay was part Alexander Hamilton and part John Q. Adams, combining the economic concerns of the former with the expansionism of the latter. In terms of China, Clay worked to counter the prevailing notion that, "the China Trade in exports from this country is... confined wholly to Specie as was declared in Congress at the time of revising the Tariff on Silk Goods, and which opinion *prevailed*; and led to the laying on of a discrimination Duty... which, if continued, will destroy the Trade in China manufactured Silks."[86] While this was certainly a serious economic concern in Europe, Clay argued that not only did specie payments, or hard currency, not make up the majority of American trade flowing into China as feared by Loudon, Jefferson and others, but that duties on silk would merely erode trade between the two countries further. This is all the more interesting considering that Clay was one of the most prominent pushers of tariffs on the national level from 1816 to the 1840s.

The Jackson and van Buren presidencies, from 1829 to 1841, were years of Democratic Party rule that saw little overall change in relations with China. But trade continued unabated, much as it had during the Jeffersonian Era. In his Third Annual Message to Congress, Jackson summarized his efforts with regard to China in purely economic terms. "To China and the East Indies our commerce continues in its usual extent, and with increased facilities which the credit and capital of our merchants afford by substituting bills for payments in specie."[87]

Unsurprisingly, the Democratic president continued to focus on the issue of the drainage of hard currency from the United States.

The declining stability of the Manchu-ruled Qing Dynasty and the growing aggression of the United Kingdom in the region was noticed and commented upon by John Shillaber, the American consul at Batavia. In December 1831 he pressed Jackson to "provide a sufficient force to visit occasionally the Indian and Chinese seas."[88] Yet the White House seems to have had little interest in the idea, only dispatching one frigate to the region, the *USS Potomac*, following a pirate attack on the merchantman *Friendship* off Sumatra. Shillaber went on to write additional letters to the president and various cabinet officials in 1834, highlighting the growing tensions in the region and recommending a more forceful American presence. Once again, there was little response to these pleas, and when an American warship was finally dispatched, its main function was to restrict the opium smuggling. Likewise, various merchants at Canton were pushing for Jackson and Van Buren to dispatch a representative to negotiate a trade agreement with the Chinese. Despite a formal memorial being presented to Congress in 1839, no action was taken by the Democrats.[89]

The Whigs Open China
The period from 1841 to 1853 represents the highpoint of Whig political ascendency. Twice the party was elected to the White

House and for several years controlled or significantly contested power in Congress as well. Though both Presidents Harrison and Taylor died prematurely and the era was dominated more by the administration of James K. Polk and his Mexican War, a number of important steps towards advancing relations with China were taken.

Shillaber's fears of British aggression in China came to fruition during the presidency of Martin Van Buren. The outbreak of the Opium War was a concern for Democarts for a number of reasons, most notably economic. The onset of aggression threatened to curtail trade, while the potential of a British victory could produce a monopoly for London following an enforced peace treaty. Shillaber himself had predicted that war between England and China will result in the former, "taking possession of and fortifying one or more islands upon this coast for concentrating trade there."[90] Likewise, the party's tendency towards non-interventionism abroad and anti-British leanings would tend to restrict America's direct involvement. In 1840, as war raged on the Chinese coast, the House of Representatives thrice requested information from the president regarding American trade with China and ongoing relations between the two countries. In his Fourth Annual Message to Congress, delivered in December 1840, Van Buren reported that in order to protect American interests, two ships, the nearly fifty-year-old USS Constellation and the USS Boston, both under the command of Commodore Lawrence Kearny, were being sent to the region. Yet by this point Van Buren had already been handily defeated in his attempt at re-election and did little else regarding the conflict. In addition, one of the main elements of Kearny's mission was to curtail the American opium trade rather than protect the merchants. Interestingly, amidst his letter writing campaign in 1834, Shillaber himself had also cautioned against direct involvement on either side in the war, merely recommending that it would be, "well if the United States take an observing attitude, combining a naval force, and a diplomatic agent."[91] The fear of British victory in China rested upon the anticipated disruption of trade that would certainly accompany war as well as increased potential trade opportunities for England that America would miss out on.

The early and tragic death of William Henry Harrison so soon after his inauguration thrust into the presidency John Tyler of Virginia. While more politically active than his predecessor, Tyler was not actually a member of the Whig party. Despite this, his time in office witnessed several important interactions with the region thanks to his own unique view on Asia, rapidly evolving conditions on the ground in China, and a Whig-dominated cabinet and legislature.

The Opium War was at its height as Tyler was sworn in, and with the Whigs eager to secure more trade opportunities with China, the stage was set for active American involvement in the conflict. The presence of the small squadron under Kearny that had been dispatched a year before by Van Buren served as the means for the United States to do so.

The Qing government had officially banned opium in 1800, but British and American traders continued to ship the product into Canton and clandestinely into other ports along the China coast. As previously mentioned, many famous individuals in the United States at the time made their fortunes off of the drug. Most American consuls to Canton dealt in the trade and numerous political families as well, including the Delanos. Not all merchants or politicians agreed with the practice however, and Commodore Kearny's original orders included a provision to put an end to Yankee merchants smuggling in opium.

Those Whigs who were not personally in favor of opium attempted to justify the English war in other terms. This is perhaps best epitomized by several speeches and letters given by John Quincy Adams concerning the event. The former president argued that opium was a mere symptom of a much larger cause of the war. Writing to James Brook in 1842, Adams somewhat sarcastically stated that,

"Perhaps the children of the celestial empire in their superiority to the rest of mankind may ultimately compel the outside barbarians to become again reverently submissive and tributary to the great emperor of the flowery land to perform the Kowtow with nine knocks of the forehead on the floor to supplicate subalterns by a Pin for the privilege of purchasing and paying for Bohea tea; and to sign bonds that they shall be strangled by their own consent, if they should ever attempt to bring a chest of opium within sight of the celestial empire. Should the Britons, on the other hand, prove themselves as far above their adversaries in the art of war as a Christian nation of Freemen is in the career of human improvement above an atheist nation of slaves, I hope - would I could promise, that the free Christian Warrior will sheath his sword in mercy and in moderation."[92]

Despite initial fears of the immediate effect of war on trade in the region, Adams, and many other Whigs, in direct contrast with the Democrats, viewed the British war as justified due the despotic and "uncivilized" nature of the Chinese with regards to both diplomacy and trade. A successful campaign would not only serve to safeguard American trade but also help to open up the nation to cultural and social modernization as well. China, despite its great technological innovations and monumental endeavors, was now largely viewed by most in Western nations as barbaric, a shift from the largely idyllic perceptions of the eighteenth century. This was not simply ethno-chauvinism, as exemplified by the Terranova Incident of 1821. In that year an accidental drowning caused by a careless American sailor led local Qing officials to demand that a sailor be turned over to face punishment. The captain of the vessel, the *Emily*, initially refused, but in the face of Chinese threats to terminate trade, American officials arrested Francis Terranova and handed him over. He was sentenced to death and executed by strangulation. This and other similar incidents shocked the Enlightenment and Christianity-grounded ideals of Westerners.

Upon arriving in China in March 1842, Commodore Kearny soon exceeded his orders and informed Vice Consul Warren Delano that he intended to sail his vessel up the river to Whampoa, becoming the first American warship to do so. By this time, however, the war in the south of China had already come to a close. The British had sailed up the coast and were quickly approaching Nanjing where the war would soon end. Kearny's actions were in keeping though with the views of Tyler's Whig cabinet. Secretary of State Daniel Webster had written that same year to Dr. Peter Parker, a missionary in Canton, regarding the presence of American naval power in the region. "The subject had been neglected and that a strong force would be sent."[93]

Harrison's greatest contribution to the broadening of relations with China before his early death had been his appointment of Daniel Webster to head the State Department. The latter hailed from an area heavily influenced by the China Trade and had risen through the ranks of the Whig party from 1827 to 1841 due in part to his support for Clay's economic system and the protective tariffs that would benefit New England manufacturing while not restricting its trade with China.

While Webster was quite successful at negotiating treaties with England over a number of issues, his time in office was short. Tyler's decision to veto the majority of legislation passed by the Whigs, when combined with issues over his exact role as an ascendant president, caused the mass resignation of his cabinet by the end of 1841. The one exception was Webster, who remained in office to continue negotiations with the British over the Maine border. Yet even he was eventually compelled to give up his position in May 1843. Interestingly, as his last act on his last day in office, he dispatched a letter with instructions for a mission to China to negotiate with the Qing court.

The mission was launched in response to British efforts to force a peace treaty and new concessions out of the Chinese. Webster and others saw an English triumph in the Opium War as inevitable at this point, and wisely sought to protect American interests from the English as much as expand them with the Chinese. Tyler, in a special message to Congress given in December 1842, argued that,

"It can not but be interesting to the mercantile interest of the United States, whose intercourse with China at the single port of Canton has already become so considerable, to ascertain whether these other ports now open to British commerce are to remain shut, nevertheless, against the commerce of the United States. The treaty between the Chinese Government and the British commissioner provides neither for the admission nor the exclusion of the ships of other nations. It would seem, therefore, that it remains with every other nation having commercial intercourse with China to seek to make proper arrangements for itself with the Government of that Empire in this respect."[94]

Three months later, in March 1843, Webster issued a circular asking for help from anyone with knowledge of or experience with the Chinese. His belief in the importance of the mission is made clear in a letter he penned to Thomas Curtis that same month. "I consider it a more important mission than ever proceeded from this country, and the more important than any other, likely to succeed it, in our days."[95]

Though some preferred placing former president John Quincy Adams in charge of the delegation to Peking, Tyler eventually settled on Caleb Cushing. Hailing from a shipbuilding family and representing a portion of Massachusetts heavily dependent upon the China Trade, Cushing advanced through Congress, becoming the chairman of the House Committee on Foreign Affairs in the early 1840s. These factors, combined with his support for Tyler in his move to veto most of the economic programs of the Whigs, led him to be selected to represent the nation before the Emperor of China.

As part of his final instructions for Cushing, Webster informed him that while the mission was essentially peaceful, its main objective was, "to secure the entry of American ships and cargoes into these ports, on terms as favorable as those which are enjoyed by English merchants."[96] These ports included Amoy (Xiamen), Ningbo, Shanghai, and Fuzhou and closely paralleled the demands of both the British and French at the time. Furthermore, though Webster was quick to remind Cushing that the mission was completely pacific in nature, he urged him in the strongest terms not to kowtow to the emperor, despite Qing demands to the contrary, and that American receive equal treatment to other nations. President Tyler personally paid a visit to the ship carrying the diplomatic expedition, the *USS Missouri*, as it cruised off of Hampton Roads, Virginia. After spending several hours aboard, he disembarked and the vessel proceeded across the Atlantic. Nineteen days later, the *Missouri* anchored at Gibraltar in order to fill its coal bins. That night, however, due to the carelessness of a crew member, a fire broke out aboard which soon reduced the ship to a charred wreck. Cushing survived the disaster, fleeing the burning ship with his official letters and instructions. The disaster itself was mentioned in Tyler's Third Annual Message to Congress, delivered later that year.

With Dr. Parker as his interpreter, Caleb Cushing was eventually able to negotiate a treaty with the Qing at Wanghia just outside of Macau. At a small stone table inside the courtyard of the Kun Iam Temple, Cushing and the Chinese minister Qiying signed a treaty on July 3, 1844. Qiying had previously represented the Qing at the Treaty of Nanjing, so it is not surprising to find similarities between the two documents.

As per the hopes of the Whigs and the instructions of Webster, Cushing secured the standard array of demands that were seen as beneficial to both the political standing and economic advantage of the United States. Among the highlights of the treaty were a standardization of tariff rates (Article II), the opening of additional ports (Article III), the establishment of free trade within the ports (Article XV), the allowing of Americans to learn Chinese (Article XVIII), a promise by the Qing to defend American nationals and their property against mobs and rioters (Article XIX), and the granting of extraterritoriality (Article XXI).

The free trade and open ports idea of the Whigs served as the opening salvo of the much later Open Door Policy of the Republican Party. While some speculation has existed that this idea arose merely in an attempt to level the playing field after the division of China by the various European powers by the 1890s, its roots stretch much further back to at least the time of the Treaty of Wangxia. Additionally, the Whigs hoped to avoid a repetition of the *President Adams* incident in 1812, by requiring through Article XXVII of the treaty that the Qing were responsible for all damage to or looting of American merchantmen in Chinese waters.

Though the Treaty of Wangxia is often grouped in with the various European treaties of the time and considered to be one of the "Unequal Treaties", its undertaking and provisions show it to be far from a tool of oppression. The vast majority of articles within the agreement were meant to either simply place America on the same level of trade as England or else require China to conform to basic, international norms of behavior. The United States even went so far as to agree to ban its citizens from the opium trade. "Citizens of the United States... who shall trade in opium or any other contraband article of merchandize, shall be subject to be dealt with by the Chinese Government, without being entitled to any countenance or protection from that of the United States."[97] Likewise, the treaty pledged that Americans who attempted to trade beyond the five assigned ports, "shall, with her cargo, be subject to confiscation to the Chinese government."[98] Additionally, the newly appointed American consuls, "will carefully avoid all acts of unnecessary offence to, or collision with, the officers and people of China."[99]

The approval of the treaty by President Tyler on January 17, 1845, two months before he left office, served as the continuation of a new direction set in place by the president concerning American interests in the Far East. The Tyler Doctrine aimed at securing America's boundaries, pushing its interests to the Pacific and beyond, and garnering respect abroad. In terms of the Pacific, President Tyler focused much energy on ensuring the independence of the Hawaiian Islands. Then called the Sandwich Islands, the chain held a strategic location in the Pacific Ocean, allowing for the refueling and refitting of both merchantmen and warships as they transversed between America and Asia. Due to his concerns that another country may try to seize the islands and due to the fact that, "the United States possesses so large a share of the intercourse with those islands, it is deemed not unfit to make the declaration that their Government seeks, nevertheless, no peculiar advantages, no exclusive control over the Hawaiian Government, but is content with its independent existence and anxiously wishes for its security and prosperity," Tyler moved to neutralize the islands,[100] couching much of this announcement in terms of its benefit to American economic interests in China. In fact, over half of his address to Congress concerned the recent British success in the Opium War, his belief in the need to launch what would become the Cushing Mission, and the ever-increasing trade between the two nations.

Tyler's concern for Hawaii was proven correct only four months later in February 1843 in what became known as the Paulet Affair. Captain George Paulet of the *HMS Carysfort* occupied Honolulu for six months in response to complaints from several British nationals. King Kamehameha III issued a formal protest but could do little against the guns of the British warship. In July 1843, Commodore Kearny sailed the *USS Constellation* into Hawaii, finally returning from his three-year mission to China. Kearny was soon joined by the *USS United States* under the command of Commodore Thomas ap Catesby Jones and the two issued a strong renunciation of Paulet's action. Luckily, London had already decided against their captain's course of action and the arrival of the *HMS Dublin* a few weeks later settled the matter peacefully.

Taylor and Fillmore
President Polk's administration was second only to Jefferson's in its enthusiasm for seizing on the idea of Manifest Destiny. By the end of his four years in office, he had secured the border of Texas, defeated Mexico, acquired all of the province of California, and finally divided the Oregon Territory with the United Kingdom in 1846. But apart from overseeing the dispatch of the countersigned Treaty of Wangxia to China, Polk took little direct action in regards to relations with that country. He did, though, couch

his acquisition of California in economic terms that portrayed the seizure as favorable to trade between the two nations. In his Third Annual Message to Congress he proposed that, "The Bay of San Francisco and other harbors along the Californian coast would afford shelter for our Navy, for our numerous whale ships, and other merchant vessels employed in the Pacific Ocean, and would in a short period become the marts of an extensive and profitable commerce with China and other countries of the East."[101]

Zachary Taylor's election brought the Whig Party back into power, yet his short time in office due to his early death, left him with few accomplishments to speak of and none concerning China. His replacement, Millard Fillmore, attempted to expand American economic interests in East Asia by forcibly opening up the empire of Japan. Having largely closed itself off to the rest of the world following Tokugawa Ieyasu's seizure of power, Japan had remained economically isolated and aggressive towards those few unwary sailors who landed or were washed up upon its shores. As Fillmore emphasized in his Third Annual Message to Congress in late 1853, "Our unfortunate countrymen who from time to time suffer shipwreck on the coasts of the eastern seas are entitled to protection."[102] Commodore Matthew Perry was duly dispatched to "obtain from the Government of that country some relaxation of the inhospitable and antisocial system which it has pursued for about two centuries. He has been directed particularly to remonstrate in the strongest language against the cruel treatment to which our shipwrecked mariners have often been subjected and to insist that they shall be treated with humanity."[103]

The opening of Japan in 1854, under the guns of American warships, also benefited the China Trade, providing coaling stations and ports at which to buy provisions.

DAVID PETRIELLO

One of the more forgotten parts of Perry's expedition was his diversion to Taiwan while awaiting a response from the Japanese government. The island began to appear in various American reports and texts sporadically beginning with William Shaler's mention in 1808. Taiwan was blessed with many natural resources which were highly valued by American merchants including rice, coal, and camphor. Despite this, the fragmentary hold of the Qing government on the island, the presence of numerous, warring local tribes, and seas dominated by pirates, left it a no-man's land along the major routes of the China Trade. Attempts to trade with the island or land there for missionary work were often met with attacks and kidnappings. In 1847 the merchant ship *Paragon* was wrecked along the coast while the *USS Porpoise* which approached Taiwan in 1854 was never heard from again. It would in fact take until 1856 for the first major, foreign-controlled, long-term trading post to be opened on the island, set up by Williams, Anthon, & Company.

In a similar vein to what had occurred with Spanish Florida, due to the anarchic nature of Taiwan and the potential for trade, interest in the island therefore focused around its seizure or purchase by the American government. As early as 1834, John Shillaber, the American consul at Batavia, wrote to President Jackson broaching the idea of acquiring the island. A little over a decade later during the presidency of James K. Polk, Whig congressman Thomas Butler King of Georgia pushed a similar notion. A strong proponent of internal improvements and a champion of the US Navy, King urged the establishment of a coaling station on the island. But neither Democratic president acted upon the issue of Taiwan, once again leaving it in the hands of local merchants and interests to push American policy.

In 1851 Dr. Peter Parker, growing concerned at stories of American missionaries and sailors being held hostage on Taiwan, asked the American government to dispatch a warship in order to search for them. Though the *USS Porpoise* entered the seas off Taiwan in 1854 for that purpose, it was soon lost and never heard from again. That same year, however, Commodore Matthew Perry sent the *Macedonian* and the *Supply* south from Japan to investigate the island. He himself had read widely about the island and seems to have envisioned himself as an explorer of the Pacific, responsible for bringing American trade influence to all parts of East Asia, not merely Japan.

Writing that year to the new president, Franklin Pierce, Perry described the situation as, "This significant island, though nominally a province of China, is practically independent... yet, such is its productiveness in minerals, drugs, and the more valuable products of the genial regions." He went on to document how upon landing, the captain of the *Macedonian* was asked by the local magistrate, Li Chu-ou for assistance in putting down a revolt. Thus, Perry felt that the Qing would actually welcome an American occupation as a way to secure its own people on the island.[104]

That same year, Townsend Harris, who was preparing to travel to Japan to renegotiate Perry's initial treaty, wrote to President Pierce regarding his own view of Taiwan. Harris recommended purchasing the island for five major reasons; 1) its abundant resources, 2) to construct a trading port, 3) to Christianize it and then spread the religion throughout Asia, 4) to construct a trade depot for goods from China, and 5) to improve relations with Japan. Jefferson Davis, who was secretary of war at the time, personally delivered Harris' report to Pierce over a year later in July 1855 to Pierce. Yet, in the end, the president did nothing to forward the idea of acquiring Taiwan.

Gideon Nye, a merchant in the China Trade originally from Massachusetts, became interested in Taiwan at this time both do to its economic opportunities as well as the loss of his own brother in a shipwreck off of its coast. In fact, he had been one of the main voices in calling for Commodore Perry to dispatch the *Macedonian* to the island.[105] By 1857, Nye and Parker were regularly exchanging communications on the subject of seizing or purchasing the territory. The latter even met with Commodore James Armstrong of the US East India Squadron in Macau to discuss seizing Taiwan by force.

Both Parker and Nye wrote to President-Elect Buchanan, various members of his administration, and Caleb Cushing, who was now a private citizen. At around the same time, the British including Admiral Michael Seymour were also beginning to show interest in the acquisition of the island. Despite Nye's subsequent contact with the new American minister to China, William Read, President Buchanan's hands-on approach to foreign policy meant that he was to be the clearing house for all actions in the Far East, and he had little interest in obtaining land in Asia, risking war with China, or running into conflict with England. Therefore, in the end, no further action was taken regarding the plans of Nye and Parker.

The only reaction by Buchanan to events in China arose out of a forced response to the Second Opium War. The outbreak of war between England, France, and China in 1856 quickly brought in local Americans as well. Though President Buchanan officially kept the nation out of the war, rejecting calls by London for an alliance, several local commanders, officials and civilians became involved in the conflict. After four day of bombardment of Canton by the British, an opening was made in the city walls. As troops entered the port they were accompanied by the American consul, James Keenan, who planted a US flag on the top of the Chinese governor's home.

Shortly afterwards, a Qing fort along the Pearl River opened fire on the American ship, *Portsmouth*, possibly confusing it for an British or French vessel, or out of anger towards Westerners in general. opened In response, James Armstrong of the *San Jacinto*, along with the *Portsmouth* and the *Levant*, attacked a series of forts along the river, ultimately disabling them and taking or destroying 176 guns. Thank in part to this aggressive show of force, no further actions against American vessels took place.

The incident coincided with Pierce's decision to send Peter Parker to Canton in 1856 to renegotiate the Treaty of Wangxia . After its adoption in 1844, the treaty had stipulated that renegotiation was possible after 12 years. Though Armstrong's actions helped to ensure American neutrality in the war, Parker's mission was largely unsuccessful.

The subsequent actions of Commodore Josiah Tattnall certainly did not serve to endear the Chinese to the Americans. During the disastrous Anglo-French attack on the Taku Forts along the Pei-ho River, the American chartered ship *Toey-Wan* provided noteworthy support to the allied fleet. Commodore Tattnall, who would later command the *Merrimack* during its famous Civil War encounter with the *Monitor*, rowed over to the *HMS Plover* under fire to offer to evacuate the wounded from the ship. Several American sailors even climbed aboard the English warship and helped to man the understaffed cannon. To explain his actions, Tattnall made the now-famous statement that, "blood is thicker than water".

Though American involvement in the Second Opium War was peripheral, the nation still sought to leverage increased economic opportunities with the negotiation of a new treaty. William Bradford Reed focused on using diplomacy to establish essentially the same rights as those achieved by the British and French at the point of a cannon. But the resulting Treaty of Tianjin, signed in June 1858, struck a very different tone from that adopted by the English. The first article itself laid out the atmosphere of friendship and cooperation that existed between the two.

"There shall be, as there have always been, peace and friendship between the United States of America and the Ta Tsing Empire, and between their people, respectively. They shall not insult or oppress each other for any trifling cause, so as to produce an estrangement between them; and if any other nation should act unjustly or oppressively, the United States will exert their good offices, on being informed of the case, to bring about an amicable arrangement of the question, thus showing their friendly feelings."

The provisions set out in the treaty were generally aimed at aiding and promoting communication and trade between China and the United States. Articles IV and V laid out the right of envoys to both visit the capital and interact with their respective opposites. Still further on, the treaty established mutuality between the leaders and envoys of both nations, ending the traditional, inferior treatment and forms of degradation forced on Western diplomats by the Qing court. Finally, the United States achieved promises of protection for its citizens and vessels with regard to mob violence and pirates, a long sought-after demand.

"All citizens of the United States of America in China, peaceably attending to their affairs, being placed on a common footing of amity and good will with the subjects of China, shall receive and enjoy for themselves and everything appertaining to them, the protection of the local authorities of Government, who shall defend them from all insult or injury of any sort. If their dwellings or property be threatened or attacked by mobs, incendiaries, or other violent or lawless persons, the local officers, on requisition of the Consul, shall immediately despatch a military force to disperse the rioters, apprehend the guilty individuals, and punish them with the utmost rigor of the law."

This defense was likewise extended to include those who openly practiced their religion within the country.

Overall, relations between America and China as conducted by the National Republican and Whig parties was primarily aimed at increasing economic access to the Asian country. Apart from a small number of misunderstandings and accidents, little to no physical or martial confrontations erupted between the two nations. Indeed, the only major incursions in terms of force by the United States took place in and around the island of Taiwan due to the perennial issue of pirates. Yet, despite the promised wealth of the Orient, all of these increases in the ability to trade took place against the backdrop of a general decline in the number and variety of exports from China to America. While economic relations between the two nations could have simply continued on a minor scale, the arrival of a new party in American politics, the Republican Party, instead ushered in a new era in Sino-American relations.

4

BURLINGAME AND THE GILDED AGE IN CHINA

SINO-AMERICAN RELATIONS FROM 1860-1896

MANY SEGMENTS OF the China Trade continued to decline as the nineteenth century wore on. The ascent of manufacturing in the northern states especially removed much of the early impetus for trade between the two nations. A rising standard of living and falling prices meant that the northern factories could outperform those in China for many basic textiles. Meanwhile the opium trade started to shrink as many Western governments turned against the sale of the drug, especially once migrating Chinese began to bring it with them to America. Additionally, a ginseng rush in Minnesota in 1859 only further helped to devalue the commodity and collapse prices. Overall, it seemed in the latter half of the nineteenth century as if the once-promising China Trade was going nowhere.

Abraham Lincoln
The onset of the Civil War likewise served to distract American interests from developments in Asia. Locally-based US diplomats, military officers, and merchants continued to control most of the nation's policy towards China. Taiwan especially, with its long history of pirates and hazardous sailing conditions, would frequently see rescue attempts and punitive expeditions

launched by local Americans.[106] The best examples of this include the Formosa Expedition of 1867 and Charles Le Gendre's invasion of the island later that same year.

Abraham Lincoln's only concrete action with regard to China was the appointment of a new consul, Anson Burlingame. A resident of Massachusetts, he was a strong proponent of trade with China. Yet at the same time, Burlingame had to contend with the Qing Empire's slow slide towards chaos as well as continued piracy against American ships off the coast.[107] While the new consul made little progress on the latter issue, he did manage to usher in one significant shift in Sino-American relations, a change that was to characterize the Republican Party's handling of China for the next century.

Upon his arrival in China, Burlingame decided to depart from the port cities and consular buildings usually haunted by foreign diplomats and instead traveled around the country. He observed firsthand the deprivation caused by both the Qing government as well as the impact of the Unequal Treaties. He soon began to take a more active role in Chinese affairs, far beyond the traditional maintenance of trade relations that had characterized the actions of his predecessors. Burlingame recognized that the modernization of China was necessary for it to avoid complete collapse. In order to accomplish this, he believed, China would need an outside benefactor as a source of guidance, materials, capital and technology. At the very least, the new American diplomat felt that the various Western powers should refrain from stripping away control of Chinese ports from the Qing government and respect its territorial integrity. While serving as part of a Qing embassy to Boston in 1868, Burlingame summarized this new doctrine as a "cooperative policy... that policy substituted for the old doctrine of violence one of fair diplomatic action."[108]

The Burlingame Doctrine was largely a continuation of the capitalist approach towards China that had characterized Sino-American relations for the previous ninety years. The man himself had represented a mercantile district in Massachusetts and had been a staunch opponent of slavery, once famously accepting a challenge from Preston Brooks of South Carolina to a duel following a heated exchange on the House floor. Thus the concept of free trade and an aversion to the oppression of a minority people were pillars of his personal as well as diplomatic philosophy.

In April 1863, Burlingame renegotiated the Treaty of Tianjin signed five years earlier. Through his efforts, the double taxation of American ships trading goods between Chinese ports was eliminated. A year later, in February 1864, President Lincoln and the US Senate approved the new treaty, helping to expand trade opportunities with East Asia. This decision by Lincoln was the only major diplomatic action he took with regard to the Qing Empire during his time in office.

Burlingame himself soon returned to the United States, touring the country giving speeches on Chinese history and on the need for improved Sino-American relations. Yet in only a short time, he was once again pressed by William Seward to return to China. His subsequent time in the country so impressed the Qing government, that in 1867, when he was concluding his assignment, he was asked by Peking to head a Chinese diplomatic mission to the United States. He arrived in America in March 1868 accompanied by two Chinese ministers and six students from China, as well as several other notables.

Thanks in part to his pre-existing connections within Congress, the Johnson administration, and the Republican party, Burlingame was by July able to obtain a modification of the Treaty of Tianjin. China's right to its own integrity was secured, trade was further expanded, and perhaps most importantly, its citizens were permitted to travel to and settle permanently in America. Finally, the document ended the enslavement and sale of Chinese laborers, known as coolies, to businesses along the West Coast. Certainly the Republicans' aversion to slavery pushed them towards eliminating this trade. Burlingame perhaps best summarized this point in a speech he gave in 1868. "This treaty strikes down or reprobates—that is the word—the infamous Coolie trade... it invites free immigration into the country of those sober and industrious people by whose quiet labor we have been enabled to push the Pacific Railroad over the summit of the Sierra Nevada."[109] Not only was the enslavement of the Chinese ended, but they were to take their place in Republican eyes as the Irish immigrants of the West.

A month later, Burlingame was in Boston attending a banquet for the Chinese delegation. He stated that the city was chosen for a visit due to the fact that it "was the first to establish relations with China," and because, "my associates... have desired to make themselves acquainted with the systems of learning in the West," although his own connections to the region were more likely the reason.[110] Burlingame laid out an argument for closer cooperation between the two nations built upon trade, cultural exchanges, student exchanges, immigration and the spread of Christianity. He prophetically envisioned a Pacific Century, "when all travel between these two mighty nations shall be over the justly named Pacific Ocean... when we shall be the east and China the west."[111] This view of global realignment would come to dominate the Republican world view for many years. "The land of Washington has greeted the land of Confucius."[112]

Perhaps the best evidence of the new connection between the two nations was the communication received from China following the assassination of President Lincoln. Prince Gong, the architect of Chinese modernization in the nineteenth century, wrote to his opposite number in America that he had received, "communication informing me that the President of the United States had been removed by death, an announcement that inexpressibly shocked and startled me."[113]

Gong's role in the improvement of relations between the two countries was essential to the modernization of China. The successful development of the Qing empire required both external aid as well as internal impetus. Interest by Burlingame and others in his party, along with promises of increased trade and student exchanges seemed to bode well for the former requirement. Gong and his openness to the West and its technologies, along with the modernizing ideas of Zeng Guofan, helped to promote the latter.

The efforts by these two men began in earnest in 1850 with the enrollment of a man born in a village in southern China, Yung Wing, in college at Yale. He was the first Chinese person to ever go to an major US college. After graduating in 1854 and returning to China, he worked with various missionary groups as a translator before being tasked with returning to America to purchase machinery to manufacture modern rifles, which the Qing needed to battle the Taiping Rebellion. He arrived at the height of the US Civil War with the 68,000 taels of silver given to him by Zeng, and was eventually able to obtain orders of machines from Putnam Machine Company and Warner and Whitney of Fitchburg.[114]

Returning to China, Yung Wing employed the newly-arrived American technology to upgrade the Qing weapons factories in Shanghai. Zeng Guofan undoubtedly watched in delighted wonder and satisfaction as modern rifles began to be produced at the Kiangnan Arsenal. Success was quickly met with duplication and expansion. In 1868, with further help from Western experts and the local scholar and technician Xu Shou, the Chinese finally were able to construct a series of steamships including the *Auspicious* (Tianqi), *Dignity and Tranquility, Controlling the River,* and *Fathoming the Sea.* Following the success of Kiangnan, Zeng Guofan proceeded to set up an additional arsenal and shipyard at Fuzhou. Yung was eventually sent back to America in 1872. Entrusted with $100,000 he personally opened negotiations with Dr. Richard Jordan Gatling to purchase his famed rapid-fire guns. This was complemented at the time by the Tianjin Arsenal, which in the 1880s began to produce ammunition under license from both Krupp and Remington. Soon after, it began to mass-produce the guns themselves. By the 1890s, the Tianjin Arsenal was the single largest industry in China, employing over two thousand workers.

The hallmarks of the modernization efforts by Gong and Zeng revolved around the two elements of acquiring Western weapons technology and the dispatching of students on educational trips to the West. The Chinese Educational Mission would ultimately send 120 young men abroad to America between 1872 and 1875. Yun first proposed the idea to Zeng during a meeting between the two men in 1863, but as was symptomatic of the bureaucratic troubles confronting the Qing, it would take almost a decade for the plan to be approved by the throne. Even after it was accepted, few Chinese families showed interest in their sons taking partt, no doubt in part due the entrenched prejudices against all things Western.

Eventually enough students were recruited, especially from the southern provinces, to allow the first ship to sail in 1872. Overall, the entire mission unfolded quite successfully, with the vast majority of students graduating from Yale. However, their return to China was shrouded in suspicion, jealousy, and a conservative reaction against the Self-Strengthening Movement. Immediately upon their return they were shunted into an abandoned building and most never saw their Ivy League education put to any use above operating telegraphs. The Chinese Educational Mission, like many other elements of Zeng and Gong's reform movement failed from the top down, not the bottom up.

Ulysses S. Grant

With the relative peace and prosperity that returned the United States following the end of the Civil War, American interests moved towards economic matters which helped to usher in the Gilded Age. Relations with China continued to be largely economic, though with an ever-growing concern on the part of the United States for China's territorial integrity and the need for modernization. President Grant made both points clear in his First Annual Message to Congress in December 1869. With regards to the issue of trade, Grant proposed that, "Our neighbors south of us and China and Japan, should receive our special attention. It will be the endeavor of the Administration to cultivate such relations with all these nations as to entitle us to their confidence and make it their interest, as well as ours, to establish better commercial relations."[115]

Likewise, concerning the development of China he opined that

"Through the agency of a more enlightened policy than that heretofore pursued toward China, largely due to the sagacity and efforts of one of our own distinguished citizens, the world is about to commence largely increased relations with that populous and hitherto exclusive nation. As the United States have been the initiators in this new policy, so they should be the most earnest in showing their good faith in making it a success. In this connection I advise such legislation as will forever preclude the enslavement of the Chinese upon our soil under the name of coolies, and also prevent American vessels from engaging in the transportation of coolies to any country tolerating the system."[116]

To help accomplish the latter, Grant recommended "that the mission to China be raised to one of the first class."

The incident of greatest significance to occur in China during Grant's tenure was the Tianjin Massacre of 1870. As was typical of the time, the arrival of foreigners in the city after the opening of the treaty ports led to fear and rumors. Most of the local anger was focused on a foreign church-run orphanage which was accused of kidnapping children and murdering them as part of its religious practices. Following the arrest of several man who claimed to have worked as kidnappers for the church, a riot erupted in the town. Dozens of Western buildings were burned down, the French consul was murdered, a number of nuns were raped and killed, and over fifty other people were butchered by the mob. Zeng was recalled in an attempt to mollify the anger of the West, but the incident only further hardened positions on both sides.

President Grant made mention of the occurrence in his Second Annual Message to Congress in December 1870. The administration seems to have wished to downplay the incident, either to calm public fears that could affect trade opportunities or out of a desire to support the Qing government.

"The massacres of French and Russian residents at Tien-Tsin, under circumstances of great barbarity, was supposed by some to have been premeditated, and to indicate a purpose among the populace to exterminate foreigners in the Chinese Empire. The evidence fails to establish such a supposition, but shows a complicity between the local authorities and the mob. The Government at Peking, however, seems to have been disposed to fulfill its treaty obligations so far as it was able to do so."[117]

Grant went on to express some fear that the then-ongoing Franco-Prussian War would extend to Asian waters, which would "neutralize the Christian influence and power, and that the time was coming when the superstitious masses might expel all foreigners and restore mandarin influence."[118] The president then sought to play the role of mediator, helping to establish a truce in the region in order to provide for "the future protection in China of the lives and properties of Americans and Europeans."[119]

Grant, like many American leaders before him, sought to emphasize the economic importance of China to the US. His presidency saw the onset of a disastrous recession that would last well into the 1890s and came to be termed the Long Depression. The president looked to encourage any outlet for trade in order to reduce unemployment at home and increase government revenues. "Our depressed commerce is a subject to which I called your special attention at the last session, and suggested that we will in the future have to look more to the countries south of us, and to China and Japan, for its revival. Our representatives to all these Governments have exerted their influence to encourage trade between the United States and the countries to which they are accredited."[120]

Several years later, Grant touched once more upon the issue of the almost slave-like importation of Chinese workers, termed the "Coolie Trade". Ever since Burlingame had first endeavored to confront the practice in the 1860s, Republicans had sought to connect the issue with slavery in the South. The president mentioned the attempts at abolishing the practice in his Fifth Annual Message to Congress in 1873 that coincided with the ascension of the three-year-old Guangxu Emperor to the Qing throne. "Some advance, although slight, has been made during the past year toward the suppression of the infamous Chinese cooly trade. I recommend Congress to inquire whether additional legislation be not needed on this subject."[121]

Grant's final interaction with China came during a time of heightened tension between the Qing and Japan. In keeping with the growing concern for the territorial integrity of the Qing Empire as well as fear of the rising power of Japan, in 1874 the president sought to intervene in a territorial dispute between the two. "During the past year the fear of hostilities between China and Japan, growing out of the landing of an armed force upon the island of Formosa by the latter, has occasioned uneasiness. It is earnestly hoped, however, that the difficulties arising from this cause will be adjusted, and that the advance of civilization in these Empires may not be retarded by a state of war."[122] The president was likewise concerned about the alleged involvement of private American citizens in the affair, many no doubt still expressing interest in the acquisition of Taiwan for the US. "In consequence of the part taken by certain citizens of the United States in this expedition, our representatives in those countries have been instructed to impress upon the Governments of China and Japan the firm intention of this country to maintain strict neutrality in the event of hostilities, and to carefully prevent any infraction of law on the part of our citizens."[123]

Yet perhaps the most interesting actions undertaken by Ulysses S. Grant with regards to China actually occurred in the years after his presidency. In an attempt to remove himself from the public eye, especially after his Republican successor failed to achieve outright victory in the 1876 contest, Grant departed on a worldwide tour. The former leader was greeted as a hero and man of honor at every destination, being met with parades and seas of American flags. His initial impressions of China were less than flattering. He wrote that Peking was "but for the nave of the thing, it was not worth the trouble of a visit."[124] Grant was even more unimpressed with the southern part of the empire, saying of Amoy, "The city, if possible, is more filthy than Swatow."[125]

As for the people, though, Grant was readily impressed by both the general population and its leaders. "The Chinese seem to be a most industrious and frugal people."[126] He later commended Viceroy Li Hung-chang for being, "the most intelligent and most advanced ruler – if not man – in China."[127] He did, however, turn down a chance to meet with the eight-year-old emperor, stating that he would have found it demeaning.

Though Grant was quick to acknowledge the mistreatment of the Chinese by Westerners, he largely placed the blame for this on their own shoulders. "I am satisfied that the Chinese are badly treated at home by europeans [sic] as well as when they emigrate. I blame them for submitting to such dictation."[128] In fact the former president went so far as to state that he would, "not blame them if they were to drive out all europeans [sic] – Americans included – and make new treaties in which they claim equal rights."[129]

Overall, Grant was not opposed to the modernization of China, but recommended that the Chinese first focus on improving their internal condition, much in keeping with the approach decades later of Chiang Kai-Shek, Mao and others. "They seem to possess the shrewdness to realize that their safety consists in holding back in modern civilization & progress until they can educate their own people to take the management in building roads, constructing machinery, etc. and until it can be done with their own capital."[130] Grant also pressed for political reform for China, especially a strengthening of central power. "The present form of government gives no state power whatsoever."[131]

Foreshadowing the view of many others of the late twentieth century, Grant opined that, "My impression is that the day is not very far distant when they will make the most rapid strides towards modern civilization, and become dangerou[s] rivals to all powers interested in the trade of the East."[132]

His greatest contribution to Sino-American relations arose out of a dispute between China and Japan over the Ryukyu Islands. Due to Grant's position as an outsider, or out of hopes that China and the United States would find a common enemy in Japan, Viceroy Li sought his help in resolving the matter. Though Grant expressed his concern that he would be of little practical help, he promised to address the issue upon his arrival in Japan. In the end, while meeting the Meiji Emperor, with whom he allegedly became the first Westerner to shake hands, Grant recommended that a joint commission be formed to establish whether China or Japan held sovereignty over the islands. Japan annexed the entire archipelago shortly after Grant's return home. Nevertheless, the event marked a more prominent role for the United States, not only internationally, but more specifically in terms of playing a more protective and helping role in terms of the future of China.

Rutherford B. Hayes

The previous century of Sino-American relation had seen active Federalist, Whig, and Republican involvement in China while the Democratic Party had largely expressed passive disinterest. This began to change with the administration of Rutherford B. Hayes from 1877 to 1881, during which time a generation of unrestricted Chinese immigration transformed Democratic disinterest into vehement opposition.

The movement of Chinese people across the Pacific had begun in earnest shortly after the discovery of gold in California. While several hundred arrived in 1848 and 1849, by 1852 this number had climbed to over 20,000. Only a generation later, people of Chinese descent accounted for ten percent of the entire population of California, a level that holds constant to the modern day. As the gold rush dried up, however, the Chinese immigrants began to be employed on the railroads that were quickly growing across the region. From 1866 to 1869 the Central Pacific Railroad alone employed 10,000 Chinese workers.

Fears of this alien culture with its non-Western philosophy were augmented by the various financial panics of the 1870s. The animosity even erupted in a number of riots throughout California. On October 24, 1871, allegedly in response to the shooting of a white police officer, a large-scale riot broke out in the Chinese quarter of Los Angeles. In what one East Coast newspaper termed "a disgraceful crusade," the mob hanged or killed upwards of twenty Chinese residents and attempted to burn most of the section of the town to the ground.[133]

Denis Kearney, a recent Irish immigrant who only moved to California around 1873, became an outspoken critic of the influx of Chinese. His following soon grew and by the end of the decade he formally organized it into the Workingmen's Party of California. Followers of the group were largely concerned with the economic impact of the Chinese rather than cultural or political issues, in keeping with the more famous Know-Nothing party of the 1830s. Kearney was infamous for recommending violence as a solution to the "Chinese problem", and was arrested on a number of occasions. His influence was significant for over a decade, with a later newspaper referring to him as "very nearly dictator of California."[134]

Democratic fears of Chinese immigration had first combined with Republican concerns at the end of Grant's administration over the virtual enslavement of Chinese men and women. As previously mentioned, President Grant had sought action from

Congress regarding the continuing trade in Chinese workers across the Pacific during his Fifth Annual Message in 1873. A little over a year later the House and Senate pieced together the Page Act, sponsored by Republican Congressman Horace Page of California. The legislation increased fines and proposed jail time for anyone attempting to import Chinese laborers into the country against their will. Furthermore, it set up strict entry requirements for females in an effort to cut back on prostitution. By 1870, around sixty-one percent of all Chinese women in California worked as prostitutes, servicing the massively skewed male population that had migrated to the state.[135] Despite the perhaps noble aims of the various Republican legislators who signed on to the law, others hoped to use it to simply reduce the presence of Chinese in the nation by eliminating the chance for them to establish families and gain citizenship for their children under the Fourteenth Amendment.

Yet this minor but notable victory was not enough for Kearney and other likeminded Democrats. Following a speech by several members of the fledgling socialist party outside of city hall in San Francisco in July 1877, a small riot broke out among citizens disconcerted with the speakers' lack of resolve to address the issue of the Chinese. After two days of trouble, the deaths of four Chinese, and the destruction of over $100,000 worth of property, order was finally restored to the city thanks to the efforts of the police and city fathers. In fact, it was this event and the failure of the socialist party to actively deal with the issue of the Chinese which led Kearney to formally establish his Workingmen's Party of California.

Kearney's rhetoric and organizational skills allowed his group to even play a role in the 1878 California Constitutional Convention. Article XIX of the adopted document, the culmination of their efforts, was aimed at restricting the immigration and rights of the Chinese:

Section 1. The Legislature shall prescribe all necessary regulations for the protection of the State, and the counties, cities, and towns thereof, from the burdens and evils arising from the presence of aliens who are or may become vagrants, paupers, mendicants, criminals, or invalids afflicted with contagious or infectious diseases, and from aliens otherwise dangerous or detrimental to the well-being or peace of the State, and to impose conditions upon which persons may reside in the State, and to provide the means and mode of their removal from the State, upon failure or refusal to comply with such conditions; provided, that nothing contained in this section shall be construed to impair or limit the power of the Legislature to pass such police laws or other regulations as it may deem necessary.

Section. 2. No corporation now existing or hereafter formed under the laws of this State, shall, after the adoption of this Constitution, employ directly or indirectly, in any capacity, any Chinese or Mongolian. The Legislature shall pass such laws as may be necessary to enforce this provision.

Section. 3. No Chinese shall be employed on any State, county, municipal, or other public work, except in punishment for crime.

Section. 4. The presence of foreigners, ineligible to become citizens of the United States is declared to be dangerous to the well-being of the State, and the Legislature shall discourage their immigration by all the means within its power. Asiatic coolieism is a form of human slavery, and is forever prohibited in this State, and all contracts for coolie labor shall be void. All companies or corporations, whether formed in this country or any foreign country, for the importation of such labor, shall be subject to such penalties as the Legislature may prescribe. The Legislature shall delegate all necessary power to the incorporated cities and towns of this State for the removal of Chinese without the limits of such cities and towns, or for their location within prescribed portions of those limits, and it shall also provide the necessary legislation to prohibit the introduction into this State of Chinese after the adoption of this Constitution. This section shall be enforced by appropriate legislation.

That same year at meeting in Toledo, Ohio, the Greenback Labor Party for the first time included as a key component of its platform complete opposition to Chinese immigration.

President Hayes could do little regarding the growing animosity towards the Chinese on the West Coast, but he did do his best to counter it on a national level. While not as famous as his veto of the controversial Bland-Allison Act, Hayes also refused to pass a piece of legislation restricting the shipping of Chinese immigrants. The Democratic Congress had cobbled together a bill which sought to limit the number of Chinese that could be brought to the West Coast onboard a ship to only fifteen per vessel, a far cry from the hundreds of Irishmen that had transited the Atlantic on each boat a generation before. "As this number was not fixed in any proportion to the size or tonnage of the vessel or by any consideration of the safety or accommodation of these passengers, the simple purpose and effect of the enactment were to repress this immigration to an extent falling but little short of its absolute exclusion."[136]

Unlike his veto of the Bland-Allison Act, Hayes' decision was not overturned by Congress. Hayes couched his veto in the notion that any such piece of legislation would be a unilateral abrogation of the Burlingame Treaty with China which had specifically allowed for immigration.

"I am convinced that, whatever urgency might in any quarter or by any interest be supposed to require an instant suppression of further immigration from China, no reasons can require the immediate withdrawal of our treaty protection of the Chinese already in this country, and no circumstances can tolerate an exposure of our citizens in China, merchants or missionaries, to the consequences of so sudden an abrogation of their treaty protection."[137]

The Democratic Party's reaction to the veto was overwhelmingly hostile. A move was made to impeach the president, which was defeated only by the Republicans refusing to vote, thus depriving the session of its necessary quorum.

Yet public opinion was slowly turning against the views of the earlier generation of Republicans. The same year that he vetoed the Democrats' attempt to restrict the immigration of Chinese labor, Hayes himself began to address the issue. In his Third Annual Message to Congress, delivered on December 1, 1879, the president stated that, "The Government of China has signified its willingness to consider the question of the emigration of its subjects to the United States with a dispassionate fairness and to cooperate in such measures as may tend to prevent injurious consequences to the United States. The negotiations are still proceeding, and will be pressed with diligence."[138] With the establishment of the first permanent Chinese embassy in Washington in September 1878 by Yung Wing, communication between the two nations had become much more regular.

Hayes dispatched a new minister to China in 1880, James B. Angell, along with William H. Trescott of South Carolina. Over the summer and fall of that year, Angell and his Qing counterparts cobbled together a treaty aimed at reducing Chinese immigration into the United States. By November 1880, the Angell Treaty was finalized in Peking and in May 1881 was officially signed by President Garfield. Overall, the treaty was a compromise between the open, unlimited immigration of the Burlingame Treaty and the complete moratorium sought by West Coast Democrats. Article I of the treaty stated that:

Whenever in the opinion of the Government of the United States, the coming of Chinese laborers to the United States, or their residence therein, affects or threatens to affect the interests of that country, or to endanger the good order of the said country or of any locality within the territory thereof, the Government of China agrees that the Government of the United States may regulate, limit, or suspend such coming or residence, but may not absolutely prohibit it. The limitation or suspension shall be reasonable and shall apply only to Chinese who may go to the United States as laborers, other classes not being included in the limitations. Legislation taken in regard to Chinese laborers will be of such a character only as is necessary to enforce the regulation, limitation, or suspension of immigration, and immigrants shall not be subject to personal maltreatment or abuse.

The exclusion of white collar workers, professionals and students once again served to show that for Hayes and his party, this was a labor and economic issue rather than a cultural or racial one.

Article II of the treaty sought to reinforce the various provisions of the earlier Burlingame Treaty aimed at protecting those Chinese who had settled here:

Chinese subjects, whether proceeding to the United States as teachers, students, merchants or from curiosity, together with their body and household servants, and Chinese laborers who are now in the United States shall be allowed to go and come of their own free will and accord, and shall be accorded all the rights, privileges, immunities, and exemptions which are accorded to the citizens and subjects of the most favored nation.

A second treaty adopted at the same time also gave China the same tonnage duties as America's primary trading partner, the United Kingdom, and also once again outlawed the opium trade between either country. Truly compromise documents, these treaties did not completely betray the earlier ideals of Burlingame, nor did they allow the continued unabated flow of Chinese laborers into the United States. The *Helena Weekly Herald* expressed the view of many Democrats along the West Coast when it said that, "the new treaty on the subject of immigration will be entirely satisfactory to the Pacific Coast sentiment."[139] Yet, the same article also hinted at what was very soon to become reality, saying that the Angell Treaty "broadly clears the way for Congressional action to restrict immigration of Chinese laborers *to any extent* (italics added)."[140]

Garfield and Arthur
Overall, Rutherford B. Hayes presided over both the seizure in 1878 of Congress by Democrats for the first time since 1858 and the associated rise in anti-Chinese bias and legislation. Though Republicans would hold onto the White House in 1880 and once again secure control over the Senate, the Democrats would maintain a hold on the House until 1895 and continued their focus on reducing both trade with, and immigration from, China.

James A. Garfield gave tacit approval to the Angell Treaty in his acceptance speech in July 1880:

"The recent movement of the Chinese to our Pacific coast partakes but little of the qualities of such an emigration, either in its purposes or its result. It is too much like an importation to be welcomed without restriction; too much like an invasion to be looked upon without solicitude. We cannot consent to allow any form of servile labor to be introduced among us, under the guise of immigration. Recognizing the gravity of this subject, the present administration, supported by Congress, has sent to China a commission of distinguished citizens, for the purpose of securing such a modification of the existing treaty as will prevent the evils likely to arise from the present situation. It is confidently believed that these diplomatic negotiations will be successful, without the loss of commercial intercourse between the two powers, which promises great increase of reciprocal trade and the enlargement of our markets. Should these efforts fail, it will be the duty of Congress to investigate the evils already felt, and prevent their increase by such restrictions as, without violence or injustice, will place upon a sure foundation the peace of our communities, and the freedom and dignity of labor."[141]

Yet an additional letter which emerged at the same time seemed to show a different side of the candidate.

On October 20, 1880, two weeks before the date of the presidential election, Garfield was delivered a telegraph asking for comment upon a letter he had written back in January on the issue of Chinese immigration. *Truth*, a New York penny periodical had published what amounted to a hit piece on the candidate, a letter that he had supposedly written taking a far different stance on the issue. "The question of employees is only a question of private and corporate economy, and individuals or companys [sic] have the right to buy labor where they can get it cheapest. We have a treaty with the Chinese government that should be religiously kept... until our great manufacturing and corporate interests are conserved in the matter of labor."

Despite being written on House stationary and bearing his signature, it was quickly made evident that the Morey Letter, as it was termed, was a clumsy forgery. Democrats dispatched thousands of copies of it to Oregon and California, hoping to swing voters in those states away from the Republican Party. Though Garfield's party did end up losing California for the first of only two times before 1916, the loss of these five electoral votes was hardly felt in the overall election. Nor was this the only attempt by the Democrats to tie Garfield into the pre-Angell thinking of the Republicans. In March 1881, the *Stark County Democrat* published an article claiming that, "Garfield will take the Chinese under his wing. In Congress he was always the friend of the Chinese, and in his inaugural he dilates on the importance of general education in this country, and in this he does not except the 'heaten Chinee'."[142]

The importance of the issue actually arises in the lengths to which Republicans went to deny the allegations, or more actively tie themselves, to limits on Chinese immigration. Garfield and his people quickly published his acceptance letter, running it side by side in newspapers to not only demonstrate the differences in handwriting but to also drive home his devotion to limiting mass immigration of Chinese laborers to the United States. John Isaacs Davenport went so far as to write a detailed book on the letter in an attempt to debunk it, though it was not published until 1884.

While his official signature was placed on the Angell Treaty on May 9, 1881, Garfield did little else in connection with China itself. He was subsequently shot only seven weeks later while waiting to board a train at the B&O Railway Station in the capital district. During the agonizing two months that followed, the Chinese minister to the United States, Chin Lan Pin, arrived at the White House in full ceremonial dress to visit Mrs. Garfield and deliver a formal letter of condolence and well-wishes from the Qing Emperor.

Garfield's death brought Chester A. Arthur to the presidency, a man known more for his rise through the corrupt political machine of New York than for his dealings with China. Yet his presidency was to see the culmination of efforts by the Democratic Party to stop the migration of Chinese people to America.

The Democratic Congress moved in 1882 to pass a bill that would practically end Chinese immigration to America for twenty years. The initial piece of legislation called for a twenty-year moratorium on Chinese immigration into the United States, largely predicated on the year-old Angell Treaty, whose Article I provision, as many Republicans feared, was utilized to restrict the arrival of laborers. The various economic and social concerns of the Democrats along the West Coast were used to justify the section of the agreement which allowed for this modification "...whenever in the opinion of the Government of the United States, the coming of Chinese laborers to the United States, or their residence therein, affects or threatens to affect the interests of that country, or to endanger the good order of the said country or of any locality within the territory thereof."

In fact, for many residents of California the already harsh bill did not go far enough. "In order to bring about a radical change in the Pacific coast labor market a law would have been needed which provided for the deportation of the Chinese now domiciled on the coast."[143] What had once been a minority opinion among some elements around San Francisco Bay and Los Angeles had now achieved a considerable level of national acceptance. "The anti-Chinese demonstration on Saturday has probably satisfied Congress that the opposition to Chinese immigration on this coast is not confined to the unthinking element of society, but is endorsed by the community generally."[144]

Yet despite the support the measure received in both Congress and among many segments of American society, there still existed a number of Republican voices who opposed the bill. One of the most important was George F. Seward, nephew of the more famous William H. Seward. The younger Seward had served in various diplomatic roles in China since 1861, and had been made the official minister to that nation in 1876. It was he who had actually been tasked by Hayes with negotiating with the Qing court what would eventually become the Chinese Exclusion Act. Due to his stringent opposition to the idea, Seward worked on a modified version of the proposal, eventually convincing Peking to agree to prevent various unwanted groups such as the sick, poor or prostitutes from migrating to America. However, many within the State Department disagreed with Seward, and with rumors of corruption and financial irregularities surrounding his time in China, he was subsequently recalled by Hayes in 1880.

Senator George Frisbie Hoar, a Republican from Massachusetts, gave an impassioned speech on the Senate floor denouncing the bill and its intentions. He began his exhortation by reminding his fellow Congressmen that, "our people, 100 years ago, founded this nation upon the moral law, affirming that all men were equally derived from their creator."[145] Hoar went on to attack the law as abrogating the Burlingame and Angell treaties in a way that was inconsistent with international law and general decorum. He pointed out that, "China offers to modify the Burlingame treaty so as to permit the exclusion of prostitutes, criminals, diseased persons, and imported coolie laborers. This offer was rejected by our government and a treaty substituted which does permit the exclusion of the three first named classes, but only permits their exclusion of laborers."[146] Finally, Hoar challenged even the notion of a "Chinese problem", asserting that at present their immigration was dwindling and they represented no more than, "the 500[147] part of the whole population."[147] To him, the treaty was, "nothing less than the legalization of racial discrimination."

Yet the full support of Democrats and a number of Republicans allowed the bill to pass through Congress. President Arthur almost immediately vetoed the legislation, drafting a lengthy message to the House and Senate as to why he chose to do so. Much like Hoar, Arthur largely focused on the idea that the passage of this bill both violated the pre-existing treaty and showed bad faith to the Chinese government:

"A nation is justified in repudiating its treaty obligations only when they are in conflict with great paramount interests. Even then all possible reasonable means for modifying or changing those obligations by mutual agreement should be exhausted before resorting to the supreme fight of refusal to comply with them. These rules have governed the United States in their past intercourse with other powers as one of the family of nations. I am persuaded that if Congress can feel that this act violates the faith of the nation as pledged to China it will concur with me in rejecting this particular mode of regulating Chinese immigration, and will endeavor to find another which shall meet the expectations of the people of the United States without coming in conflict with the rights of China."[148]

Arthur went on to highlight the many accomplishments of the Chinese who had immigrated to America.

"No one can say that the country has not profited by their work. They were largely instrumental in constructing the railways which connect the Atlantic with the Pacific. The States of the Pacific Slope are full of evidences of their industry. Enterprises profitable alike to the capitalist and to the laborer of Caucasian origin would have lain dormant but for them. A time has now come when it is supposed that they are not needed, and when it is thought by Congress and by those most acquainted with the subject that it is best to try to get along without them. There may, however, be other sections of the country where this species of labor may be advantageously employed without interfering with the laborers of our own race."[149]

Finally, the president urged Democrats and residents of the Pacific coast to look towards the future, suggesting that the temporary gains to be acquired from banning a few thousand Chinese workers would pale in comparison to the advantages that could be garnered over the next few centuries from strong trade with East Asia.

"Experience has shown that the trade of the East is the key to national wealth and influence. The opening of China to the commerce of the whole world has benefited no section of it more than the States of our own Pacific Slope. The State of California, and its great maritime port especially, have reaped enormous advantages from this source...San Francisco has before it an incalculable future if our friendly and amicable relations with Asia remain undisturbed. It needs no argument to show that the policy which we now propose to adopt must have a direct tendency to repel Oriental nations from us and to drive their trade and commerce into more friendly lands."[150]

Only two days after Arthur penned his veto message, the Senate took up a vote to pass the bill over his protest. However, the test vote fell short of the required two-thirds majority with 29 voting for its passage and 21 opposing it. Of those Democrats who voted for the measure, all 23 were in the affirmative, joined by only six Republicans. The *New Ulm Weekly Review* praised the moral strength and stopping-power of Arthur, crediting him with, "a trait of character which very few had given him credit for possessing."[151]

Yet Arthur was far from an ideologue on the "Chinese Question". Even his stringent veto message was softened by a final sentence. "It may be that the great and paramount interest of protecting our labor from Asiatic competition may justify us in a permanent adoption of this policy; but it is wiser in the first place to make a shorter experiment, with a view hereafter of maintaining permanently only such features as time and experience may commend."[152]

A new version of the bill was introduced to the House on April 12, 1882, unsurprisingly by Horace F. Page, the Republican congressman from California who had produced the Page Act in 1875. This amended law included a few key changes to the original legislation, most notably reducing the time period of exclusion from 20 years to 10. After overwhelmingly passing through Congress, President Arthur finally signed the bill into law on May 8, 1882. Though he had made his case eloquently and forcefully, he knew he lacked the political or popular will to stand in its way much longer.

President Arthur also became one of the first American leaders to address the prospect of American capital being used in China to fund the growth of industry. In his Third Annual Message to Congress he expressed concern that, "The transference to China of American capital for the employment there of Chinese labor would in effect inaugurate a competition for the control of markets now supplied by our home industries."[153] The view fit in well with both the Democrat's fear of losing jobs to the Chinese as well as classic Republican view on tariffs and the protection of domestic industry.

Later Republicans

The changing attitudes of the Republican Party towards China was made evident in its 1884 platform. The recent laws passed against Chinese immigration were reinterpreted as being in keeping with traditional Republican views against slavery:

> "The Republican party, having its birth in a hatred of slave labor and a desire that all men may be truly free and equal, is unalterably opposed to placing our workingmen in competition with any form of servile labor, whether at home or abroad. In this spirit, we denounce the importation of contract labor, whether from Europe or Asia, as an offense against the spirit of American institutions; and we pledge ourselves to sustain the present law restricting Chinese immigration, and to provide such further legislation as is necessary to carry out its purposes."[154]

Benjamin Harrison likewise gave a tepid level of acceptance to the new norm in his letter accepting the nomination as presidential candidate for the Republican Party in 1888. "The objections to Chinese immigration are distinctive and conclusive, and are now so generally accepted as such that the question has passed entirely beyond the stage of argument."[155]

Perhaps due to these changes, the Republicans were able to handily sweep the Pacific states in the 1884 election. California, especially, returned to the Republican column by a large margin, voting for James G. Blaine and against northern Democrat Grover Cleveland. Yet despite these victories, Cleveland was able to secure victory for himself in the election and his party was able to maintain its hold on the House and come within striking distance of seizing the Senate.

An additional series of anti-Chinese riots at various locations along the Pacific coast in 1885 and 1886 only further convinced Cleveland and his party of the need to permanently remove the Chinese presence from this country. Not surprisingly, Democrats quickly moved to pass another series of laws aimed at curtailing the presence of the Chinese in America. Fearing for the safety of its citizens, the Qing court made the first move, requesting talks between the two nations in August 1886. By January of the next year, Charles Harvey Denby had begun negotiating on behalf of Cleveland.

The demands of the Democratic Party were quite extreme – a moratorium on all migration for thirty years and a promise that any Chinese who returned home would not be allowed to ever come back to America. Predictably appalled by the demands, the Qing court was in no position to anger the United States having only just emerged from a disastrous war with the French. A year later, on January 1, 1888, both sides agreed in principle to the Bayard-Zhang Treaty under which the Chinese agreed to halt all immigration for twenty years as well as to limit those Chinese living in America who were allowed to return home. Yet the terms proved to be a bitter pill for the Chinese public and Chinese Americans to swallow. Faced with few prospects for obtaining a Qing signature to the treaty, Congress acted unilaterally and on October 1, 1888, President Cleveland signed into law the Scott Act. Championed by William Lawrence Scott of Pennsylvania, the chair of the Democratic National Committee, the bill effectively forbad Chinese residents from ever re-entering the country if they left. Despite several legal challenges to the law by Chinese residents, most notably Chae Chan Ping v United States, even the Republican-dominated Supreme Court upheld the right of the government to regulate and restrict settlement in the nation. All of this culminated in the Geary Act of 1892 which required the use of internal passports to provide identification and prove residency for all Chinese in the United States.

Overall, the period from the presidency of Lincoln to the second term of Cleveland saw a curious shift in relations between the two countries. Despite growing interest in the modernization of the Qing Dynasty by Burlingame and other Republicans, the corruption in the court and the untenable position of the empire in the age of New Imperialism dashed hopes for this project. Likewise, declining bilateral trade combined with increased cross-Pacific migration to both concern New England Republicans and enrage Northern Democrats. It would take the advent of American imperialism in the 1890s, the downfall of the Qing Dynasty and the emergence of America on the world stage during the World Wars to once again spark Republican involvement in China.

THE REPUBLICAN PARTY AND THE RISE OF CHINA

5

RE-ENGAGING CHINA

SINO-AMERICAN RELATIONS FROM 1896-1949

REPUBLICAN ENGAGEMENT in China was slow to rekindle from the 1890s through the early part of the twentieth century. In keeping with the imperialist thinking of the day, the interests of the United States in China were viewed as a combination of economic opportunities, security fears and notions of the White Mans' Burden. Just as Democratic fears of the Yellow Peril restricted the acceptance of Chinese into America, so the corruption and incompetence of the Qing court discouraged American government involvement and private industry investment in the modernization of the empire. Yet the rise of William McKinley and the Open Door Policy inaugurated by his secretary of state, John Hay, marked the return of Republicans to their original philosophy of free and open commerce and interaction with China.

William McKinley

The election of William McKinley to the presidency in 1896 saw not only the return of the Republican Party to the White House, but the emergence of a number of other factors which would prove to be ideal for the growth of trade and cooperation between the two countries. One of these factors was certainly the return of the Republican Party to power in Congress. While McKinley himself had voted in favor of the Chinese Exclusion Act, the new speaker of the house, Thomas Brackett Reed, had staunchly opposed it.

The slow, violent decline of the Qing Dynasty necessitated some sort of intervention by the United States in order to protect its citizens. As early as his Second Annual Message to Congress in December 1898, McKinley made note of the frequent riots in various Chinese cities and specifically cited the attack on an American Methodist bishop, Earl Cranston, a month previously. Over the course of the next year, these riots and attacks increased, prompting the president to dispatch a contingent of Marines to guard American interests in Peking over the winter of 1899-1900. "The interests of our citizens in that vast Empire have not been neglected during the past year. Adequate protection has been secured for our missionaries and some injuries to their property have been redressed."[156]

Holding true to his anti-imperialist sentiments as well as more traditional Republican attitudes towards China, McKinley withdrew the Marines once order was restored. Yet only a few months later, the full fury of the Boxer Rebellion erupted in northern China. The Boxer siege of the international legations in Peking was mentioned by McKinley in his acceptance of the Republican nomination in July 1900.

"The sudden and terrible crisis in China calls for the gravest consideration, and you will not expect from me now any further expression than to say that my best efforts shall be given to the Immediate purpose of protecting the lives of our citizens who are in peril, with the ultimate object of the peace and welfare of China, the safeguarding of all our treaty rights, and the maintenance of those principles of impartial intercourse to which the civilized world is pledged."[157]

The president duly dispatched American troops to take part in the ill-fated Seymour Expedition which left Tianjin in early June with the aim of reaching Peking and relieving the foreigners trapped in the Legation Quarter. They were forced to retreat, and it was another month before a better-organized force fought their way through and lifted the famous 55-day siege on August 14. McKinley proclaimed a day of thanksgiving to be nationally celebrated on November 29, 1900, for the numerous blessings which he felt had descended upon the nation that year, including the fact that "the lives of our official representatives and many of our people in China have been marvelously preserved."[158]

The increasing industrialization of the United States that occurred in the 1890s and the growth of global trade both lent themselves to closer economic interactions with China. In 1898, McKinley advised Congress that,

"In this relation, as showing the volume and value of our exchanges with China and the peculiarly favorable conditions which exist for their expansion in the normal course of trade, I refer to the communication addressed to the Speaker of the House of Representatives by the Secretary of the Treasury on the 14th of last June, with its accompanying letter of the Secretary of State, recommending an appropriation for a commission to study the commercial and industrial conditions in the Chinese Empire and report as to the opportunities for and obstacles to the enlargement of markets in China for the raw products and manufactures of the United States. Action was not taken thereon during the late session. I cordially urge that the recommendation receive at your hands the consideration which its importance and timeliness merit."[159]

McKinley renewed his request more emphatically the next year.

"American capital has sought and found various opportunities of competing to carry out the internal improvements which the Imperial Government is wisely encouraging, and to develop the natural resources of the Empire. Our trade with China has continued to grow, and our commercial rights under existing treaties have been everywhere maintained during the past year, as they will be in the future. The extension of the area open to international foreign settlement at Shanghai and the opening of the ports of Nanking, Tsing-tao (Kiao chao), and Ta-lien-wan to foreign trade and settlement will doubtless afford American enterprise additional facilities and new fields, of which it will not be slow to take advantage. In my message to Congress of December 5, 1898, 1 urged that the recommendation which had been made to the Speaker of the House of Representatives by the Secretary of the Treasury on the 14th of June, 1898, for an appropriation for a commission to study the commercial and industrial conditions in the Chinese Empire... I now renew this recommendation, as the importance of the subject has steadily grown since it was first submitted to you, and no time should be lost in studying for ourselves the resources of this great field for American trade and enterprise."[160]

The president's call was partially in response to the efforts of the American China Development Company which had begun operating in East Asia in 1896. Among the many men involved in this enterprise were conservative Bourbon Democrat Calvin Brice of Ohio and Charles Denby, then the US Minister to China. Closely associated with the State Department during the administrations of Cleveland, McKinley and Roosevelt, the company focused most of its efforts on railroad projects. In 1898, it was granted the right to build and operate a line from Canton to Hankow over which it was to have sole control for fifty years. The project soon experienced difficulties, and by 1904 was all but dead. The State Department effectively cut ties with the American China Development Company that year and the Qing government canceled plans for the railroad. After a number of changes, J.P. Morgan bought a controlling share of the company in 1905 and at its urging, President Roosevelt dispatched former minister Conger to Peking in an effort to restart construction of the railway line.[161]

Anger over the Chinese Exclusion Act had resulted in a boycott in China of American goods which threatened to upset larger trade interests between the nations. Regardless of the ultimate failure of the ACDC to construct its railroad, it was the first major example of the direct involvement of the United States government in the modernization of China that had been envisioned by Burlingame a half century before.

McKinley himself, like many Republican leaders at the time and like many observers within China itself, saw the corrupt and decaying imperial monarchy as the primary reason for the backwardness of the empire.

"Our purposes should be pronounced in favor of such course as would hasten united action of the powers at Peking to promote the administrative reforms so greatly needed for strengthening the Imperial Government and maintaining the integrity of China, in which we believed the whole western world to be alike concerned. To these ends I caused to be addressed to the several powers occupying territory and maintaining spheres of influence in China the circular proposals of 1899, inviting from them declarations of their intentions and views as to the desirability of the adoption of measures insuring the benefits of equality of treatment of all foreign trade throughout China.

For the real culprits, the evil counselors who have misled the Imperial judgment and diverted the sovereign authority to their own guilty ends, full expiation becomes imperative within the rational limits of retributive Justice. Regarding this as the initial condition of an acceptable settlement between China and the powers, I said in my message of October 18 to the Chinese Emperor:

'I trust that negotiations may begin so soon as we and the other offended Governments shall be effectively satisfied of Your Majesty's ability and power to treat with just sternness the principal offenders, who are doubly culpable, not alone toward the foreigners, but toward Your Majesty, under whose rule the purpose of China to dwell in concord with the world had hitherto found expression in the welcome and protection assured to strangers.'"[162]

Perhaps the greatest advancement by the McKinley White House in terms of Sino-American relations was the Open Door Policy. William W. Rockhill, an expert on Sino-Tibetan languages and culture, had first proposed the idea to then Secretary of State John Hay in 1899. While Rockhill was certainly motivated by of a genuine concern for the territorial integrity and cultural survival of China to develop the concept of all nations freely trading in China with no claims on the nation itself, the past failure of the United States to acquire land there as well as fears for the safety of its recently purchased Philippines Territory drove the McKinley administration to take note of the policy. On September 6, 1899, Hay formally submitted the idea to President McKinley, who himself forwarded it to Congress in March of the following year. Only three months later, the Party itself included the notion as a plank of its platform for the 1900 election. "Every effort should be made to open and obtain new markets, especially in the Orient, and the Administration is warmly to be commended for its successful efforts to commit all trading and colonizing nations to the policy of the open door in China."

Following his victory in the 1900 contest against William Jennings Bryan, McKinley further acknowledge the new direction in Sino-American relations in his annual address to Congress. As with the efforts by previous presidents to connect the core tenets of the Chinese Exclusion Act to more traditional Republican ideals, so too did McKinley attempt to establish a distant lineage for the Open Door Policy:

"The United States from the earliest days of foreign intercourse with China had followed a policy of peace, omitting no occasions to testify good will, to further the extension of lawful trade, to respect the sovereignty of its Government, and to insure by all legitimate and kindly but earnest means the fullest measure of protection for the lives and property of our law-abiding citizens and for the exercise of their beneficent callings among the Chinese people."[163]

Theodore Roosevelt

The ascension to power of Teddy Roosevelt following the assassination of President McKinley in 1901 brought to the White House a man who was both interested in an active foreign policy and also young and energetic enough to carry it out. Yet his proactive approach would endanger the future of China and indirectly aid in the rise of Japanese imperialism in the region.

It was largely the outbreak of the Russo-Japanese War in 1904 that propelled Roosevelt and America more deeply into Chinese affairs. While American and British public opinion was supportive of Tokyo in the war, following as it did so closely upon the first Sino-Japanese War (1894-5) led the American government to fear Japan's expansionist approach. Early on in the war, in fact, Roosevelt and other world leaders moved to limit the scope of the conflict in an effort to respect Chinese territory. Russia had traditionally been an American ally, referred to at one point by Roosevelt himself as a beneficial civilizing and modernizing influence on the Qing Empire. "I feel that an immense boon to humanity has been conferred by... Russia when she expanded over Turkestan, and for the matter of that, over Manchuria. It was a hard task but a task for the benefit of the provinces taken... I am glad to see Russia expand in Asia."[164]

Apart from the pro-Russian sentiment that had dominated American foreign policy for years, fear of the rapid modernization of Japan was a more significant driver of Roosevelt's efforts to exert influence in the region. As the president had stated during his First Annual Message to Congress in 1901, "owing to the rapid growth of our power and our interests on the Pacific, whatever happens in China must be of the keenest national concern to us."[165]

In order to relieve American concerns, the Japanese likewise sought to portray themselves as a civilizing influence in China. In 1905 the *New York Times* published a speech by Prime Minister Katsura Taro in which he stated, "The introduction of the blessings of modern civilization into the East Asiatic countries, that is our Far Eastern policy... China and Korea are atrociously misgoverned. These conditions we will endeavor to correct." Katsura made sure to emphasize as well that his nation was simply following the example of both Britain and the United States.

In the end, Roosevelt mediated a treaty between both Russia and Japan that aimed to balance both powers in northeast Asia. Though Japan gained a more secure foothold in the Korean peninsula, the removal of Russia from Manchuria seemed to bode well for the continued integrity of the Qing empire. Perhaps predictably though, Japan soon began to play a more influential role in the internal politics of the waning Qing Dynasty. American officials largely blamed Japan for Chinese moves in 1905 to put an end to the US-backed Canton-Hankow Railroad. "Japan could have no more effective means in her play for the leadership among the yellow race of the Far East than by controlling the railroads of China."[166] In typical Roosevelt fashion, the president resorted to gunboat diplomacy to successfully end the boycott, anchoring the Asiatic Squadron off Shanghai as a show of force.

Roosevelt also oversaw American participation in the suppression of the Boxer Rebellion and the peace process that followed. In keeping with the Republican concept of the Open Door Policy, he discouraged the territorial partitioning of China by the victors. Various measures were implemented to ensure the safety of foreigners in the empire as well as to punish some of those responsible for the anti-foreigner uprising. A number of provisions of the treaty, while appearing to aid the foreign powers, also benefited the development of China. A prime example was the requirement that the Qing court "participate financially in the work of bettering the water approaches to Shanghai and to Tientsin, the centers of foreign trade in central and northern China, and an international conservancy board, in which the Chinese Government is largely represented, has been provided for the improvement of the Shanghai River and the control of its navigation."[167] These civil works progress would increase not only the trade of China, but would allow for the more rapid entrance and diffusion of foreign technology and ideas. Tariffs on foreign goods flowing into the nation were also reduced, lowering prices for Chinese consumers and limiting the effects of famine. Roosevelt reiterated his party's view during his First Annual Message to Congress:

"During these troubles our Government has unswervingly advocated moderation, and has materially aided in bringing about an adjustment which tends to enhance the welfare of China and to lead to a more beneficial intercourse between the Empire and the modern world; while in the critical period of revolt and massacre we did our full share in safe-guarding life and property, restoring order, and vindicating the national interest and honor. It behooves us to continue in these paths, doing what lies in our power to foster feelings of good will, and leaving no effort untried to work out the great policy of full and fair intercourse between China and the nations, on a footing of equal rights and advantages to all. We advocate the «open door» with all that it implies; not merely the procurement of enlarged commercial opportunities on the coasts, but access to the interior by the waterways with which China has been so extraordinarily favored. Only by bringing the people of China into peaceful and friendly community of trade with all the peoples of the earth can the work now auspiciously begun be carried to fruition."[168]

Commercial relations between the two nations still remained a priority for Republicans, with Roosevelt pushing new negotiations with the Qing in 1903. The resulting Conger Treaty of October 8, 1903, not only reinforced the majority of elements from previous treaties, but removed all internal tariffs on goods transiting throughout the empire and opened up additional ports and cities in Manchuria to American business. Yet Roosevelt once again recognized the need for political and internal reform before these developments would bear fruit for China: "The full measure of development which our commerce may rightfully expect can hardly be looked for until the settlement of the present abnormal state of things in the Empire; but the foundation for such development has at last been laid."[169]

During the election of 1904, Roosevelt and the Republicans doubled down on their more active foreign policy in general and their involvement in China in particular. To that effect, the party platform contained the following plank: "Our great interests and our growing commerce in the Orient render the condition of China of high importance to the United States. We cordially commend the policy pursued in that direction by the administrations of President McKinley and President Roosevelt." As part of this, Roosevelt saw to involve the country once more in the modernization of China. In order to increase trade between the two countries and bring the economy of China into line with the modern world, the president dispatched a commission to Peking in 1905. It helped achieve the goal of slowly moving the country from the silver standard over to the gold standard which had only recently been adopted by the United States during the administration of McKinley.

Roosevelt also sought to turn the Boxer Protocol into a way to push China forward. Rather than accept its share of the indemnity owed by the Qing to the foreign governments, the president, upon the urging of numerous ministers and educational leaders, proposed to Congress that a portion of the money be remitted back to China. Yet rather than simply give the money back to the Qing or use it for projects preferred by the Chinese, the money would fund a number of scholarships and educational programs in order to train young, promising Qing students in the United States "This Nation should help in every practicable way in the education of the Chinese people, so that the vast and populous Empire of China may gradually adapt itself to modern conditions. One way of doing this is by promoting the coming of Chinese students to this country and making it attractive to them to take courses at our universities and higher educational institutions. Our educators should, so far as possible, take concerted action toward this end."[170] One of the education programs which grew out of this money was the famed Tsinghua University in Beijing. The school was to serve as a preparatory school from which distinguished students would transfer to American universities to finish their education. Some of the more notable graduates of the college include Hu Jintao, Xi Jinping, Zhu Rongji, Qian Zhongshu, and Min Chueh Chang, one of the inventors of the modern birth control pill.

The Senate approved the measure in 1908 and, thanks to subsequent efforts by John Dewey and Paul Monroe, the China Institute was formerly established in New York in 1926 following a second remission of Chinese debt from the Boxer Protocol. Thousands of students and many future leaders of China would directly benefit from this decision, with the Institute itself being led for thirty-seven years, auspiciously, by a direct descendant of the philosopher Mencius, Meng Chih.

Roosevelt couched part of his most famous accomplishment, the construction of the Panama Canal, in terms of its impact on Sino-American relations as well. As early as 1884, Chester A. Arthur had proposed the idea for a Nicaraguan canal to a lame duck Congress, stating that:

"It will bring the European grain markets of demand within easy distance of our Pacific States, and will give to the manufacturers on the Atlantic seaboard economical access to the cities of China, thus breaking down the barrier which separates the principal manufacturing centers of the United States from the markets of the vast population of Asia, and placing the Eastern States of the Union for all purposes of trade midway between Europe and Asia. In point of time the gain for sailing vessels would be great, amounting from New York to San Francisco to a saving of seventy-five days; to Hong Kong, of twenty-seven days; to Shanghai, of thirty-four days, and to Callao, of fifty-two days."[171]

In characteristic fashion, Congress moved exceptionally slowly on the proposal, with little to no concrete progress for the next sixteen years. Republicans once again broached the topic in their platform for the 1900 election, from whence it became a mainstay in the subsequent Roosevelt administration and through to its completion over a decade later.

Roosevelt also became the first Republican president in a generation to seek to modify the Chinese Exclusion Act, taking to task some of the more stringent components of it. During his Fifth Message to Congress in 1905, the president started by repeating the standard Republican message of eliminating coolie labor as a means by which to benefit the Chinese: "Not only is it to the interest of this country to keep them out, but the Chinese authorities do not desire that they should be admitted."[172] He then called for a return to the Angell Treaty era where non-Chinese laborers were welcomed into the nation:

"But in the effort to carry out the policy of excluding Chinese laborers, Chinese coolies, grave injustice and wrong have been done by this Nation to the people of China, and therefore ultimately to this Nation itself. Chinese students, business and professional men of all kinds--not only merchants, but bankers, doctors, manufacturers, professors, travelers, and the like--should be encouraged to come here, and treated on precisely the same footing that we treat students, business men, travelers, and the like of other nations. Our laws and treaties should be framed, not so as to put these people in the excepted classes, but to state that we will admit all Chinese, except Chinese of the coolie class."[173]

Roosevelt further couched his proposal in terms of the Open Door Policy as well as hinting at economic or social repercussions that could result from the continued exclusion and mistreatment of the Chinese:

"As a people we have talked much of the open door in China, and we expect, and quite rightly intend to insist upon, justice being shown us by the Chinese. But we cannot expect to receive equity unless we do equity. We cannot ask the Chinese to do to us what we are unwilling to do to them. They would have a perfect right to exclude our laboring men if our laboring men threatened to come into their country in such numbers as to jeopardize the well-being of the Chinese population; and as, mutatis mutandis, these were the conditions with which Chinese immigration actually brought this people face to face, we had and have a perfect right, which the Chinese Government in no way contests, to act as we have acted in the matter of restricting coolie immigration. That this right exists for each country was explicitly acknowledged in the last treaty between the two countries. But we must treat the Chinese student, traveler, and business man in a spirit of the broadest justice and courtesy if we expect similar treatment to be accorded to our own people of similar rank who go to China. Much trouble has come during the past Summer from the organized boycott against American goods which has been started in China. The main factor in producing this boycott has been the resentment felt by the students and business people of China, by all the Chinese leaders, against the harshness of our law toward educated Chinamen of the professional and business classes."[174]

As much as Roosevelt sought to help in the reform China and reduce the debilitating effect of both American domestic policy and European and Japanese territorial expansion towards the nation, he ultimately placed much of the blame for China's dire situation squarely on the shoulders of the Qing court. This was largely in keeping with his belief in individual responsibility for success. Roosevelt in fact referenced the deleterious foreign policy of the Qing in 1908 as part of his appeal to Congress to fund the construction of four battleships.

"They are blind to what has happened in China... For centuries China has cultivated the very spirit which our own peace-at-any-price men wish this country to adopt. For centuries China has refused to provide military forces and has treated the career of the soldier as inferior in honor and regard to the career of the merchant or of the man of letters. There never has been so large an empire which for so long a time has so resolutely proceeded on the theory of doing away with what is called 'militarism.' Whether the result has been happy in internal affairs I need not discuss; all the advanced reformers and farsighted patriots in the Chinese Empire are at present seeking (I may add, with our hearty good will) for a radical and far-reaching reform in internal affairs. In external affairs the policy has resulted in various other nations now holding large portions of Chinese territory, while there is a very acute fear in China lest the Empire, because of its defenselessness, be exposed to absolute dismemberment, and its well-wishers are able to help it only in a small measure, because no nation can help any other unless that other can help itself."[175]

China likewise became a model for Roosevelt of the failure of a nation to properly conserve resources.

"All serious students of the question are aware of the great damage that has been done in the Mediterranean countries of Europe, Asia, and Africa by deforestation. The similar damage that has been done in Eastern Asia is less well known. A recent investigation into conditions in North China by Mr. Frank N. Meyer, of the Bureau of Plant Industry of the United States Department of Agriculture, has incidentally furnished in very striking fashion proof of the ruin that comes from reckless deforestation of mountains, and of the further fact that the damage once done may prove practically irreparable. So important are these investigations that I herewith attach as an appendix to my message certain photographs showing present conditions in China. They show in vivid fashion the appalling desolation, taking the shape of barren mountains and gravel and sand-covered plains, which immediately follows and depends upon the deforestation of the mountains. Not many centuries ago the country of northern China was one of the most fertile and beautiful spots in the entire world, and was heavily forested. We know this not only from the old Chinese records, but from the accounts given by the traveler, Marco Polo.

This ruthless destruction of the forests in northern China has brought about, or has aided in bringing about, desolation... In northern China the mountains are now such as are shown by the accompanying photographs, absolutely barren peaks… the Mongol Desert is practically extending eastward over northern China. The climate has changed and is still changing…Almost all the rivers of northern China have become uncontrollable, and very dangerous to the dwellers along their banks, as a direct result of the destruction of the forests. The journey from Pekin to Jehol shows in melancholy fashion how the soil has been washed away from whole valleys, so that they have been converted into deserts."[176]

After a long diatribe on the damage caused by the Qing to their own territory, Roosevelt warned Congress that, "In northern China this disastrous process has gone on so long and has proceeded so far that no complete remedy could be applied."[177]

William Howard Taft

Taft's time in the White House saw a continuation of the now decades-old Open Door Policy. In keeping with the actions of previous presidents, much of this focused on the territorial integrity and economic openness of the nation. As Taft summarized it in his First Annual Message to Congress in 1909, "In the Far East, this Government preserves unchanged its policy of supporting the principle of equality of opportunity and scrupulous respect for the integrity of the Chinese Empire, to which policy are pledged the interested Powers of both East and West."[178] In fact, Taft was quite a bit more aggressive than Roosevelt in expressing support for preserving China's independence and restricting Japanese expansion in the region.

The growing need for an American presence on the world stage was quickly confronted by its military limitations. Taft and his secretary of state, Philander Knox, developed the notion of Dollar Diplomacy as a way to exert influence upon other nations without requiring the commitment of direct force. The application of public and private capital would be directed towards influencing the domestic affairs of other countries. One of the earliest examples concerned Knox's attempts to insert American influence into the Manchurian railway. The overarching goal was to restrict Russian and Japanese expansion into the region, though in the end the plan had little impact.

Much of the focus of American business interests in China at this time remained the construction of railroad lines throughout the empire. Apart from being a profitable enterprise in and of itself, the extension of transportation into the interior of East Asia would increase commerce and hasten development and modernization as well. After the failure of Dollar Diplomacy in Manchuria, the Taft administration took personal interest in the Hukuang Loan which was finally negotiated in 1910 to finance the railway line between Hankow and Canton. An international group was formed to finance the project consisting of various British, French, and German banks. Knox pressured the Chinese to allow an American consortium to claim a 25% share in the undertaking to continue the spirit of the Open Door Policy. As Taft commented in his Second Annual Message to Congress in 1910, "The policy of this Government in these matters has been directed by a desire to make the use of American capital in the development of China an instrument in the promotion of China's welfare and material prosperity without prejudice to her legitimate rights as an independent political power."[179] Finally, in May 1910, the European banks relented and allowed the various American business interests to join the group. Despite subsequent apprehension on the part of Peking, the agreement was pushed through and formalized by 1911.

Likewise, Taft continued the recent Republican efforts to promote monetary reform in China. Building upon McKinley's own commitment to the gold standard in 1900, various administrations had attempted to right the monetary issues of the Qing. "The confusion which has from ancient times existed in the monetary usages of the Chinese has been one of the principal obstacles to commercial intercourse with that people."[180] The process had first been undertaken in 1903 as part of the Conger Treaty. After careful study of the prospects, the Qing government finally approached the United States for a loan of $50 million in 1910 to help implement the change which Taft supported. Yet a lack of capital available to the various American banks within the Hukuang Consortium led them to invite the European banks to invest as well. By 1911, the Hankow Railroad, the currency reform project, and the Manchurian Railroad were being grouped into one massive foreign intervention that soon attracted concern from the Russians and Japanese. The Open Door Policy, instead of preventing the slow dismemberment of China by singular powers was now opening up the borders of the empire to a collective onslaught.

Another interest of the Taft administration was the political modernization of China. The 250-year-old Manchu-ruled Qing apparatus had proved to be unable to prevent many disastrous rebellions during the nineteenth century as well as all the foreign encroachments. The president applauded the establishment of provincial assemblies in 1909, the first step towards a national legislative body. "It is a matter of interest to Americans to note the success which is attending the efforts of China to establish gradually a system of representative government."[181] The widespread use of opium remained one of the largest stumbling blocks to social reform in China, and Taft applauded the nation's participation in the Shanghai Opium Commission that same year. With the Qing Empire producing some 85% of the world's supply of the product, its eradication would benefit Western nations as well.

Building upon exchanges of diplomatic officials a generation before, the early twentieth century also saw high-level visits by various political and military advisors. In 1910, the Manchu princes Zaitao and Zaixun toured a number of countries, including the United States. Zaixun served as the Naval Minister in the Imperial Cabinet and used the opportunity abroad to study the various ships and weapons of the Western powers, while his older brother focused on land forces and fortifications. Zaitao arrived in San Francisco aboard the *Chiyo Maru* in April 1910, to be greeted with, "every possible honor and token of respect, maintained exclusively for blood royal...to make momentous his coming."[182] The ostentatious welcome stood in sharp contrast to the city's attitude towards the arrival of non-royal Chinese citizens. Despite the tremendous welcome, various newspapers reported his, "uninterested... placid sense of boredom".[183] In fact, the extreme brevity of his itinerary led some to speculate that his subsequent meeting with President Taft had more to do with American demands regarding the Hukuang Loan rather than an in-depth study of the nation's military. Despite this, Taft would remark in his annual message to Congress that year that, "This exchange of friendly visits has had the happy effect of even further strengthening our friendly international relations."[184] Prince Zaitao's visit also indirectly helped to further the assimilation of the Chinese into American society. The queue hairstyle was a Manchu-imposed requirement on Chinese males. Even when abroad they were required to wear their hair in this style or else face the possibility of retribution against their families back in China. During the waning days of the dynasty, however, Peking relaxed this demand. Prince Zaitao had cut off his own queue while traveling in Europe and word of this soon sparked similar actions among Chinese in New York, California, and Hawaii.

A year later, the first – and last – Qing warship to ever visit the New World, the *Hai Chi*, docked in New York City. It was greeted with the friendly interest of New York residents although the visit became tied to the Torreon Massacre of Chinese residents in Mexico more than to Sino-American relations. Reflecting the awkwardness of Chinese exclusion by the Scott and Geary Acts, city authorities had to grant special permission to allow the sailors to enjoy shore leave.

The expansion of foreign constructed and financed railroads, rather than push China towards modernization, was instead seen by many as simply another step in the continued territorial degradation of the empire. In seeking to increase the pace of modernization within the nation, Peking had begun to encourage provincial governments to fund and construct their own railroad projects as early as 1905. The previously mentioned Hankou Railroad had first emerged as a local project almost entirely funded by the people and government of Sichuan. Zhan Tianyou, who had been educated in America as part of the Chinese Educational Mission, had even been brought aboard to accelerate the project. Yet despite this, local corruption and poor management eventually drove the Qing government to seize control of the project and seek the foreign funding that would eventually become the Hukuang Loan.

In September 1911, protests and riots against the construction of railroads broke out in Chengdu. They were put down with bloody force by the local authorities, but the Railway Protection Movement spread, requiring more troops, which denuded the Qing military in other provinces. Revolutionaries in Wuchang then seized upon the opportunity and launched an armed insurrection that sparked the Xinhai Revolution that toppled the Qing empire, leading to the establishment of the Chinese republic in 1912. Taft, rather than unilaterally recognize the newly-forming republican government, preferred instead to continue with the international cooperative approach of the Open Door Policy:

"Especially important at the present, when the ancient Chinese Empire is shaken by civil war incidental to its awakening to the many influences and activities of modernization, are the cooperative policy of good understanding which has been fostered by the international projects referred to above and the general sympathy of view among all the Powers interested in the Far East. While safeguarding the interests of our nationals, this Government is using its best efforts in continuance of its traditional policy of sympathy and friendship toward the Chinese Empire and its people, with the confident hope for their economic and administrative development, and with the constant disposition to contribute to their welfare in all proper ways consistent with an attitude of strict impartiality as between contending factions."[185]

Apart from the dispatch of nineteen American warships to various ports along the Chinese coast, the nation largely followed the trend of international cooperation with regards to China.

"A policy of international cooperation was accordingly adopted in an understanding, reached early in the disturbances, to act together for the protection of the lives and property of foreigners if menaced, to maintain an attitude of strict impartiality as between the contending factions, and to abstain from any endeavor to influence the Chinese in their organization of a new form of government."[186]

Following the success of the Chinese revolution and the establishment of republican rule, Taft felt not only vindicated in his previous neutrality, but praised the political modernization in progress, saying he hoped it would be quickly followed by social and economic modernization as well. "The natural sympathy of the American people with the assumption of republican principles by the Chinese people was appropriately expressed in a concurrent resolution of Congress on April 17, 1912...the United States is, according to precedent, maintaining full and friendly de facto relations with the provisional Government."[187]

The government of the United States under Taft and other friendly powers then began to issue loans to the new government to both fund its administrative activities as well as push forward modernization. The various countries included certain provisions, much in keeping with the Platt Amendment in Cuba, "to safeguard and strengthen China's credit by discouraging indiscriminate borrowing and by insuring the application of the funds toward the establishment of the stable and effective government necessary to China's welfare."[188] Unfortunately, the loan was not finalized until after the 1912 US election and the new Democratic president Woodrow Wilson opposed many elements of the relationship between the bankers and the government as well the conditions offered to China:

"The conditions of the loan seem to us to touch very nearly the administrative independence of China itself... The responsibility on its part which would be implied in requesting the bankers to undertake the loan might conceivably go the length in some unhappy contingency of forcible interference in the financial, and even the political, affairs of that great Oriental State, just now awakening to a consciousness of its power and of its obligations to its people.

The-Government of the United States is not only willing, but earnestly desirous, of aiding the great Chinese people in every way that is consistent with their untrammeled development and its own immemorial principles. The awakening of the people of China to a consciousness of their responsibilities under free government is the most significant, if not the most momentous, event of our generation. With this movement and aspiration the American people are in profound sympathy. They certainly wish to participate and participate very generously in the opening to the Chinese and to the use of the world the almost untouched and perhaps unrivaled resources of China.

The Government of the United States is earnestly desirous of promoting the most extended and intimate trade relationship between this country and the Chinese Republic. The present Administration will urge and support the legislative measures necessary to give American merchants, manufacturers, contractors, and engineers, the banking and other financial facilities which they now lack and without which they are at a serious disadvantage as compared with their industrial and commercial rivals. This is its duty. This is the main material interest of its citizens in the development of China. Our interests are those of the Open Door — a door of friendship and mutual advantage. This is the only door we care to enter."[189]

With these words, Wilson effectively terminated the possibility of government-backed loans to the Chinese. Instead, China's new leader, Yuan Shikai, turned to the same British, German, French, Russian, and Japanese consortium that had furnished much of the railroad money to the country. These subsequent loans and the stringent conditions attached to them would help to eventually topple Yuan's government.

Roaring Republican Twenties

Two decades of progressivism, internationalism, and unfettered immigration helped to usher in the reactionary election of Warren G. Harding in 1920. Though the subsequent decade long return of the Republican Party to power ushered in fresh prospects for interactions with China, the onset of the Warlord Era in the latter country served to sever most economic ties and weaken the political resolve in the White House to effect the modernization of the country.

The administration of Warren G. Harding saw a return to the traditional milestones of Sino-American relations, focusing on upholding the Open Door Policy and helping to aid in the modernization of the country. As part of Harding's platform of a Return to Normalcy, the president hoped to move the country away from the imperialism and internationalism that had characterized most administrations since 1898. Part of the Republican rationale for this move was financial, as the massive arms buildup prior to 1914 in Europe had done much to overburden the taxpayers of those nations. Thus, early on Secretary of State Charles Evans Hughes worked closely with Secretary of the Treasury Andrew Mellon to find common ground. The culmination of this strategy would be the Washington Naval Conference of 1921 to 1922.

Though the larger American goal was to reduce the possibility of war with either the United Kingdom or Japan, part of the effort to restrain the latter involved reaffirming the Open Door Policy in China. One of the more contentious sticking points in Asia during the Versailles Conference was the fate of the Shandong Peninsula. China had utilized Germany in 1895 to expel Japan from Liaoning, in return Berlin received Shandong. With the ending of the war, both China and Japan saw an opportunity to once more acquire the territory.

The new Chinese government began to play a dangerous game with regards to Japan, with Beijing secretly granting them concessions in Shandong while the Chinese delegates to the Conference impassionedly demanded it be returned. In fact, it now appears that the Chinese ambassadors had never been informed of these dealings before they were dispatched to Paris.[190] Diplomat Wellington Koo spoke forcefully for the return of the ancient land of Confucius to the Chinese people, likening it to the European admiration for Jerusalem. Yet at the end of the day, the matter was to be decided in secret by the major allies. Japan was to receive the peninsula with the understanding that she would then return it to China, a solution that the Chinese found wholly unacceptable.

The response in China to this perceived betrayal by Wilsonian idealism in particular and the West in general was profound. A series of protests and demonstrations by students erupted in what became known as the May 4th Movement. Officials were called on to resign, Japanese goods were burned, and a call was made to not sign any agreement at Versailles. Though the protests eventually died down, the new republic refused to sign the Treaty of Versailles, though whether this was due to the influence of the May 4th Movement or merely an attempt to use it as a convenient cover is unknown. More importantly, the sense of betrayal felt by many Chinese who were in favor of modernization led them to turn towards other sources of technology and funding, most notably the Soviet Union which in 1919 sent its first delegation to Beijing.

The issue of status of Shandong itself was finally put to rest on February 4, 1922, when Charles Evans Hughes was able to produce the Shandong Treaty between Japan and China at the Washington Naval Conference. Though the peninsula was returned to the latter it only delayed Japanese hopes for expansion in the slowly disintegrating nation.

Two days later on February 6, Hughes achieved the culmination of John Hay's 1899 proposal for an international Open Door Policy in China through the passage of the Nine Powers Treaty. The United States, United Kingdom, France, Japan, China, Italy, Belgium, Netherlands, and Portugal all agreed to uphold the territorial integrity of China and promote free trade with the nation. Combined with the Shandong Treaty, the two documents reduced international pressure on the nation for almost a decade until the Japanese invasion of Manchuria in 1931.

Apart from these efforts to continue to ensure the territorial integrity of China, Harding also worked towards relieving the effects of the slowly developing civil war in the country. An excessive drought in 1919 led to a failure of the 1920 harvest in the northern part of the country. In response, famine soon began to ravage areas of China north of the Yellow River. As the Warlord Era had only recently begun, the central Chinese government was still able to mount a relatively effective relief campaign. In the United States, President Harding joined with former presidents Taft and Wilson to call for the collection of aid for the famine victims. The collaboration between the three men was notable for being the, "first time in the history of the country", that three presidents had joined together in any such endeavor.[191] A China Famine Fund was subsequently established under the command of President Taft and Thomas Lamont. Its main course of action was the issuance and sale of China Life Saving Stamps at 3 cents each in order to raise money for the relief effort. Though half a million lives would be lost in all in northern China, thanks to both local and international efforts a larger disaster was averted.

Finally, in keeping with the pro-modernization policies of his Republican predecessors, Harding met with Chinese President Xu Shichang to discuss the opportunity for industrialization. Xu was the head of the largest coal company in China, the Chunghain Coal and Mining Company based in Shandong. While in New York during the first leg of his visit to the United States, Xu announced that, "Geologists have declared that the deposits of coal in the Province of Shanghai alone could supply the entire world for a hundred years."[192] Much as with England's success with industrialization in the late 1700s, coal was to be a vital component for the modernization of China.

The continuing deterioration of China would become a pressing issue for the Coolidge administration. As early as June 1923, President Harding had assured the Chinese that he was willing to work for the unification of the country along with a consortium of American banks.[193] Cao Kun was subsequently able to claim the presidency of China largely by bribing the 590 members of parliament with 5,000 silver dollars each. Coolidge preferred to remain as neutral as possible, sending no military support to any particular clique, nor recognizing any side as legitimate. Following the collapse of Qirui's government in 1926, United States' warships were called to the area, but only to ensure the safety of American lives.

The wars and chaos of the Warlord Era saw a number of naval incidents which resulted in the presence of American vessels off the China coast. In July 1918, despite having joined World War I on the Allied side, Chinese soldiers opened fire on the USS Monocacy as it sailed on the Yangtze River. Two years later, the Monocacy was again engaged by Chinese fighters during the Alice Dollar Incident. During this minor flare up, the Monocacy was again fired upon by Chinese militants who had hours before attacked the steamship *Alice Dollar*. Suffering only two wounded, the American warship was able to drive off the local fighters, thought the consul still subsequently demanded both an apology and reparations. Perhaps the most serious was the Nanking Incident of 1927. As the National Revolutionary Army approached the city of Nanking in March of that year, the retreating soldiers of the Beiyang Army proceeded to loot and attack many of the Chinese and Western residencies of the city. Many people were assaulted and several were killed including Dr. John Elias Williams, the vice president of Nanking University. In response, British and American warships in the area opened fire on the city to drive off the attackers and protect Westerners. Speaking shortly after the event to the United Press, Coolidge reiterated the desire of America to remain neutral in the conflict and to simply protect its own people:

> "Weeks ago we saw this situation developing and sent a suggestion to the contending factions that they exclude the foreign quarters of the city of Shanghai from the area of military operations. This they failed to do, making the dispatch of our forces necessary. In a public statement issued by our Secretary of State on the 27th of January we indicated that we were ready to negotiate a treaty giving China complete tariff autonomy and to negotiate the release of extraterritorial rights as soon as China is prepared to give protection to American citizens and their property. The friendship of America for China has become proverbial. We feel for her the deepest sympathy in these times of her distress. We have no disposition to do otherwise than to assist and encourage very legitimate aspiration for freedom, for unity, for the cultivation of a national spirit, and the realization of a republican form of

government. In the turmoil and strife of the present time we realize fully that forces may be let loose temporarily beyond their power to control, which may do injury to American nationals. It is to guard against that eventuality that our forces are in Chinese waters and to do what China itself would do if peace prevailed. We do not wish to pursue any course of aggression against the Chinese people. We are there to prevent aggression against our people by any of their disorderly elements. Ultimately the turmoil will quiet down and some form of authority will emerge, which will no doubt be prepared to make adequate settlement for any wrongs we have suffered. We shall of course maintain the dignity of our Government and insist upon proper respect being extended to our authority. But our actions will at all times be those of a friend solicitous for the well-being of the Chinese people."[194]

Coolidge's belief in small, limited government also impacted his efforts to aid in the modernization of China. While little federal money or effort was apportioned to the process, he was quick to encourage the involvement of private industry. In October 1925, Coolidge praised the efforts of the Young Men's Christian Association for, "the help that is likely to be given in China through the access which these associations have to the students promises to be important, far-reaching, and beneficial."[195]

Efforts by Coolidge himself to help modernize China remained limited to participation in international groups promoting modern financial practices and laws. As such, in October 1925 he dispatched representatives to the Chinese Customs Conference as well as the Commission on Extraterritoriality. Both of these had emerged from the Washington Conference and were seen as a further way to pull China into the international order. But just six months after the representatives arrived in China, the then-current government of Duan Qirui was overthrown. The president later informed Congress that, "It became impossible under the circumstances to continue the negotiations."[196] Yet he was quick to reassure that, "We are prepared to resume the negotiations thus interrupted whenever a Government representing the Chinese people and acting on their behalf presents itself."[197]

Following the completion of the Northern Campaign by Chiang Kai-shek and the establishment of a stable national government for the Republic of China in Nanjing, American economic and social interests quickly again turned towards China. Coolidge reiterated the interest of America in participating once more in the China market. "We have recognized this Government, encouraged its progress, and have negotiated a treaty restoring to China complete tariff autonomy and guaranteeing our citizens against discriminations. Our trade in that quarter is increasing and our forces are being reduced."[198] As part of this, the two nations signed the Tariff Relations Treaty in 1928. Despite the document consisting of only two, short articles, its larger implications were noteworthy. Secretary of State Frank Kellogg's negotiations, which allowed for tariff autonomy for China, not only continued the Open Door Policy but fulfilled the promises made during the Washington Naval Conference several years prior. Chiang Kai-shek's new government was treated as an equal, a move that heralded the end of the Unequal Treaties era.

Despite the more well-known association of Herbert Hoover with the Stock Crash of 1929 and the onset of the Great Depression, his interactions with China are also of historical importance. In 1898 at the age of 24, Hoover had traveled to China while working for the Ming concern, Bewick, Moreing and Company. While there, he helped to establish coal mines, build adequate port facilities, and even tried his hand at mining for gold. But then Hoover became caught up in the Boxer Rebellion of 1900 and was amongst the foreigners besieged in Peking. He was rescued when the siege was lifted, and his time in China forever impacted his view of government action and the treatment of refugees.

Hoover's first interactions with China after becoming president came with regards to the famine of 1928-1930. A massive drought in northern China led to crop failures which would eventually kill an estimated three million people. As Chiang Kai-shek's government was still not firmly established, the official response to the crisis was both delayed and ineffective. Having seen conditions in China firsthand earlier in his life, and having been responsible for food supplies to Belgium and other nations during and after World War I, Hoover naturally felt the need to engage. In May 1929, only two months after taking office, Hoover contacted the American Red Cross and requested that they dispatch a mission to China to investigate conditions with regards to the famine so that the president could properly organize a response.

In August 1931, despite the worsening recession in America, Hoover worked with the Federal Farm Board to negotiate the sale of cheap wheat to China. As its original mission involved aiding in the sale of surplus food so as to increase prices, the humanitarian nature of the move was balanced out by the economic benefits to the United States. In the end, the Farm Board negotiated the sale of fifteen million bushels of wheat to China to help with the continued famine in north China as well flooding along the Yangtze.

A believer in the promise of effective communication, Hoover continued and expanded upon the presidential radio broadcasts that had begun under Coolidge. During his time in office, the first direct radiotelegraphic service was established between the United States and China, with Hoover broadcasting a message directly to Chiang Kai-shek on December 6, 1930. American companies had introduced the radio to China as early as 1922 with varying degrees of success until the arrival of the Kellogg Switchboard Company in 1924.

The advent of the Depression curtailed any hopes of increased American investment in China. At the same time, the growing power of Japan in the region provided a serious test of the US commitment to the Open Door Policy and the decisions of the Washington Conference. The Mukden Incident of September 1931 was used by Tokyo to justify the invasion and seizure of Manchuria. In a special message to Congress delivered in December 1931, two days after his formal State of the Union Address, Hoover expressed concern about the situation. "As parties to the Kellogg-Briand Pact and to the Nine Power Treaty, we have a responsibility in maintaining the integrity of China and a direct interest with other nations in maintaining peace here."[199] Due to a lack of public interest, however, and a quickly decaying economy at home, Hoover did little more than hide behind the League of Nations and the language of the Kellogg-Briand Pact. "In the recurring efforts of the nations to bring about a peaceful settlement, this Government has realized that the exercise of the utmost patience was desirable, and it is believed that public opinion in this country has appreciated the wisdom of this restraint."[200]

Following little to no concrete action by the League of Nations, the Hoover administration would have found itself alone in opposing Japanese expansion by force. However, with little desire to become involved in a war and the economic necessity of maintaining trade with Japan, the President and his secretary of state, Henry L. Stimson, issued a note to the Japanese government in January 1932. The Stimson Doctrine, as it was termed, announced that the United States would not recognize the conquest of Manchuria. "It cannot admit the legality of any situation *de facto* nor does it intend to recognize any treaty or agreement entered into between those Governments, or agents thereof, which may impair the treaty rights of the United States or its citizens in China, including those that relate to the sovereignty, the independence, or the territorial and administrative integrity of the Republic of China, or to the international policy relative to China, commonly known as the open door policy." Predictably, this half-hearted response to the situation and superficial nod to the Open Door Policy did nothing to slow the continued onslaught of Japan which took Harbin only a few weeks later in February. Despite this, the Republican platform of 1932 praised the actions of Hoover and the application of the Doctrine, while quite tellingly the Democratic Party failed to mention the subject entirely.

The subsequent two decades from 1933 to 1953 of Democratic Party dominance of US politics coincided with the slow dismemberment and conquest of China by the Japanese Empire. Little effort was made by Roosevelt to curtail this process and by 1937, the Nine Powers Treaty itself was in shambles following the failure of a conference at Brussels. Subsequent action to slow the progress of Japan was made more out of self-interest due to the safety of the Philippines and America's position in the Pacific than out of any genuine desire to aid China.

6

FROM CLOSED DOOR TO OPEN DOOR

SINO-AMERICAN RELATIONS FROM 1949-1980

THE TWO DECADES that the Republicans were out of power in both the White House and Congress from 1933 to 1953 witnessed immense changes both in the domestic and the international sphere. The New Deal ushered in an era of big government which would drastically change the nation. Likewise, the outbreak of World War II would reshape the balance of world power and see the advent of the Cold War. Nor did China escape from the forces of change that swept the world during the Roosevelt era. A hands-off approach to the Open Door Policy by Roosevelt and Truman, as well as their failure to see its value at the start of the Cold War left the Nationalists largely unsupported from abroad and the Communists in firm control of the nation by 1949. China as a political partner, an experiment in modernization, and an economic opportunity for the United States had been lost.

Republican Voices in the Wilderness
Perhaps the greatest Republican voice from the wilderness during the Roosevelt-Truman years was Robert A. Taft. Son of the former president, the younger Taft had spent time in Asia as a boy and soon developed into one of the most conservative opponents of both the New Deal and growing American internationalism.

In keeping with his Ohio Republican roots, Taft initially took a more protectionist approach towards trade with China. "Free trade is a beautiful theory, and probably means a greater average prosperity for the entire world, but it seems obvious to me that it tends to level standards of living, so that while the Chinese may be benefited, the American standard is reduced."[201]

Likewise, his belief in isolationism initially made him wary of extending military aid to China in its war with Japan. Yet, as usual, his bigger concern in the matter was Roosevelt's extralegal attempts at obtaining such funding. In December 1940, Treasury Secretary Morgenthau attempted to use the Stabilization Fund to grant a loan of $50 million to Chiang Kai-shek. As the Fund had been set up at the height of the Depression as an emergency reserve for use in foreign exchange intervention and not for war aid, Taft strenuously protested to Roosevelt against the plan.[202] By this point, he had begun to favor the granting of direct aid to China, but only if approved by Congress, not through the unilateral action of the executive branch. Finally, his belief in the limited role to be played by the government in the economy of the United States influenced his view of the role of the nation in modernizing China. "No outside nation can insure India or China freedom from want. They have never had it, and they probably never will. But we can render them friendly assistance in meeting their own economic problems. They are the only ones who can solve these problems."[203]

Yet with the onset of the Cold War, Taft's view of the importance of China began to change. Fearful of both the spread of communism and Soviet influence as well as wary of extended and wasteful American commitment abroad, Taft became a harsh critic of Truman's policy in China. "Today in China, we continue a policy that threatens to undo in the Far East everything the Marshall Plan is trying to do in Western Europe."[204] He saw most of the actions being taken by the administration in China as serving to directly aid in the rise of the communist party to power. Chief among his concerns was Truman's desire to see the CCP included in a unified government in China. By 1948, Taft saw himself pushing for substantial amounts of military aid to Chiang Kai-shek in order to liberate Manchuria, in opposition to calls from General Marshall for only limited involvement. Truman continued to push for restrained effort in China despite Marshall expressing the view to the House of Representatives during questioning that should Chiang be defeated, northern China, Korea, and probably Japan would all fall to communism as well, pushing the United States out of East Asia.[205]

Despite Republican efforts however, Truman did little more to help Chiang and by 1949 the mainland had finally succumbed to communism. To Taft, the blame for this loss fell largely on the shoulders of the State Department. "In the State Department there's been a strong Communist sympathy, as far as the Chinese Communists are concerned." Taft continued to pressure the White House on action in East Asia, commenting during an interview in 1950 that, "I myself have always urged a much more determined attitude against communism in the Far East and China and the President's new policy moves in that direction."[206] Yet Truman still neglected the advice of Taft and others, rarely if ever consulting Congress regarding China, Taiwan, Korea, or Indochina. Only in 1950 did the President belatedly position American naval ships in the Taiwan Strait. Tellingly, the administration had ridiculed Taft for suggesting the same tactic several months earlier.[207]

Taft placed much of the blame for the outbreak of the Korean War on Truman's failed foreign policy as well. "Certainly the cause of the attack which they made was the Chinese policy of the Administration giving basic encouragement to the North Korean aggression. If the United States was not prepared to use its troops and give military assistance to Nationalist China against Chinese Communists, Koreans thought why should it use its troops to defend Nationalist Korea against Korean Communists?"[208]

Two years later, during the lead-up to the 1952 election, Senator Taft drew a sharp contrast between himself and the more liberal members of his party by openly endorsing a Nationalist Chinese invasion of the mainland. Truman's war in Korea had largely settled down to a stalemate and Mao was still focusing on invading Taiwan. While delivering an address at the Lincoln Day banquet in Seattle, Taft suggested that, "Now that a Communist assault in southeast Asia is on the horizon, it should be clear to our government that the only chance to stop it is by a Chinese Nationalist invasion of Communist-held territory. An invasion, well organized, might snowball rapidly."[209] Taft went so far as to state that, if elected president, he would return the recently fired Douglas MacArthur to the front lines to help secure victory against North Korea. While some, such as Schlesinger, saw Taft's departure from his more traditional view of isolationism during the 1920s and 1930s as following the evolution of both popular opinion in America as well as the thinking of Truman and others, it was actually well in keeping with the Open Door Policy of the Republican Party. Taft had always been for supporting the freedom and integrity of traditional China, but staunchly shied away from committing American forces to the region.

"I have never felt that we should send American soldiers to the Continent of Asia, which, of course, included China proper and Indo-China, simply because we are so outnumbered in fighting a land war on the Continent of Asia that it would bring about complete exhaustion even if we were able to win.... So today, as since 1947 in Europe and 1950 in Asia, we are really trying to arm the world against Communist Russia, or at least furnish all the assistance which can be of use to them in opposing Communism."[210]

Another Republican voice in the wilderness during the Roosevelt and Truman years was Henry Luce. The son of a Protestant missionary, Luce spent much of his youth in China during the last decade of the Qing Dynasty. He became an adherent to the philosophy that the Far East needed American monetary aid and leadership in order to both survive and modernize. A staunch Republican, Luce began publishing *Time* magazine during the 1920s and quickly turned it into the mouthpiece for increased American involvement abroad, especially in China. Luce often took to task both Roosevelt and Truman for failing to save Nanking from the advancing Japanese as well as Korea from communism. As early as 1940, *Time* was pushing for more concentrated efforts to save China, arguing that it was, "far more important even than speedy aid to the Allies." Luce himself even visited the nation in 1941 as the personal guest of Chiang Kai-shek, a trip that only further cemented his view of the need for Washington to accept its role in the upcoming "American Century".

The Republican nominee for president in 1940, Wendell Willkie, would himself play an interesting part in Chinese history during World War II. Dispatched by Roosevelt in 1942 to serve as his personal envoy to Chiang Kai-shek, Willkie toured Chongqing, greeting crowds and meeting Chiang and his wife. According to several sources, most notably his traveling companion Gardner Cowles, Willkie subsequently had a tryst with the Chinese first lady, Soong Mei-ling. In his biography, Cowles went on to state that Soong plotted to have Willkie elected president of the United States in 1944 so that, "he and I would rule the world, I would rule the Orient and Wendell would rule the western world." Unfortunately for the ambitions of Soong,

Willkie would show poorly during the Republican primaries that year and would soon after succumb to a heart attack.

A final powerful force that emerged at this time in an effort to alter the China policy of the Roosevelt-Truman era was the China Lobby. This name was given to an informal group of Republicans in the government, private citizens, and employees and diplomats in the State Department who sought to push back against the abandonment of China. Notable members of the group included Henry Luce, Alfred Kohlberg, Frederick McKee, Walter Judd, William Knowland, and Joseph R. McCarthy of Virginia. Its actions were both cultural — helping to broaden the interest of Americans in China — as well as political. In the latter vein they pushed an Asia First policy, seeking to refocus the interests of Truman and Eisenhower from the European battlefield of the Cold War to Asia. The group was largely responsible for the continuation of aid to Chiang Kai-shek, the continued focus on Korea, and early involvement in Southeast Asia as well.[211]

Eisenhower

The Republicans rode to victory in the 1952 election in large part due to fears of communism expanding both abroad and at home. The Republican platform that year again criticized Truman's failure to save China or solve the situation in Korea:

> "They required the National Government of China to surrender Manchuria with its strategic ports and railroads to the control of Communist Russia. They urged that Communists be taken into the Chinese government and its military forces. And finally they denied the military aid that had been authorized by Congress and which was crucially needed if China were to be saved. Thus they substituted on our Pacific flank a murderous enemy for an ally and

friend."[212]

Ike pledged to resolve the stalemate in Korea and was seen as a leader who would prevent further communist expansion.

As explained in his first state of the union address, delivered in February 1953, one of his initial decisions aimed at reversing the mistakes of the Truman administration involved rededicating the American naval presence in the Strait of Taiwan towards the defense of that island. The Democrats had previously positioned the Seventh Fleet in the Strait during the Korean War to both prevent a communist invasion of Taiwan as well as a Nationalist invasion of mainland China. To Ike and the Republicans, "This has meant, in effect, that the United States Navy was required to serve as a defensive arm of Communist China."[213] This policy was particularly nonsensical as the Chinese were currently engaged in fighting UN and US forces in the Korean peninsula. While Eisenhower may not have supported the strategy of a cross-strait invasion by troops from the Republic of China, he saw no reason to make the communists think he was actively preventing it. "I am, therefore, issuing instructions that the Seventh Fleet no longer be employed to shield Communist China. This order implies no aggressive intent on our part. But we certainly have no obligation to protect a nation fighting us in Korea."[214] Thus while this change in policy would have almost no impact on American force allocation, it did show a symbolic return to pre-war Republican Sino-American relations vis-à-vis Taiwan.

The greatest challenges facing Eisenhower during his time in office with regards to China were certainly the two Taiwan Strait Crises. In his second annual message to Congress, the President announced that the United States would continue to provide both military and economic aid to the Republic of China government in Taipei. Much of the impetus for this arose from the concern that Beijing would soon become involved in the crisis in Indochina, much as it had in Korea. Yet, as the war in the peninsula was winding down, Mao Zedong began to reposition his forces to areas across from Taiwan. In August 1954, Premier Zhou Enlai issued a formal statement that the island must be liberated. President Eisenhower was questioned about the buildup on August 17th and responded that, "Well, in January or February of 1953 instructions went out to the Seventh Fleet. Those instructions regarding the defense of Formosa merely reaffirmed orders that had been in force in that fleet since 1950. Those orders are still in force. Therefore, I should assume what would happen is this: any invasion of Formosa would have to run over the Seventh Fleet."[215] Just under a month later, the PRC began an artillery bombardment of Quemoy and soon after the Dachen Islands.

Under NSC 162/2, better known as 'New Look', Eisenhower's military advisors recommended using nuclear weapons as a show of force against China, yet the President himself was not convinced that such an escalation was necessary or well-advised. Employing a more tactful approach, he had Secretary of State John Foster Dulles hint at using nuclear weapons against the mainland while he himself pursued a formal mutual defense treaty with the Republic of China in early December. Eisenhower's strategy was manifold, formally committing the United States to the defense of only Taiwan island proper, while he allowed Mao to save face by threatening the smaller, less valuable islands directly off the coast of China which, if conquered, would simply allow Taiwan to pull back its dispersed forces and shorten its defensive perimeter. At the same time, he was preparing both the American public and larger world population for what many saw as an inevitable nuclear war with China.

In mid-January 1955, the PLA landed troops and conquered

the Yijiangshan Islands, a move that prompted Congress only nine days later to pass the Formosa Resolution. The bill granted the president broad latitude to protect the Republic of China and its various territories. Immediately the American government along with Nationalist Chinese forces launched Operation Pullback to evacuate Nationalist forces from the Dachen Islands, consolidating Chiang Kai-shek's defensive perimeter. Though shelling by the communist Chinese forces would continue for the next four months, by the end of April, Mao announced that he was willing to negotiate. All attacks ended on May 1, 1955, with the Yijiangshan and Dachen islands remaining under communist control.

Three years later, in August 1958, the communist Chinese again began a bombardment of Quemoy Island. Secretary Dulles announced on September 4 that the President was looking into the situation to determine whether to utilize force as allowed by the Formosa Resolution. A week later, the President himself delivered a radio and television address to the American people laying out the background of the Quemoy Crisis. Eisenhower relied heavily on the imagery of a modern day Munich Accord in which China was allowed to devour island after island until Taiwan itself was taken. At the same time, he was in correspondence with Khrushchev, attempting to utilize the Russian leader to curtail the Chinese aggression. Interestingly, the US Air Force again recommended the use of atomic weapons in Amoy in order to drive back the communists. While Ike again rejected the first strike use of nuclear armaments, he did authorize the Seventh Fleet to escort and protect Nationalist Chinese ships and approved the secret shipment of AIM-9 Sidewinder missiles to Taiwan as part of Operation Black Magic. The latter helped to change the course of the air war, giving a distinct advantage to the Nationalist pilots. Additional military equipment, including

203 mm and 155 mm howitzers, were sent to the area as well as a Nike missile battery. These determined measures by Eisenhower ground the communist operation to a halt, and though periodic shelling continued until 1979, it served more of a propaganda purpose than a military one.

Eisenhower also became the first, sitting American president to visit the China region, making a trip to East Asia in June 1960. As he departed from Andrews Air Force Base on June 12, Ike released a recorded speech where he highlighted the reasons for the tour. Though he only briefly mentioned the value of each of the nations he was to visit while in the region, his statement on the Philippines clearly echoed both the classical ideals of the Republican Open Door Policy as well as hinted at its prospective use in Taiwan. "Because with the Republic of the Philippines we have the closest ties of association beginning six decades ago, and because it was in the Philippines many years ago that we launched our first major program to help a developing people achieve a prosperous independence."[216]

Upon arriving at Sungshan Airport in Taipei six days later, Eisenhower highlighted the traditional American commitment to China and its people. "The ideals that we share: our common commitment to self-government in our respective countries; our aspiration for a world of freedom, justice and peace and friendship under the rule of law; all these demand of us—as they do of all the free World—increased vigilance and closer cooperation in the face of the threats posed by Communist imperialism."[217] Noticeably absent however, was mention of the economic connection between the two nations that had driven much of the interaction for the previous two centuries.

The President gave an impassioned speech to an audience in Taipei a few days later in which he once more laid out the basics of the American Open Door Policy towards East Asia over the previous century. "This concern has shaped my country's policies toward the nations of the Pacific. The realization that America's security and welfare are intimately bound up with their security and welfare has led us to foster the concept of collective defense; and to contribute money, materials and technical assistance to promote their economic stability and development."[218] The next line in the President's address highlighted perhaps the most important guiding principle of the Open Door Policy which would culminate during the administration of Ronald Reagan. "But though the United States provides assistance to the nations of the Pacific Region, many of them recently emerged from Colonial status, we have not sought to impose upon them our own way of life or system of government."[219] The United States was willing to provide the material for an organic modernization of China, with few to no political or social developmental preconditions.

Eisenhower elaborated on this point by pointing out the great economic achievements of Taiwan over the previous decade which had helped to drive political progress. Much of this was built on a system of land reform that had been a cornerstone of the philosophy of Sun Yat-sen. Though communist China undertook a "land reform" program in the early 1950s, it was far more forced, chaotic, repressive, and ultimately antithetical to economic development that what had been attempted by the Nationalist government.

"We are proud that we have been of some help technically, in carrying through your agricultural reform program... In the industrial field your friends in the United States and all over the world have watched with satisfaction your growing productivity and diversification.... free China ... has advanced to the threshold of the kind of self-sustaining economic growth that has brought other free nations to wealth and power...our partnership should demonstrate how rapid progress can be achieved by the methods of free peoples freely joined in friendship for mutual benefit."[220]

Later, after a formal meeting between Eisenhower and Chiang, the two men delivered a joint communique which reaffirmed the military alliance between the two nations and pledged the United States towards continued economic development of the island.

The modernization of Taiwan was initially made possible through both local and international efforts. The retreat of the Nationalists to the island in 1949 allowed for a fresh social, political, and economic start free of many of the institutional obstacles that had prevented modernization in mainland China. Likewise, the Nationalists brought with them a sizeable portion of China's gold reserves, which helped to quickly establish a stable currency and banking system. Finally, the United States pledged $4 billion each to both South Korea and Taiwan during the Eisenhower administration, helping to provide external funding for their development. Taiwan was thus able to transition from being an agricultural export-dominated region in the 1950s to a manufacturing powerhouse by the 1960s. By 1970, Taiwan under the Republic of China was itself providing aid to 24 and technical assistance to 27 other nations around the world.[221]

The Republican commitment, therefore, to both trade with China and to aid in the modernizing of that nation did not end with the communist victory in 1949. Taiwan became a shining example of this continued ideal over the next few decades. Yet with the onset of the Vietnam War, Johnson's focus on a domestic agenda, and the increasingly fractious domestic situation at home, the Democratic 1960s again saw a reduction of political interest and efforts in East Asia.

The growing Sino-Soviet split was largely ignored by the administrations of Kennedy and Johnson, and the 1960s represented another lost decade in relations with China. The Taiwan Strait was briefly mentioned during the Nixon-Kennedy debates, but the two men merely quibbled over which particular offshore islands to defend. Not surprisingly, Nixon supported Eisenhower's defense of Quemoy and Matsu while Kennedy felt that only Taiwan itself and the Pescadores were in America's strategic interests. The only other topic of interest regarding China was the frequent vote by the member states of the United Nations to allow the People's Republic of China to take the seat then held by the Republic of China. Republicans stood firmly opposed to the idea while Kennedy was more wavering. As late as the 1964 election, the official Republican platform proclaimed that, "We are opposed to the recognition of Red China. We oppose its admission into the United Nations. We steadfastly support free China." Senator Barry Goldwater once famously compared sitting Beijing in the United Nations to, "inviting Al Capone to a Sunday evening social". The Senator had worked closely with many Chinese during World War II, helping to train Nationalist pilots in Burma and maintained a firm commitment the Republic of China throughout his life.

The advent of active American involvement in the second Indochina War from the mid-1960s once again brought China to the forefront of American thinking. Yet in this it became a question of how best not to repeat the Korean situation in late 1950 when the People's Volunteer Army crossed the Yalu River. Johnson and other Democrats often couched their trepidation in terms of direct action in North Vietnam in terms of fearing Chinese involvement. Understanding both the history and the geography of the region to a greater degree, Goldwater dismissed these notions and argued for a more aggressive strategy towards the North. He believed the Chinese would never become involved in the conflict due to the mountainous terrain separating the two nations, the animosity between China and Vietnam stretching over two thousand years, the drift of Beijing towards Washington's orbit, and the fact that Mao was to be almost solely focused on the Cultural Revolution for the next decade.[222]

Richard Nixon

Nixon's quick rise to power in the late 1940s came about in part due to his rabid anti-communism. His involvement with both HUAC and the prosecution of Alger Hiss made him a household name and established him as a good counterbalance for Eisenhower in the latter's successful run for the presidency in 1952. As an early show of continued commitment to US allies and to broaden Nixon's credentials, President Eisenhower sent him on a tour of nineteen countries and territories, including Hong Kong and Taiwan, in 1953. Apart from its importance to Sino-American relations, the excursion helped to further elevate the office of vice-president, much as Garret Hobart had done in the late 1890s. The trip itself was a remarkable success, with Nixon being greeted by crowds and dignitaries at every stop.

Yet for all his political speeches denouncing communist China and extolling America's commitment to both isolate and suffocate it, Nixon early on formulated a more nuanced approach to the nation. Shortly after his return from the Far East, he began to express doubts during National Security Council meetings that whether the policy of containing and economically isolating mainland China would bring down Mao's government. At one meeting on December 23, 1953, Nixon proposed continuing to isolate Beijing, but recommended opening trade with the country.[223] He undoubtedly hoped that apart from offering an economic boon to the United States in keeping with the nineteenth century China Trade, the move would do more to weaken communism by continuing to expose the population to Western ideas and products.

Nixon's eventual rapprochement with China was not as sudden or revolutionary as has been portrayed. As seen above, as early as 1953 he was already proposing economic links to the communist nation. Likewise, both in that year and in 1960 he proposed visiting Beijing in a formal fashion, though the State Department moved quickly to quash the idea.[224] Once elected president in 1968, he continued to suggest expanding relations with China, though always shying away from full recognition of the country. "I believe it would be a mistake for the United States to change its policy with regard to Communist China in admitting it to the United Nations."[225]

Nixon was far from being an idealist and was always realistic and pragmatic when it came to relations with China. In March 1969, following the breakdown of unofficial talks in Warsaw between representatives of the two countries, Nixon confided that, "Looking further down the road, we could think in terms of a better understanding with Red China. But being very realistic, in view of Red China's breaking off the rather limited Warsaw talks that were planned, I do not think that we should hold out any great optimism for any breakthroughs in that direction at this time."[226] At the same time, the President continued the construction of the Sentinel ABM system that had begun under Johnson, aimed at countering a limited nuclear attack from China. Yet Nixon's version of the system, rechristened Safeguard, was a reduced program. This was largely due to public concerns about its cost and placement as well as his own belief in the limited threat posed by China.

Nixon continued to publicly downplay the aggressive nature and military capability of Red China. When asked during a visit to Guam about Beijing's ability to export communism, Nixon replied that, "Red China's capacity in this respect is much less than it was five years ago, even ten years ago. Because of its internal problems, Red China is not nearly as effective in exporting revolution as it was then. I think a pretty good indication of that is the minimal role that Red China is playing in Vietnam as compared with the Soviet Union. Three years ago, Red China was furnishing over 50 percent of the military equipment, the hardware, for the North Vietnamese. Now it is approximately 80-20 the other way around. There may be other reasons for that coming about, but part of it is that Red China has enough problems within."[227]

Nixon took the opportunity of speaking before the United Nations General Assembly in September 1969 to publicly call for increased talks with China. "Whenever the leaders of Communist China choose to abandon their self-imposed isolation, we are ready to talk with them in the same frank and serious spirit."[228] These calls intensified in 1970 when Nixon laid out his view on the future of Sino-American relations for Congress during his First Annual Report on Foreign Policy. "The Chinese are a great and vital people who should not remain isolated from the international community. In the long run, no stable and enduring international order is conceivable without the contribution of this nation of more than 700 million people... The history inherited by the Chinese Communists, therefore, was a complicated mixture of isolation and incursion, of pride and humiliation. We must recall this unique past when we attempt to define a new relationship for the future."[229]

Overall, the President sought to avoid "dramatic gestures which might invite dramatic rebuffs."[230] Instead, in keeping with his view of the nineteenth century commercial opening of China to the West, Nixon sought to expand cultural and economic ties with mainland China. Apart from their strategic value, these were actions that the president could take independently of Congress. The actions undertaken by Nixon in 1970:

- Made it possible for American tourists, museums and others to make non-commercial purchases of goods from China without approval.
- Automatically validated passports for travel to China for members of Congress, journalists, teachers, students, scientists, medical doctors, and members of the Red Cross.
- Permitted subsidiaries of American companies abroad to engage in trade between China and third countries.

Nixon continued to push his China strategy in 1971 directly to that country's leaders themselves, pointing out for the sake of Beijing that two decades of socialist economic policies had only caused it to fall further behind the free nations of East Asia. "The remarkable success of the Chinese people within the free economic setting of Taiwan and Singapore, and the contributions of the overseas Chinese to growth elsewhere in Asia, stands as an eloquent rebuttal to Peking's claim of unique insight and wisdom in organizing the talents of the Chinese people."[231]

Likewise, Nixon opined that China's claim of being a world leader of the less-developed nations could only become credible once she exposed herself to the larger world. Finally, he argued that, "an international order cannot be secure if one of the major powers remains largely outside it and hostile toward it... A clash between these two great powers (China and the USSR) is inconsistent with the kind of stable Asian structure we seek."[232]

The President asserted that, "Our desire for improved relations is not a tactical means of exploiting the clash between China and the Soviet Union. We see no benefit to us in the intensification of that conflict, and we have no intention of taking sides. Nor is the United States interested in joining any condominium or hostile coalition of great powers against either of the large Communist countries. Our attitude is clear-cut, a lasting peace will be impossible so long as some nations consider themselves the permanent enemies of others." But the truth was more complicated.[233] This was likewise hinted at during Nixon's Second Annual Report to Congress on United States Foreign Policy, delivered in 1971. "Of much greater importance, however, the USSR has a vital strategic desire to secure herself and her territories against a China whose current enmity and potential growth make serious, indeed, the possibility of a future policy of irredentism."[234]

The beginning of an opening up of China to the West in the early 1970s actually had more to do with Vietnam than with either the Soviet Union or China. The Cold War was at its height as Nixon swept into the White House in 1968. As a candidate he had promised to not only restore law and order within the nation, but also achieve an honorable victory in Southeast Asia. Despite his later scandalous involvement in Watergate, he largely kept his campaign promises.[235] Nixon's strategy for Vietnam, and for the larger Cold War, eventually changed from one aimed at outright victory to a more complicated "peace with honor." In order to achieve this goal, the president required North Vietnam to both attend a peace conference as well as to agree to end the war once there. As the years wore on, and domestic support for the conflict dwindled both in South Vietnam and the United States, Hanoi was unlikely to agree to such a peace settlement.

Nixon's much-heralded détente with China was a two-pronged strategy. On the one hand, it was a gambit aimed at bringing about a closer relationship with the U.S.S.R. for the express purpose of ending North Vietnamese intransigence toward peace.[236] On the other hand, Nixon sought to continue the initial Kennan-Truman-Eisenhower objective of containing communism (the initial proclaimed reason for involvement in Vietnam), by bypassing Vietnam and pushing back the frontline of the East-West confrontation to the Mongolian border.[237] Success in this endeavor would offset the possible, and indeed likely, loss of all of Vietnam to communism once America departed. In essence, Nixon was seeking to trade Vietnam for China, a pawn for a queen. As Kissinger himself pointed out to the President during a discussion on April 27, 1971, regarding the opening of China, "Mr. President, I have not said this before but I think if we get this thing working, we will end Vietnam this year."[238]

Apart from the immediate strategic value of this move, Nixon was effectively simply resurrecting the Republican Party's Open Door Policy of the nineteenth century. The original concept of the policy was that, regardless of the internal chaos or corruption of the Qing Dynasty, opening up China economically, socially, and politically to the larger world would benefit all nations. Likewise, it was hoped that this strategy would in the end help to modernize and Westernize the country. Nixon largely hoped for a similar long term result from his own adherence to the policy.

His partner in this endeavor was Mao Zedong. The latter's ideas on modernization evolved over the time he was China's paramount leader from 1949 until the early 1970s. As head of the party, he held enormous sway over various aspects of China's economy and military. Mao's essential strategy of modernization revolved around two points, acquiring foreign aid and securing national unification and control. Having been isolated by Washington following the takeover of the mainland in 1949 and the Korean War, Mao had no choice but to rely on the Soviet Union in large part for technology, capital and military equipment. But overall, the results of this alliance were limited, and Sino-Soviet cooperation collapsed in the late 1950s with

Mao becoming increasingly paranoid. Mao's achievement was his drive to unify the state of China in order to establish what he saw as the necessary base upon which subsequent leaders could build. Mao's initial strategy of opening up China to the United States was similar to Nixon's in that it was more strategic than economic, in this case as a protective measure against Soviet hegemony.

Nixon's eventual "opening of China" began in both Pakistan and Poland. Unofficial contacts between American ambassadors and their Chinese counterparts as well as the efforts of Pakistani president Yahya Khan, helped to open up formal dialogue between the two nations. On the Chinese side, during an interview with Edgar Snow on December 18, 1970, Mao expressed his interest in welcoming Nixon to China as either a leader or private citizen. Several months later the famous Ping Pong Diplomacy visit occurred that marked a significant thaw in relations between the two countries.

In 1971, during the 31st World Table Tennis Championship in Nagoya, Japan, American athlete Glenn Cowan missed his bus from a training facility and was stranded. He was subsequently invited onto the Chinese bus and a player named Zhuang Zedong struck up a friendship with him. Photos of the two men exchanging gifts became an international sensation and led Mao to extend an invitation to the United States national ping pong team. The subsequent visit which occurred in April 1971 followed precisely Nixon's notion of socially and economically opening up communist China.

A week later, Nixon received a letter from Yahya Khan of Pakistan expressing Zhou Enlai's desire to, "receive publicly in Peking a special envoy of the President of the U.S. (for instance, Mr. Kissinger) or the U.S. Secretary of State or even the President of the U.S. himself for direct meeting and discussions."[239] The stage was now set for an official trip to China, yet the question of who to send plagued Nixon and Kissinger. Names such as Rockefeller, Haig, and Bush were bandied about, but each had negatives that stood in the way. The administration eventually decided to send Kissinger himself for an initial meeting with the Chinese, with Nixon giving him full authority to discuss any and all issues between the two countries.

In July 1971, Kissinger traveled to Pakistan where he secretly boarded a flight and was brought to Beijing. In meeting with Zhou Enlai, Kissinger worked hard to lay the groundwork for Nixon's subsequent and successful trip. Unlike in previous exchanges, the topics raised were mostly strategic, dealing with the various hotspots of the Cold War including Taiwan, Indochina, and the USSR. As Kissinger explained to Zhou, "It is no accident that our two countries have such a long history of friendship."[240] Kissinger laid out clearly the Nixon administration's preference for allowing Sino-Taiwanese relations to naturally evolve while at the same time stating that the United States was prepared to fully withdrawal from Indochina provided a general ceasefire could be enforced. Yet clearly the most important element of the mission was the finalization of plans to host Nixon in Beijing.

President Nixon addressed the nation on July 15, announcing Kissinger's trip to Beijing and his acceptance of an invitation to go there himself. Perhaps his most ardent critic in this was not the Democratic Party, but Senator Barry Goldwater. This staunch opponent of communism in general and communist China in particular had based part of his 1964 platform upon rejecting "the notion that Communism has abandoned its goal of world domination, or that fat and well-fed Communists are less dangerous than lean and hungry ones. We also reject the notion that the United States should take sides in the Sino-Soviet rift."

Kissinger personally called Goldwater hours before

Nixon's announcement to both notify him of the address as well as to beseech him to avoid making any public statements disapproving of the trip which may potentially jeopardize it. The Arizona senator maintained his silence and was invited to a meeting at the White House with Kissinger on August 5. There he was assured that the rapprochement with China was already producing positive results as the Soviet Union had requested a visit by Nixon and North Vietnam was once more pushing for peace talks.

Continuing this pattern of keeping close tabs on critics of his new Open Door Policy, Nixon invited William F. Buckley Jr. to accompany him to China in February 1972 along with various other media personalities. Buckley remained unmoved by Nixon's "real politick" attitude towards Beijing, opining that, "It is unreasonable to suppose that anywhere in history have a few dozen men congregated who have been responsible for greater human mayhem than the hosts at this banquet and their spiritual colleagues, instruments all of Mao Tse-tung. The effect was as if Sir Hartley Shawcross had suddenly risen from the prosecutor's stand at Nuremberg and descended to embrace Goering and Goebbels and Doenitz and Hess, begging them to join with him in the making of a better world."

Overall, the visit was a complete success for Nixon politically and strategically. His decision was heralded by the American public and undoubtedly played at least some role in his landslide reelection later that year. Strategically, Nixon's resurrection of the Republican Open Door Policy would eventually help allow for the modernization of China itself. At the same time, it produced the détente with the Soviet Union that would both allow for an American withdrawal from Indochina and lessen the hostility of the Cold War.

The most notable agreement to emerge from the various

confabs undertaken by Nixon with Mao and Zhou was the Shanghai Communique. Apart from each side committing itself to establishing official contacts, reducing tension, and pledging to not seek hegemony in East Asia, the document addressed the larger issue of Taiwan. The United States agreed to the "one China" principle solution put forward by Beijing while refraining from stating which one was the legitimate one. It promised a gradual drawdown of American forces in the region, though Nixon made sure to emphasize that the final solution of the problem must be, "a peaceful settlement of the Taiwan question by the Chinese themselves." Finally, in keeping with the intent of the original Open Door Policy, the two nations announced that, "Both sides view bilateral trade as another area from which mutual benefit can be derived, and agreed that economic relations based on equality and mutual benefit are in the interest of the peoples of the two countries. They agree to facilitate the progressive development of trade between their two countries." Buckley remained opposed to the agreement, stating that, "We have lost – irretrievable – any remaining sense of moral mission in the world."[241]

Despite his primary aim of using China to leverage contact with the Soviet Union, upon returning from Beijing, Nixon continued to push for increased trade and exchanges with China. In a March 16, 1972, address to Congress on the future of science and technology in America, Nixon linked the nation's own success with that of the larger world, particularly China. "One result of my recent visit to the People's Republic of China was an agreement to facilitate the development of contacts and exchanges in many fields, including science and technology. I expect to see further progress in this area."[242]

Likewise, several further sport and cultural exchanges took place between the United States and China. Notable among these was a visit to the United States by a Shenyang acrobatic troupe in January 1973. The importance of the performance as a form of continued diplomatic exchange between the two countries led Nixon to address it during a press conference that month. As a tactic to end American involvement in Vietnam and counter the U.S.S.R., the opening up of China worked brilliantly; as a means to open China to economic engagement with America and achieve rapid modernization, it would ultimately be a minor failure at best.

While opening up commerce between the two nations, total trade between the United States and China remained below $1 billion from 1970 until almost the end of the Carter administration. When examined in the light of total American trade commitments during the decade, the new China trade amounted to roughly 0.6% of American exports. Though some may posit that as a new trade outlet, initial volume should be expected to be small, a careful look at the products being sent by Nixonian America to China further deflates the initial economic impact of the United States upon that nation.

Grain amounted to 20% of total average American exports to the rest of the world during the 1970s. In contrast, during the early 1970s grain accounted for 80% of all American exports to China.[245] Even as the decade continued and other items such as aircraft parts were also sent across the Pacific, wheat and soybeans remained the single largest items being traded between the two nations. Despite Mao's own theories on the importance of the peasant farmer to the state, grain is far from being a tool of modernization. The United States was merely using China as a market for its excess produce, whereas China was still attempting to recover its agriculture from the ravages of the Great Leap Forward and Cultural Revolution while in the midst of sharp population increases. Finally, Foreign Direct Investment (FDI) by Western corporations was virtually non-existent. Chinese regulations heavily restricted the influx of foreign capital until 1979. As Kissinger pointed out during a question and answer session with White House staff in 1971, "they are not interested in trade for trade's sake."[246]

Likewise, the visit by a Congressional delegation to China the next year returned with a similar report for Nixon. "The Chinese side is prepared to have trade between our countries develop in some measure, but slowly. We did not find among our hosts the same high degree of enthusiasm for early and measurable increase in trade which has stimulated the interest of American businessmen."[247] Without an inflow of hard currency, it would be virtually impossible for China to modernize.[248] Overall, Nixon's larger economic outlook for the United States did not involve China, thus no legislative groundwork was laid to allow easier access to the Asian giant for American businesses and investors. The instability of China during the Cultural Revolution and Cold War antagonisms were still fresh in the minds of many Americans. Internal stability in the United States combined with encouragement and incentives from the executive and legislative branches would be necessary before anyone would become interested in the nation as a place to invest.

Likewise, the cultural and educational connections that Nixon hoped would materialize remained extremely modest in reality. In 1970 alone, following the relaxation of travel restrictions by the White House, 270 Americans were approved to visit China, bringing to one thousand the total number approved since the establishment of the PRC. Yet despite this, Beijing only allowed three Americans to enter the nation that year. Contacts remained extremely limited for the rest of the decade.

Drawing China closer to the Western orbit was certainly something of a diplomatic coup for Washington. Though some in the Nixon-Ford White House thought that China should be employed as more of an ally against the U.S.S.R., this path was not fully pursued, and in some ways it could not be. Nixon's overall strategy toward China can best be described as one of *possible* alliance. Kissinger, when speaking with Zhou Enlai in 1973, spoke of two ways in which the United States could aid China against the Soviet Union, "One, if war should be prolonged in the obvious way, we could be helpful by supplying equipment and other services... One problem any country has is early warning... We would be prepared to establish a hotline between our [military satellites] and Beijing by which we could transmit information to you in a matter of minutes."[249] China *could* be America's newest, frontline ally in the war against the Soviet Union. Yet Nixon's larger goal was détente and peaceful coexistence with the U.S.S.R. Once China was securely in his camp and the Russians were at the bargaining table, the reinforcement and modernization of China proved to be less than urgent. This was also undoubtedly handicapped by the outbreak of the Watergate investigation which consumed the president, Congress and the nation for much of these years.

As the United States and Soviet Union allegedly drifted closer together during the 1970s as part of the policy of détente, Washington's prospective alliance with China was never fully exploited. Yet Nixon still did cooperate with Beijing on a few small occurrences both tactically and strategically. Kissinger, during his many conversations with the Chinese, offered access to various types of defense-related technology and data, such as satellite imagery, super computers, and even a Washington-Beijing hotline, though there is no evidence that Mao accepted any of the offers.[250] In one meeting on February 23, 1972 between Kissinger, Vice-Chairman Ye Jianying, and Vice-Foreign Minister Qiao Guanhua, Kissinger went so far as to reveal American intelligence on the dispositions of all Soviet units along the Chinese border. Strategically, Nixon did back up China during its confrontation with the U.S.S.R. over the border of Mongolia and did not stand in the way of Beijing claiming the China seat in the United Nations and on the U.N. Security Council, a goal it had sought since 1949.

Yet despite initial hopes, the 1970s détente with China produced questionable results. As shown above, little economic connection occurred. In strategic terms, though Nixon's "opening up" of China was seen at the time as a game-changer, some have argued that in the long run it was a failure due to the lack of any real further economic, political, social, or military cooperation between the two for the next decade.[251] Overwhelmingly, American economic and technological support continued to flow almost solely into the Republic of China, that is, Taiwan. The offer of friendship with Beijing had produced few tangible results, and the stumbling block of Taiwan was still there.

Gerald Ford
Gerald Ford's first major interaction with China came about in 1972 when, as House Minority Leader, he traveled as part of a Congressional delegation to mainland China. He was in many ways favorably impressed by both the nation and its potential, turning his analysis into a 27-page report for the US Congress upon his return. Most notably he reported to President Nixon that the extremes that the communist government went to in order to impress the members of the diplomatic mission boded well for Nixon's desire to expand relations with the country.[252]

Upon becoming president after Nixon's resignation, Ford largely continued his predecessor's policies towards Beijing. Speaking before the United Nations General Assembly in September 1974, he largely echoed Nixon's similar address. "We will seek out, we will expand our relations with old adversaries. For example, our new rapport with the People's Republic of China best serves the purposes of each nation and the interests of the entire world."[253] A month later, during a press conference, Ford challenged Congress to continue the new foreign policy direction towards China. "If we have a runaway Congress that does not understand the need and necessity for the broadening of détente, that does not understand the need and necessity for a continuation of our policy vis-à`-vis the People's Republic of China, then it is going to make it much harder for a President to carry out a policy of peace abroad."[254]

The following year, Ford undertook his own presidential visit to mainland China. Most of those who accompanied him were Nixon appointees who had joined the previous president on his trip to the nation. Ford met first with Deng Xiaoping and talked in depth about their common concern of growing Soviet expansionism. Deng, whose title then was Vice-Premier, broached the subject as, "how should we deal with this bastard," portraying a friendly informality that both Ford and Kissinger appreciated. The President also had a meeting with the sickly Mao, who spoke succinctly about the weakness of China in the face of Russian power. But the concern and the weakness declared by each power in the face of Soviet aggressiveness was perhaps more theatrical and strategic for the establishment of friendly relations than actually representative of real conditions.

Overall, Ford's trip sought to find common ground with the Chinese on confronting and containing Russia during the Cold War. As he summarized during a speech at the University of Hawaii in December of 1975 while en route home:

"The center of political power in the United States has shifted westward. Our Pacific interests and concerns have increased. We have exchanged the freedom of action of an isolationist state for the responsibilities of a great global power. As I return from this trip to three major Asian countries, I am even more aware of our interests in this part of the world.

The security concerns of great world powers intersect in Asia. The United States, the Soviet Union, China, and Japan are all Pacific powers. Western Europe has historic and economic ties with Asia. Equilibrium in the Pacific is absolutely essential to the United States and to the other countries in the Pacific."[255]

Ford's time in office was too short to see much change from Nixon's initial China policy. Instead he continued the efforts towards cultural exchanges and worked towards increased coordination in strategic planning. In the vein of the former, the President welcomed China's National Women's Basketball team in November 1975 which played five games against American teams in California, New York, Tennessee, and Maryland.

Goldwater vs Carter

As Jimmy Carter entered office as president in 1977, the United States began a new phase in Sino-American relations. Détente with the Soviet Union had proven to be a failure as shown by Soviet actions in Ethiopia, Angola and Afghanistan. Instead, based upon a concept of tri-polarity, the Carter administration chose to view China as an equal to both the Soviet Union and the United States, a view that China had long held of itself. It was thought by people in the Carter administration that recognizing and engaging the three sides of the Cold War struggle might serve to either lessen overall tensions or strengthen America's position through a potential Sino-American alliance.[256]

Carter initially rode into office on a foreign policy platform based upon human rights. Just as the new president began to distance the country from such authoritarian regimes as South Africa and the Somoza's Nicaragua, so too did he seek to distance himself from a direct alliance with the People's Republic of China. But as Zbigniew Brzezinski rose to prominence over Cyrus Vance, the importance of China increased and Carter and Brzezinski promoted China to equal status with the Soviet Union in terms of US strategic thinking. This strategy vastly inflated the economic and military power of China at the time.

The larger hurdle to the above strategy concerned Taiwan, specifically the quarter century old American military alliance and history of economic involvement with the island. Though unofficial Sino-American relations had been in effect since Nixon's 1972 talks, the Chinese attitude toward Taiwan kept formal links in abeyance. In fact, the question of the island's status had been a major component of both Nixon and Kissinger's meetings with Mao and Zhou. Following Mao's death in 1976, Beijing hinted at concessions on the Taiwan question and Carter quickly moved to permanently resolve the issue with official recognition of the People's Republic of China from January 1, 1979. President Carter subsequently followed this move by abrogating the Sino-American Mutual Defense Treaty of 1954 and withdrawing American forces from the island, which was immediately followed by Congress passing the Taiwan Relations Act. The legality and wisdom of many of these decisions by the president were called into question both then and since. Yet nonetheless, Carter's move opened the door for further economic and technological cooperation with the C.C.P.[257] Much of his impetus for doing so was based upon fear of the growing power of the Soviet Union rather than any sort of "dissatisfaction with Taiwan."[258] One of the most outspoken critics of Carter's renunciation of Taiwan was Goldwater. As early as April 1977, the conservative senator had traveled to Taiwan and, in a departure from tradition, delivered a speech criticizing the President's decision not to allow the ambassador from the Republic of

China to have a formal meeting. If Goldwater was suspicious of Carter's longterm plan for Taiwan, his fears became reality following the President's unilateral recognition of mainland China. The move so outraged Goldwater that he formally sued President Carter, arguing that the latter had violated the US Constitution by nullifying the treaty without consulting Congress. The case eventually reached the Supreme Court where in December 1979 a divided court found that the matter was a purely political question and thus not within the purview of the judiciary. Congress subsequently failed to formally protest the President's action, thus indirectly approving of the ending of the American-Taiwan alliance.

When President Carter left office in early 1981, trade between the US and China had grown to $4.8 billion annually. Yet, China ranked only 24th among all American trading partners, placing it somewhere between Switzerland and Malaysia.[259] The growth of trade between the two nations had largely slowed from the opening of China until the inauguration of President Carter in 1977. As seen in figure three, the average annual increase in trade dropped sharply from 1972 until 1977 before leveling out to an average 200% increase a year around 1979.

In addition, the largest single traded commodity from the United States to China remained wheat for the better part of the decade. In return, China shipped mainly textiles, shoes and rugs across the Pacific This was far from the fantastic "China trade" touted in the 1800s or the current global emporium that the nation represents.

The overall effect of the introduction of the American market into China also had little economic impact on the Asian nation. The nation's Gross Domestic Product took an average of 10 years to double, and its slope did not vary to a large degree between 1955 and 1980.

This can be compared to the GDP growth of Japan, which doubled in the same time period every five years. China's GDP per capita, though, did grow by a considerable percentage between 1965 and 1980 when compared to the US in the same era. Even taking into account the often spurious figures that emerge from China at the time and since, the country was slowly recovering economically after decades of failed policies.

It should be recognized, though, that any increase in GDP was not spread equally across the nation, but tended to remain among the existing upper class and within cities. In addition, the American economy at the time was suffering through one of its worst periods of economic strain since the 1930s. One positive change that did take place was that while the Soviet Union was the source of 70% of China's imports in 1960, by 1980 China traded with over 150 nations, and over 90% of its trade involved non-communist countries.[263] Economically, Carter opened the door slightly more to the PRC, yet the result in aiding in the development of China was little greater than that achieved by Nixon.

In terms of cooperation against the Soviet Union, Carter's accomplishments with regard to China were once again mixed. The most notable foreign action for China during the time was undoubtedly the Sino-Vietnamese War of 1979. Launched in response to Hanoi's invasion of Cambodia the previous year, China sought to reduce the pro-Soviet power of Vietnam in order to secure its southern flank. Despite mutual interests, American assistance did not materialize. President Carter dispatched the *Constellation* carrier group to the Gulf of Tonkin to monitor Soviet naval activity but did little more of value. The Chinese armed forces ravaged the countryside of northern Vietnam, but soon withdrew as quickly as it had entered after announcing an unprecedented victory. Yet to appreciate this "victory," one must first analyze China's original objectives in declaring war. If China sought to protect Cambodia or chasten Vietnam, it failed. If, however, China was seeking to demonstrate to the West its arrival on the world stage as an anti-Soviet ally, then it succeeded.[264] More importantly for China's leaders, the results of the war emphasized the continued inherent weaknesses in both the Chinese economy and military. Fear of losing access to Middle Eastern oil sources in the event of Soviet naval action, poor internal transportation, non-existent communication networks, doctrinal weaknesses, and antiquated military technology all became evident during the short, but bloody, war. If anything, the Sino-Vietnamese War convinced Beijing anew of the need to strengthen ties with the West in order to modernize itself. At the same time, the poor showing by Carter in the crisis also led China to doubt the ability or willingness of the United States to continue to confront the Soviet Union.[265] China would have to work more towards actively modernizing itself instead.

Experience had shown that China lacked the capital and technology to modernize on its own. Yet would the outside world respond to China's call? With the rise of Reagan, a conservative Republican candidate who, like Goldwater, had vigorously attacked what he saw as the abandonment of Taiwan, would the links between the U.S. and China forged under Nixon and Ford expand to a level helpful to push China forward, or would he instead resort to an Eisenhower model of confrontation and staunch anti-communism?

7

THE REAGAN REVOLUTION IN CHINA

SINO-AMERICAN RELATIONS FROM 1981-1989

WHILE RONALD REAGAN is perhaps best remembered for his efforts to both destabilize and topple the Soviet Union as well his strengthening of the American economy, the role he played in the modernization of China is far less well-known but equally monumental. President Reagan expanded upon Nixon's New Open Door Policy with China by returning it to the truest sense of the original nineteenth century concept. As was the case back then, Reagan not only sought to have China become a buyer of American goods, but also endeavored to play an active role in modernizing it as well. Yet Reagan's expanded outreach was only successful due to the presence in China of a leader who was equally committed to the Open Door concept. The death of both Mao Zedong and Zhou Enlai in 1976 helped to pave the way for a new generation of reform-minded leaders, most notably Deng Xiaoping.

The Secret Chinese Revolution

A quarter century had elapsed since the communist victory and the removal of the Nationalist government to Taiwan. Yet little substantial progress had been made towards the economic and technological modernization of the country long sought by the general population of China. Centralized rule and economic planning had not produced the wonders promised by Mao and others. Various reforms and modernization efforts had come and gone without significant progress. Where progress was achieved it was countered by losses of life and civil rights. In fact, China was arguably worse-off in many ways in the first half of the 1970s than it had been in 1949.

The death of Mao would bring about a radical change in Chinese politics. The debate between central planning and the gradual liberalization of the market reignited between Deng Xiaoping and Mao's successor as party chief, Hua Guofeng in the late 1970s.[266] As Vice-Premier, Deng was confronted with China's fragmented and inefficient agricultural system, which threatened at any moment to push China back into the famines of the 1950s. To solve this, he began to de-collectivize farms in 1978. Replacing them with a Household Responsibility System in which families received private plots that they paid for in kind, Deng was able to push agricultural output from 2.7% to 8.2% in under a decade.[267] The free market competition that naturally went hand-in-hand, with farmers being able to sell their surplus, reduced agricultural prices in China by up to 50%. Thanks to these and other successes, Deng would eventually triumph, stripping Hua Guofeng of his power in the early 1980s and replacing him with the reformers Hu Yaobang and Zhao Ziyang.

Zhao Ziyang first rose to prominence as the reformist party chief in Sichuan province. Thanks to his market-based reforms, production in the province rose 81% and agricultural output increased by 25% in less than three years. Regardless of his success, his methods aroused fury amongst Maoist hardliners. Deng took notice and promoted him to be a full member of the Politburo in 1979, from which he became a member of the Standing Committee in 1982. From here, Zhao was able to repeat his successes in other parts of the country.[268]

Further backed up by the new Party chief Hu Yaobang, Deng led this triumvirate of reformers who wished to depart from the Soviet economic model and employ partial market solutions for the developmental problems of China. The ideas of the Deng-Zhao-Hu clique would be summed up in the 1982 Constitution which paved the way for outside forces to participate in the modernization of China. Unlike the previous Constitution of 1978, power was to be decentralized to prevent a future Mao from rising up. In addition, the desire to work with the larger world to pursue modernization was implicitly enshrined in the document. "The future of China is closely linked with that of the whole world... and [China seeks] peaceful coexistence in developing diplomatic relations and economic and cultural exchanges with other countries."[269]

Most notable among the new additions to the Constitution was Article 18:

The People's Republic of China permits foreign enterprises, other foreign economic organizations and individual foreigners to invest in China and to enter into various forms of economic co-operation with Chinese enterprises and other economic organizations in accordance with the law of the People's Republic of China. All foreign enterprises and other foreign economic organizations in China, as well as joint ventures with Chinese and foreign investment located in China, shall abide by the law of the People's Republic of China. Their lawful rights and interests are protected by the law of the People's Republic of China.[270]

Yet by themselves Deng, Zhao and Hu would have been unable to drag China forward to modernity. In order to accomplish this, they would need outside support and capital. While Japan and various Western European states made promising overtures in this area, it would take the monetary and technological promises of the United States to truly catalyze the process.

"The conditions. . . for freedom exist to an infinitely greater degree with our Chinese friends in Taiwan [than in Beijing]."[271] Reagan's announcement to C.P.A.C. on his visions for a revitalized Republican Party's foreign policy towards East Asia during the 1970s laid out his view of the complicated Taiwan-China-United States relationship. Reagan largely distrusted the path along which Nixon and Ford had led the United Stated vis-à-vis its relationship with China. He very early on stressed reliance upon a Truman/Eisenhower line of containment running through our traditional East Asian allies, a strategy that surprised few observers once he arrived in office.

Yet that is not to say that Reagan did not appreciate the advantages to be gained from a closer relationship with China. He was always quite willing to separate the Chinese people from their government, urging relations with the latter while shunning the former. In 1967, during a debate with Senator Robert Kennedy, the-then Governor Reagan argued that for both moral and economic reasons, the United States should trade wheat with China, which was then in the grip of a famine. The Chinese people should be embraced, the Chinese economy should be accessed, yet the Chinese government should be approached cautiously. As Reagan himself summed up during his speech to the fourth C.P.A.C. in 1977:

"Our relationship with mainland China is clouded. The so-called 'Gang of Four' are up one day and down the next and we are seeing the pitfalls of making deals with charismatic personalities and living legends. The charisma fades as the living legends die, and those who take their place are interested not in our best wishes but in power. The keyword for China today is turmoil. We should watch and observe and analyze as closely and rationally as we can".[272]

As such, the first year and a half of the Reagan administration, from January 1981 to July 1982 is generally seen as a period of a continued Kissinger-Brzezinski era realist approach to the People's Republic of China. Yet this should be seen in the context of the overall Reagan policy of confronting the Soviet Union. Secretary of State Haig, a product of the Nixon-Kissinger White House, combined the previous administration's concept of tri-polarity with Reagan's goals on eliminating the U.S.S.R. In this light, China was seen by some as the most valuable of all potential American allies. With a population of about a billion people, bordering a large and vulnerable area of the U.S.S.R., and commanding respect from countries at times hostile to the United States, Haig publicly proclaimed China to be, "the most important country in the world."[273] If the price of closer ties with Beijing involved loosening those with Taiwan, the Secretary was not opposed.

Reagan's Early Confrontations with China
Despite these episodes and Reagan's agreement to augmented commerce with China, the president was not averse to being firm with the Beijing government. Reagan remained a staunch anti-communist and loyal ally to the Republic of China on Taiwan. Beijing, believing perhaps too much in Haig's statements and Carter's actions, sought both to test the resolve of a weakened United States as well as to gain concessions in exchange for their help in the fight against the Soviet Union. Reagan's first term in office would be characterized by both closer socio-economic

relationships with China as well as several virulent episodes of confrontation.

One of the first issues with China confronting the Reagan administration was the renegotiation of various Carter era trade treaties. The one which was of the greatest immediate interest to China was an agreement over textiles, the main export of China to the United States at that time. From 1970 to 1980 China had grown from producing 13.7% of the world's textiles to 17.1%, and from 4.8% of the world's clothing to 10.1%.[274] In 1982, the United States proposed an increase of 1.5-2% in the amount of textiles allowed into the American market to avoid what many saw as "dumping" by the Chinese. In contrast, China was pushing for an annual growth in textiles shipments of 6%, which Beijing saw as necessary for the continued growth of their economy. Negotiations wore on for months with little agreement between the two parties. China refused to cut its exports, and the United States, then suffering with a crippling 15% unemployment rate in the textile industry, refused to raise import levels.[275] Eventually, Washington imposed quotas on 32 specific items which originated in China in an attempt to force Beijing to compromise.

In response to what they saw as American hypocrisy over the issue of free trade, China began its first Western-style embargo. In late 1982, the government in Beijing announced that they would cease importing American agricultural products, specifically soybeans, cotton and wheat. These items, at the end of the Carter era, represented the supermajority of Sino-American trade products. It has been estimated that the United States lost $400 million in overall trade during this 1982-1983 trade war.[276]

Yet by 1982, soybeans and wheat had declined in relative importance as part of the China trade. The Reagan administration had transitioned to encouraging more valuable items of trade including petroleum products, oil drilling equipment, space and nuclear technology, arms and capital. In short, Reagan could afford to lose some agricultural trade in order to stand tough against China.

In addition, total Sino-American trade in these more profitable products did not decline during this period. In fact, China increased its importation of heavy petroleum drilling equipment and encouraged additional American capital investment at the same time that it was limiting agricultural imports.[278] In the end, the United States and China compromised on a 2-3% increase in the Chinese textile industry's share of the American market. Yet this was far from what China wished to achieve and it remained a distant fourth behind Japan, Taiwan, and South Korea as a textile supplier to the United States. China's first use of political and associated economic pressure did not yield the results that they had hoped for.

The Cold War had a long history of political asylum cases becoming notable battles between the opposing superpowers of the Soviet Union and the United States. Thus it is not surprising to find a similar occurrence once China entered the scene. In July 1982, during the above-mentioned trade spat, China's top-ranked women's tennis star Hu Na, while playing in a competition in San Francisco, defected. On the grounds that she was being forced to join the Communist Party by her occasional doubles partner, Communist Party Politburo member Wan Li, and fearing threats amid the internecine political fighting back in China, Hu Na asked for political asylum in the United States. Despite considerable sympathy from both the Reagan administration and the American public, the State Department delayed for over nine months before finally approving the request.[279] The drawing-out of the process, combined with the loss of face over such a public, high-level defection, caused a diplomatic firestorm from Beijing.

Stating that America was "conniving" to lure Chinese athletes and scholars away, China said that the incident highlighted Washington's "hegemonic ambitions."[280] China went so far as to threaten to cut recently-established cultural ties with the West. In April 1983, a series of joint concerts scheduled for the Fort Worth Chamber Orchestra and various Chinese musicians was cancelled due to the "tense climate.".[281] The China desk at the State Department even pressured Reagan to decline asylum status for Hu Na and seek a "less provocative alternative."[282]

Yet in the end, these threats and cancellations proved to be of minor importance. Only nineteen group exchanges or events were cancelled, including the Chinese premiere of the film *Star Wars*. No trade agreements were terminated, Chinese students were not withdrawn from American universities and a new Chinese high official even presented his credentials to Reagan at this time.[283] Clearly, China had underestimated the Reagan administration's belief in valuing human rights issues above its strategic relationship with the PRC. As with the previous year's textile war, America had shown China that it still held the upper position in the relationship. Contrary to what had been promised by previous administrations and by Secretary Haig, China and the United States were not to be equal partners.

Pan Am Airlines was the first and only American carrier granted access to mainland China in 1981, ending a 32-year gap in direct air services between the two nations. Less than two years later, in the spring of 1983, Pan Am announced that it was also reopening its old Tokyo to Taipei route,[284] but shortly after these flights began in June of that year, Beijing stripped the airline of certain flight privileges and issued a formal protest to the US government. It was another flexing of China's perceived political muscle to threaten commercial and cultural ties between the two nations.

China announced on June 17 a series of punishments aimed at Pan Am, including restrictions on the right to fly over southern China and revoking permission to conduct emergency landings in Guangdong. A formal request was made to Washington to name another airline to replace Pan Am as the designated US carrier to China. Beijing even went so far as to announce that President Reagan was personally responsible for Pan Am's decision and what it described as its subsequent violation of Chinese sovereignty.[285]

The Reagan administration refused to become involved, arguing that the dispute was purely a business affair. In April 1984, China granted Northwest Airlines access to the China market, undoubtedly in an effort to punish Pan Am. Yet increasing American access to China would only have a net positive effect on trade and cultural exchanges between the two nations. In any event, the argument became moot in April 1985 when Pan Am sold off its Pacific division to United Airlines after years of financial losses.

Once again, China's protests and efforts amounted to little. Beijing had both misread America's view of it and misunderstood the nature of the capitalist market system which it was entering. Air routes between the United States and China remained open and aided the various trade and cultural exchange programs begun by President Reagan.

Perhaps the largest sticking point between the United States and China during Reagan's first term in office concerned the sale of weapons to Taiwan. Reagan had entered office on a platform of re-strengthening ties with the Taiwan's Republic of China government. Shortly after the signing of the Shanghai Communiqué in 1982, Reagan announced the sale of $800 million in weaponry to Taipei. China saw the Communiqué as requiring a gradual reduction in arms sales to Taiwan, but Reagan argued that that hinged upon peaceful unification of the two which would thus end the need for weapons sales; as the two had not united, he was free to sell weapons to the island.[286] The sale included the much-desired FX and F-5G Tigershark fighter jets and was seen by the Chinese as a violation of the spirit of détente and cooperation that had been developing since the Nixon administration. In addition, an implicit fear was developing within the Chinese government of the possibility of Reagan abandoning of China for Taiwan or at least arming the island to the point that it posed a danger to the mainland.[287]

Secretary Haig shuttled back and forth between the two capitals, attempting to ease tensions and convince Reagan to end the arms sales. He eventually prevailed upon the Pentagon to release a report downgrading the military capacity of the PRC, thus eliminating the need for the sale of the FX fighter to Taiwan. Yet China still protested against any possible military sales to the island. In May, Vice-President Bush visited Deng in Beijing in an unsuccessful attempt to diffuse the situation. Senate Majority Leader Howard Baker Jr. likewise visited China to reassure the Communist Party that the Taiwan Relations Act neither required nor prohibited weapons sales.[288]

Despite threats by China to once again end trade relations with the United States and even attack Taiwan, little came of the incident. Secretary Haig resigned in June, frustrated at Reagan's inability to bend on Taiwan in favor of China. Confronted by the loss of their ally in the White House, China agreed to a vague commitment by the White House to "reduce gradually" its sales of arms to Taiwan. In fact, by September 1983, China had agreed to its own purchase of weapons with Washington, while the United States continued to arm the island. Secretary of Defense Weinberger even made a trip to Beijing only months after the Taiwan arms sales row. The results of this trip included closer military cooperation and a laundry list of items that Beijing wished to purchase from Washington. Yet again, China had backed down in its confrontations with the United States, in the end opening itself up more to the United States and to subsequent actions by Reagan that would help to modernize the nation. Reagan had thereby clearly asserted his belief on the level of importance of China to United States foreign policy.

In June 1983, China issued a formal protest to Western countries about Taiwan's practice of issuing visas. By allowing Taiwan to issue its own visas at its offices abroad, it said, Western nations were granting de facto recognition to Taiwan's separate sovereignty and status. Likewise, by using their own offices in Taiwan to issue official visas, Western nations were making a further statement about the independence of the island. The American Institute in Taiwan alone issued over 100,000 visas a year to Taiwan residents during the late 1970s and early 1980s.[289] Yet no actual Chinese actions followed the demands, and all Western nations and Japan declined to pursue the matter further. As trade with Taiwan still represented a greater share of GDP than trade with China, little could have been expected by Beijing.

A similar flare-up occurred following China's request to join the Asian Development Bank. Founded in 1966 to promote economic and social development in East Asia, the Bank served as another international link between East and West to reduce poverty in the former and promote capital investment from the latter. As with its entrance into the United Nations, GATT, and other groups, China linked its membership to the expulsion of Taiwan from the group. Yet, unlike the UN, the charter of the ADB specifically stated that it, "shall not be influenced... by the political character of the member."[290] Thus both nations could remain within the body with no need for legal compromise. Yet China still insisted upon Taiwan's removal as part of its continued efforts to ostracize the island. Many in the West feared that since Taiwan had reached a level of sustainability beyond the original concept of the ADB, it might be abandoned by Reagan in order to repair strained relations with China.[291]

Secretary of State George Shultz issued a statement saying that the United States would not turn its back on the island and furthered this declaration by directly stating that if Taiwan was removed from the ADB, American financial support for the bank would subsequently decline.[292] A few months later, the House of Representatives took a symbolic vote, putting Congress on record as supporting the termination of monetary aid to the ADB should Taiwan be removed. This threat surely was aimed at also swaying Japan, South Korea and other allies of the United States in the region. Any withdrawal of American aid would have had drastic effects on both the region's economy and those countries' own investments. Thus, once again we find China backing down, joining the ADB officially in 1986, with Taiwan also remaining within it.

Reagan Visits China

Reagan's early trips in the first few years after his inauguration mostly continued the trend of previous presidents of stressing traditional American allies such as Canada, Italy, the United Kingdom and West Germany. But Reagan's trip to East Asia in 1983 was different. Though Eisenhower had visited Korea twice and Ford had become the first sitting president to visit Japan, Reagan's trip was more in keeping with his policymaking expeditions to Europe. Asia had been a vital component of America's Cold War policy of containment since 1950, and undoubtedly Reagan wished to emphasize this.

While in South Korea, the president gave a speech in which he noted that the, "rapid progress of your economy, and the stagnation of the North, has demonstrated perhaps more clearly than anywhere else on Earth, the value of a free economic system."[293] Seoul had lagged behind Pyongyang during the 1950s in both economic and political advancement, and by the time of the Kennedy administration, South Korea had even become something of an embarrassment to American claims of Western, capitalist, democratic superiority. But from the early 1960s onwards, the United States had begun to pump capital into the nation and empowered local human capital to direct the modernization of South Korea. The strategy paid off and by the 1970s South Korea had surged ahead of the North.[294] The blueprint for this free market approach to modernization would be built upon by Reagan during his administration in regard to other nations as well.

President Reagan's thinking came through even clearer during a radio address he made from Tokyo on November 12, 1983:

"There's much talk in the Congress of protecting American jobs, but protectionism is defensive and dangerous. Erecting barriers always invites retaliation, and retaliation is a threat to the one out of every eight American jobs dependent on our exports. At the end of this vicious cycle are higher costs for consumers and lost American jobs, the exact opposite of what we all want. Let's recognize Japanese and Korean efficiency for what it is. If their products are better made and less expensive, then Americans who buy them benefit by receiving quality and value. And that's what the magic of the marketplace is all about. The best course for us to take is to take the offensive and create new jobs through trade, lasting jobs tied to the products and technology of tomorrow. I'm confident American products can compete in world markets if they can enter foreign markets as easily as foreign products can enter ours. Currently they can't. Restrictions and tariffs limit U.S. imports into Japan and Korea. In our meetings I've insisted that reciprocity and open markets are vital to our mutual prosperity. I also encouraged the Prime Minister to open his capital markets to more foreign investment. This will increase demand for Japanese yen, helping its price rise in relation to the dollar, thereby making it easier for the Japanese to buy our products and making our products better able to compete in other markets."[295]

Again, we see a man who clearly believed in the free market as the best path to prosperity and freedom for all nations. Should his handling of the People's Republic of China be any different?

The president's trip to our allies in East Asia was followed by a visit from China's Premier Zhao Ziyang to the United States in January 1984. This was the first official state visit by a Chinese leader to America since Deng's groundbreaking trip in 1979. Over the course of ten days, the Premier visited Guam, Pearl Harbor, Williamsburg, Virginia and other cities, while meeting with various US industrial and political leaders. Zhao did not seek to close any monumental agreements during his visit, but the businesslike style of both him and his entourage contrasted sharply with the more affable image Deng created during his 1979 trip when he famously donned a cowboy hat during a visit to a Texas rodeo.

During the official welcome ceremony for Zhao on January 10 on the South Lawn of the White House, President Reagan summed up his view of the relationship between the two nations with the following statement:

"China is now embarked on an exciting experiment designed to modernize the economy and quadruple the value of its national economic output by the year 2000. Premier Zhao, you eloquently described a key to achieving that end when you said that progress, and I quote, 'lies in our efforts to emancipate our thinking in a bold way -- to carry out reform with determination, to make new inventions with courage, and to break with the economic molds and conventions of all descriptions which fetter the development of productive force.' These are words of vision. Our people understand and appreciate such vitality. We welcome the opportunity to walk at China's side in this endeavor. Great strides of cooperation have already been made. In the last few years, each of our countries has tried to help the other build a better life. Our trade has flourished. The United States is now China's third largest trading partner. American investment in China exceeds that of all other countries. We're making available technology that will help open new horizons for your country. Our citizens travel, study, and live in our respective countries in growing numbers. There are more than 10,000 Chinese students enrolled in American universities and more than a hundred Chinese delegations arrive here each month. And more than a hundred thousand Americans now visit China each year. These exchanges between our countries, especially among our young people in the universities, are a source of joy for today and optimism for tomorrow. Only countries determined to be friends would be so open themselves."

Despite his battles with China during his first few years in office, Reagan was determined to continue to assist in its modernization. During the visit, the two leaders announced a preliminary agreement covering US help to build up China's nuclear energy capabilities. This represented an estimated $20-billion-dollar investment opportunity for American industry.[296] Having also visited the University of California at Berkeley and witnessed firsthand advanced American robotics, Zhao expressed his interest in seeking bilateral cooperation in the fields of science and technology. Finally, the Premier also stated that "China is willing to buy (American weapons)", if America was willing to sell.[297] Overall, Zhao's trip to the United States was pleasant, successful, and showed his willingness to engage the US government to an unprecedented extent.

To further demonstrate his commitment, President Reagan mirrored past Cold War bilateral exchanges between the United States and Soviet Union, and undertook his own trip to China following Zhao's visit, in April 1984, becoming the third American chief executive to visit China. Combined with the fact that this was Reagan's second trip to East Asia in less than six months, the administration was clearly signaling the rising importance of this region to American foreign policy. The president himself in a radio address from China on April 28, proclaimed East Asia to be the fastest growing trading market for both the United States and the world. In addition, Reagan opined that, "today China's efforts to modernize, foster the spirit of enterprise, open its doors to the West, and expand areas of mutual cooperation while opposing Soviet aggression make it a nation of increasing importance to America and to prospects for peace and prosperity in the Pacific".[298]

Yet not everyone agreed with the efforts by the president to broaden ties with Beijing. In an effort to balance out his trip to China, Reagan sent Senator Goldwater on his own state visit to Taiwan, during the week preceding the president's visit to

Beijing. This mirrored a similar trip by Reagan to Taipei in the early 1970s during President Nixon's trip to Beijing. En route to China, Reagan met in Hawaii with Goldwater who accused the White House of selling out Taiwan. Reagan himself later reminisced about "not having convinced him otherwise."[299] Despite criticism both at home and abroad, the president departed Hawaii for China with the First Lady and over 600 reporters in tow, and the nation's nuclear launch codes in hand.

President Reagan landed in Beijing to be greeted by both President Li Xiannian and a twenty-one-gun salute, and one could make the argument that the visit was receiving the same level of importance from China as had Nixon's trip a decade previously. Yet actually the Chinese had performed the same exact welcome the day before with the same bunting and flags for the president of the Seychelles. The Chinese also conspicuously failed to remove a provocative exhibition from a museum not far from the president's welcome which detailed American aid to the Kuomintang secret service during the Chinese Civil War in the late 1940s. Finally, the most enthusiastic moment detected from the small crowd of onlookers present for Reagan's welcome came at the end of his speech as the masses lurched forward to catch buses home.[300] Despite these passive signs of indifference towards the American mission, President Li actively touted the importance of the Pacific region in general and the United States in particular in the upcoming decade.

Amidst the usual diplomatic events, Reagan expressed his belief in the need for mutual respect and the advantages to China of opening up to the wonders of the free market system. Minor conversations were also held on the exchange of civilian nuclear power technology and the issue of Taiwan, but no major diplomatic breakthroughs occurred, and the People's Daily buried the story of Reagan's first day on the side of the front page whose headline piece was on the rectification of the Communist Party in Hebei Province. Reagan performed the necessary pilgrimage to various Chinese landmarks including the Great Wall. He met with Deng, and Hu Yaobang, the titular chief of the Communist Party. Reagan charmed his hosts as easily as he did the American people, even trying his hand at Mandarin. But Reagan's speeches were not carried live by any Chinese television or radio network, and no translation was provided to the public.

The president's trip ended with what seemed to be two minor visits, the first a visit to Shanghai Foxboro, one of the first Sino-American joint venture companies, set up in April 1982, and employing Chinese workers to produce American-designed computer chips. The Chinese had chosen Foxboro over various other American and Japanese companies due to its willingness to transfer technology to China and not just seek a market or a source of cheap labor.[301] By 1984, the joint venture was hailed in both nations as a success, something that would have been unattainable without the relaxed technology transfer legislation pushed through under the Reagan administration. The president made sure to reference this legislation during his address at the factory, adding that, "Shanghai Foxboro is one of the first of a growing number of joint ventures between Chinese and American firms... Business partnerships between Chinese and American companies are bound to succeed. The bonds of friendship and partnership in this fine company are a wellspring of hope and progress, of modernization and prosperity."[302]

In the final event of note during his trip, the American president met with a group of students at Fudan University in Shanghai, and his remarks neatly summarized his foreign policy towards China over his two terms in office.

Reagan began by referring to the student exchange program started in the late 1970s and drastically expanded by him, which he said represented not only an exchange of students, but also of ideas, future leaders and ideals. He gave examples of various Chinese accomplishments that Americans could learn from, including earthquake prediction and cancer research, but Reagan's thinking clearly lay in the direction of Americanizing the future generation of Chinese leaders and thinkers. The president highlighted areas that he hoped to establish connections with China in, including technology transfers, space technology, nuclear cooperation, cultural exchanges, foreign policy alignment, and most importantly the dissemination of American ideals. In essence, Reagan was laying out his belief in a free-market approach towards dealing with China. Nothing was excluded, everything was on the table.

The White House would later deny any interest in seeking a strategic partnership with China, and Reagan himself made light of "this so called communist country", but he clearly had a plan for China. It would be developed, allowed to modernize, exposed to American culture and ideals, drafted into the Cold War against the Soviet Union, and eventually overcome itself through the sheer weight of democratic capitalism. If Truman is to be regarded as "the man who lost China", and Nixon as "the man who opened China", then Reagan clearly aimed to be "the man who modernized China".

Following Reagan's visit, Premier Zhao delivered an address to the National People's Congress on May 16, 1984 in which he outlined his view for the future of China. Encouraging limited free enterprise, Zhao announced that China needed to "smash" the last vestiges of radical leftism and should specifically, aim towards four goals: Increasing the number of small businesses and allowing them more flexibility, changing state-owned enterprises which delivered their profit directly to the government to taxed businesses which could reinvest profit, streamlining of construction by incorporating public bidding, allowing the construction, sale and purchase of more private homes. Delivered so soon after Reagan's departure, this should be taken as a clear syncing up of American and Chinese strategies towards modernizing the nation.

The results of President Reagan's trip to China in 1984 were under-appreciated or misunderstood by many observers at the time. The president was criticized for not achieving a breakthrough treaty or obtaining significant high-level assurances as previous inhabitants of the White House had done. In addition, Beijing's censorship of the various addresses made by the president was inflated by the American media into a minor crisis. The implication being either that the president was unable to get his point across to the general Chinese public or that he would be unable to work with such an authoritarian nation. Yet Reagan's trip to China proved to be successful on both accounts. The president's very presence in China was an expression of his willingness to move forward and work with Beijing. Likewise, his various addresses and speeches clearly laid out his beliefs and aims. Whether the masses in China heard any of it was immaterial. Reagan was making it clear to those who mattered that he was bent upon aiding in the modernization of the East Asian giant, if the Chinese people did not hear of it directly, they would certainly feel it through its trickle-down impact.

Reagan and the New China Trade
President Reagan completed the process begun by President Nixon, of returning Sino-American relations to the Open Door Policy of the nineteenth century. Rather than seeking to draft China into the Cold War as a unique ally, Reagan simply viewed the country as yet another Asian nation which could be modernized and used as a trading partner, ally, or simply

one less enemy. This concept is perhaps best summed up in his October 1980 televised address, "A Strategy for Peace in the '80s" in which he said,

> "Our relationship with the People's Republic of China is in its beginning stages. It is one that can and will grow, and I repeat my intention to assist its rapid growth...expanded trade, cultural contact and other arrangements will all serve the cause of preserving and extending the ties between our two countries."[303]

One of the domains in which the Reagan administration not only continued, but expanded upon the accomplishments of previous American presidents was that of Sino-American trade. In 1982, trade between the U.S. and China stood at $5.19 billion, a paltry fraction of the $546.2 billion overall worldwide trade of the United States that year. As a comparison, in total, trade with mainland China at the time represented only one-thirteenth of the United States' trade with Japan. In addition, by 1983 this trade had dropped to $4.41 billion due to the trade renegotiations mentioned previously.[304] Finally, the United States ranked third behind both Hong Kong and Japan as a major trading partner of China, with its total trade being half of what Beijing received annually from Hong Kong.[305] What trade did flow into the East Asian giant tended to be agricultural products, not the technology or capital necessary for its modernization. Worse, many in the Reagan administration wished to simply continue the status quo of limited trade, whereas some sought to abandon the new US focus on China altogether and revert to its more traditional allies such as Taiwan and Japan.[306] It would be up to Reagan to plot a new course in Sino-American relations and a new course in the trade flowing between them.

Helping to bring about his economic plans relating to China, was Reagan's establishment of an executive branch that featured many experts on East Asia. Foremost among these would of course be Vice-President George H. W. Bush, who had served as Gerald Ford's envoy to China from 1974-1976. In this position, Bush was instrumental in building early relations with that country. Other appointments included, as vice-chairman of the President's Export Council, Anna C. Chennault (Chen Xiangmei), wife of the famed General Claire Chennault, as Secretary of Agriculture John R. Block, who had served on an agricultural export team to China in 1977 and 1978 as Chairman of the Development Assistance Committee of the Organization for Economic Cooperation and Development, Rutherford M. Poats, who had served both in the military and government in various positions in the Far East, and as Assistant Secretary of Commerce, William H. Morris Jr., who had recently negotiated the $439 million sale of Tennessean products to China. The president's choice for ambassador was Arthur Hummel Jr., who was raised and educated in China, fought alongside Nationalist guerrillas against the Japanese in WWII, and held various posts in the State Department related to East Asia from 1961 until the 1980s.

Some in the US government believed that the largest role China should ever serve for the United States was simply as an outlet for American grain and other farm produce, as assisting to build up or modernize a communist enemy was anathema to them. Farm surpluses were still the number one traded item with China heading into the 1980s, and they continued to be seen by many as a profitable, non-confrontational item to sell to China, much as Nixon had done with the Great Grain Deal to the Soviet Union in 1972.

While running for president, Ronald Reagan had announced

his intentions to expand US agricultural exports. Specifically on July 3 the candidate stated that, "I will, when elected, fully assess our national security, foreign policy, and agricultural trade needs to determine how best to terminate yet another of the inequitable and ineffective policies of the Carter administration".[308] This was in direct reference to Carter's decisions to place an embargo on all grain sales to the Soviets. At the same time, it was a broad statement that could have as easily applied to China as well as to the U.S.S.R.

Three months after assuming office in 1981, Reagan did lift the embargo against the Soviet Union; he then proceeded to turn his attentions to the grain trade with the PRC. Agricultural relations with Beijing started out promisingly enough with a trip by Deputy Secretary of Agriculture Richard E. Lyng to China in June 1981, and a further visit by the Secretary of Agriculture, John R. Block in October. It was on this mission that Block announced Beijing's willingness to allow American agricultural producers to establish offices in China, a necessary step towards increased sales.

As was mentioned previously, 1982 saw the United States in the midst of a small trade war with China as Beijing began to engage the capitalist West at its own game. Due to a stalled textile negotiation, Beijing begun an embargo against imports of American soybeans, cotton and chemical fibers, reducing trade in these items from $270 million in 1981 to $130 million in 1982.[309] Yet throughout this fight, China's appetite for American grain did not lessen. In fact, in May 1982, the Reagan administration sent Deputy Assistant Secretary of Agriculture Thomas Shoesmith to the U.S. Senate to argue for declaring China a "friendly nation" for the purposes of American agricultural aid. Though the Senate Agricultural Committee ultimately rejected the request, they did agree to remove restrictions in place on China since 1966 with regards to the Food for Peace program. One of America's most successful Cold War era anti-communist programs, PL-480, better known as "Food for Peace," was established in 1954 by President Eisenhower in an attempt to both alleviate world hunger and deny the U.S.S.R. poverty and famine-stricken recruiting grounds. The law allowed for the sale of foodstuffs at bargain prices to nations around the world. Excluded from this, though, were nations which were deemed to have committed human rights violations or which did not encourage free markets. Thus, Thomas Shoesmith had to claim before the Senate Agricultural Committee that it would be improper to consider China a leader of the world communist movement in 1982.[310] "There is ample evidence that a very considerable effort has been made over the last three or four years to move away from the Maoist ideology."[311]

Hardly convinced, this episode was followed by the Senate's own investigation of the situation in China through Senator Thad Cochran's (R-Miss.) trip to Beijing in October 1982 as part of the Senate's Agricultural Committee. Cochran submitted a report upon returning to the United States in February 1983 detailing the delegation's accomplishments in the two main objectives of the trip: 1) Examining and expanding the agricultural trade between the two nations, and 2) Discovering the status of China's agricultural industry. Though agricultural products as a percentage of total American trade with China had dropped from its high of 80% during the early 1970s, it still stood as the largest class of items being sent to Beijing.

Senator Cochran's trip to China reaffirmed America's commitment to the long-term grain agreement worked out in 1981. This pact pledged China to purchase six million tons of American grain a year, with the option to increase this to nine million. The agreement was set to expire in 1984 and became an important political issue in the Southern and Midwestern United States as China had become the fifth largest market for American grain.

As for the second aim of the Congressional delegation, that of examining the agricultural industry of China, the progress made under Deng and others was beginning to be evident. Total agricultural output was up 5.7% to 154 billion tons a year, grain was up 1.4% to 32.5 million tons, which represented the second best output since the end of the Civil War in 1949, and finally, cotton production was up as well.[313]

President Reagan initially continued to support the idea of using China as an agricultural market. This support was in large part a response to the recession in American agriculture that he had inherited from his predecessor. Ever the fiscal conservative, Reagan worked with Secretary of Agriculture Block to push forward the Farm Securities Act in 1985, which lowered governmental subsidies for agriculture and instead pushed exports to countries like China as a free market way to revitalize the American farm economy. The product of two out of every five acres of American cropland was sold abroad, and China represented a new, willing, and expanding market for this product.[314] Reagan was hoping to repeat Nixon's success vis-à-vis the grain deal with the USSR, with the PRC.

Communist China's early and disastrous attempts at modernization had crippled its agricultural industry. Environmental disasters and a burgeoning population only further added to the strains of feeding its own people. While the Chinese population grew, its available arable land did not, thus cheap and reliable outside food sources would be required. To the Chinese, acquiring food from America would help to growth, while at the same time reducing the percentage of the Chinese workforce needed in the farming industry. This move by the

United States, when combined with the importation of better farming technology, allowed for China's agriculture's share in the nation's total employment to fall over the next decade from 81% to 49%.[315] This increase in the available workforce then allowed for redeployment of human capital to other projects.

Finally, various American leaders saw a thriving agricultural trade with China as a way to revitalize this sector of the American economy. Reagan likewise saw the advantages to be gained from an increased agricultural trade, yet his core belief in free trade would not allow for stopping at just the sale of soybeans. He began to take an active role in the increase of trade in all products with China, far surpassing his predecessors.

Reagan's reasons for pursuing a more active role in Sino-US trade are made apparent from evidence associated with his historic 1984 trip to Beijing. A briefing book for the president written by the conservative Heritage Foundation laid out the situation in China at the time of the trip. First, it argued that both China and the United States would benefit from increased trade in products apart from agricultural products, and second that the United States should not rely upon China as a defense against the U.S.S.R. or be drawn into any defense commitments. In order to encourage the former and avoid the latter, China required both available capital as well as modern technology.[316] This, then, became the *raison d'être* for Reagan's interactions with China.

The 1980s saw a radical shift in American exports to China from a focus on agricultural products to commercial and advanced technology, military dual-use equipment and capital investment. Though the total value of American exports to China remained largely constant from 1980 until 1987, the type of goods sent to China began to be infinitely more valuable than grain or cotton. The real revolution in trade with China brought about by Reagan involved the relaxing of trade restrictions and the shift in trade items from products needed to support life to products needed to further modernization.

Two types of trade barriers stood between the US and China in the early 1980s. The first involved protectionist measures that had been at the core of the American System since the days of Hamilton and Clay. The second were more recent Cold War legislative measures aimed at weakening communist countries by promoting economic and technological isolation. Both would have to be overcome in order to further open the Chinese market.

Various American and allied protectionist tariffs and quotas existed which prevented the Chinese from effectively exploiting their cheap and abundant labor force. These tariffs dated back to 1951, in which year the Truman administration increased tariffs on the Soviet Union and its communist allies to 1930 levels. This situation would remain until the presidency of Jimmy Carter, who in 1979 announced the granting of Most Favored Nation Status to the PRC. Though this was not the first time that a communist nation had been granted MFNS (Poland received it in 1960), it was still at the time a contentious issue. Carter used his presidential authority to waive the Jackson-Vanik Amendment, which required that MFNS countries must respect emigration laws. For the next two decades, Congress would yearly stress its disapproval of this move by subsequent presidents.

Reagan and the 97th –100th Congresses continued the process begun by Carter. A series of bills passed between 1981 and 1988 lowered tariffs and encouraged trade with China in the spirit of the President's free trade perspective. Notable among these were HR 4566 and 5707 which reduced tariffs on furs, HR 6867 which suspended tariffs on cantaloupes, various chemicals, radios, dolls, toys, and some machinery.

More important for China was the Reagan administration's abandonment of numerous Cold War era bills and laws aimed at weakening communist nations. These included both restrictions on trade amounts and items, as well as limitations on fund transfers as seen in the following Congressional acts:

- HR4830- Amends the Export Administration Act of 1979 to permit the use of distribution licenses for exports to China.
- SJR 238- Declares that the Congress favors the Agreement for Cooperation with China (relating to the peaceful uses of nuclear energy). Prohibits the issuance of a license for the export, transfer, or retransfer of any nuclear materials, facilities, or components to China until: (1) 30 days after the President has certified to the Congress that such materials and facilities shall be utilized solely for peaceful purposes; (2) China has provided the United States additional information concerning its nuclear nonproliferation policies; and (3) the President submits to the Speaker of the House and a specified Senate committee a report concerning China's nuclear nonproliferation policies.
- HR 333- A resolution providing for the consideration of the joint resolution (S. J. Res. 238) relating to the approval and implementation of the proposed agreement for nuclear cooperation between the United States and the People's Republic of China.
- SA327- Expressing the sense of the Congress that, consistent with overall American foreign policy and national security objectives, the Departments of State and Commerce should take appropriate steps to increase United States/China trade with a view to improving the trade balance, increasing American jobs through export growth, and assuring significant U.S. participation in the

growing Chinese market.

- HR4848- Authorizes the Secretary of Commerce to issue distribution licenses for consignees in the People's Republic of China. Excludes China from the definition of "controlled country" for purposes of such Act.
- HR 3231- An amendment adding a provision "The export of goods and technology to the People's Republic of China should be subject to no greater restriction under this Act than the export of goods and technology to any friendly nonaligned country."
- HR2068- Expresses the sense of the Congress that the Secretary and the Secretary of Commerce should take steps to increase U.S.-China trade.
- HR2100- Expresses the sense of the Congress that the President should work with the People's Republic of China to facilitate agricultural exports to such country.

Many additional bills were proposed which, though failing to pass, showed the general trend of Republican views towards trade with China.

- HR 2761- Prohibits any Federal department or agency from recommending denial of an application to export to China goods or technology covered by national security export controls solely on the basis of their technical level if that level does not exceed a specified level. Permits denial of such applications solely on the basis of their technical level if the goods or technology: (1) are intended for a nuclear related end use or end-user; (2) could, if used for purposes other than those for which export is intended, be of significance for nuclear explosives; or (3) are otherwise subject to certain procedures established by the Nuclear Non-Proliferation Act of 1978.
- HR 6027- Grants China access to Foreign Assistance Act of

1961 and Agricultural Trade Development and Assistance Act of 1954

- S.2608- Authorizes furnishing assistance to the People's Republic of China if the President determines that such assistance is important to U.S. security.
- HR 1564- Amends the Export Administration Act of 1979 to authorize the export of goods and technology with twice the technical level allowed for exports to other communist countries to the People's Republic of China. Prohibits certain nuclear-related goods and services from being exported under the conditions of this Act.
- HR 2770- Declares that the provisions of the Trade Act of 1974 dealing with the President's authority to extend the waiver of requirements that non-market economy countries permit freedom of emigration in order to obtain most-favored nation-treatment shall not apply to Hungary and the People's Republic of China during the period between July 3, 1983 and July 2, 1988. Grants to Hungary and the People›s Republic of China for that period: (1) most-favored-nation treatment; and (2) eligibility to participate in any U.S. program that extends credits or credit or investment guarantees. Declares that specified bilateral commercial agreements between the United States and Hungary and between the United States and the People›s Republic of China shall be treated as having been renewed for that five-year period.
- HR 4873- Removes the People's Republic of China and Tibet from the list of communist countries which are prohibited from receiving foreign assistance funds.
- HJR 315- Urges the United States and the People's Republic of China to begin talks aimed at creating a jointly administered United States-People›s Republic of

China student exchange program.

- HR 5119- An amendment to include the Peoples Republic of China in the program that sales dairy products acquired by the Commodity Credit Corporation. It designates China a "friendly country".
- HR 3537- Sino-American Nuclear Verification Act of 1985 - Prohibits issuing a license for the export to China of any nuclear equipment, material, or technology and prohibits approving the transfer or retransfer to China of such equipment, material, or technology until 30 days after the President has certified to the Congress that: (1) the verification of peaceful uses on exported items covered by the Agreement for Cooperation Between the United States and China will be essentially equivalent to that provided by the International Atomic Energy Agency; (2) China has communicated its recognition that the Agreement neither favorably nor unfavorably disposes the United States toward approving any alteration of material transferred pursuant to the Agreement or material used in or produced through the use of any material or facility transferred pursuant to the Agreement; (3) China has provided a statement of its nuclear nonproliferation policies, and those policies correspond to the description of such policies contained in a specified State Department document relating to China's nuclear nonproliferation policy; and (4) China has communicated its recognition that all proposed exports of nuclear materials, equipment, or technology under such agreement are subject to U.S. laws and regulations.
- HR 4640- Changes the licensing requirements for exports to countries that are subject to national security controls in cases where foreign availability exists (the controlled

goods are otherwise available to such countries). Treats cases of foreign availability to China differently from cases involving other "controlled countries." Requires the Secretary of State, in any case in which national security export controls are maintained with respect to China or any other non-"controlled country" notwithstanding foreign availability of such exports, to pursue negotiations to restrict the export of such goods and technology. Declares that one of the goals of such negotiations shall be to restrict such exports to "controlled countries" (other than China). Prohibits the Secretary of Commerce from requiring a validated license for exports to a country which imposes export controls that, as a result of such negotiations, meet certain standards. Requires the Secretary of Commerce to respond in writing to allegations of foreign availability by export license applicants. Sets forth information to be included in such responses. Provides that if certain technical advisory committees find that foreign availability exists the Secretary of Commerce shall report to the committees and to the Congress that: (1) the Secretary has removed the validated export license requirement on account of the foreign availability; (2) the Secretary has recommended negotiations to eliminate the foreign availability to "controlled countries" (other than China); (3) negotiations are being conducted in cases of foreign availability to China or any other non-"controlled country"; or (4) the Secretary has determined that foreign availability does not exist.

- HR4708/4800/4830- Permits the use of distribution licenses for exports to China.

The Reagan administration also aimed at furthering the

transference of dual-use technologies to China. In order to bring that about, however, both legislative and executive actions were required. Reagan's part was accomplished in May 1983 when Commerce Secretary Malcolm Baldrige went to Beijing to discuss the issue, following which he announced that China was being placed in a less restrictive category for the trade of such technologies. The President personally lobbied COCOM, the Paris-based body of Western countries that was responsible for screening the exportation of dual-use technologies to communist nations, to lift further restrictions on China's acquisition of much-needed technology. Reagan's decision was criticized at the time as the United States had just less than a decade before dragged the British before a "COCOM jury of its peers... to explain the proposed sale of 800 Rolls-Royce jet engines to Peking, plus a factory in China to make more."[319]

The administration took a further step in 1984 during President Reagan's visit with Premier Zhao Ziyang. Both men signed a protocol aimed at eliminating dual taxation. The benefit to both nations of such a piece of legislation was obvious. For American banks and individuals, the ability to invest in China could produce incredible profits, whereas for China, foreign factories could be attracted. Many American allies quickly followed suit. Shortly after the Reagan-Zhao announcement, both Britain and Australia likewise signed treaties with China eliminating dual taxation.

These trade policy changes by Reagan were accompanied by a similar liberalization of economic conditions in China. In fact, the key to the success of Reagan's actions in helping with the economic modernization of China were the equally radical liberalizing steps of the Chinese government. In the sphere of trade, these consisted of a series of acts undertaken to open up the nation to the outside world, moves that would have been unthinkable only a decade prior.

The most important and far reaching of these movements involved the setup of Special Economic Zones in 1980. The concept of SEZs first came to the forefront in the United Kingdom in 1977 from the mind of Peter Hall, a British geographer and urban planner who envisioned them as a solution to the stifled economic growth of cities in the nation. Having observed the successful growth of the Asian Tigers in the 1970s, specifically Hong Kong, Singapore, and Taiwan, Hall theorized that the low taxes and low regulations present in these areas was responsible for their strong growth during the decade. He then proposed that as an "extremely last ditch solution", similar zones of pure unfettered free markets could be implemented in England to revitalize blighted urban areas. Overall, the idea ran, growth needed to be increased rather than simply just sped up or moved.[320]

America's experience with the idea can be traced back to Stuart Butler of the Heritage Foundation who wrote a paper on the topic in 1979. Butler theorized that economic zones with limited regulations and taxation could be utilized to improve the impoverished urban areas of America that had been stagnating since the White Flight of the 1950s. In essence, replace the system of central planning and subsidized growth with one founded on market principles and the creation of new wealth. Acting upon these recommendations, Representatives Jack Kemp and Robert Garcia of New York introduced the Urban Development and Enterprise Zone Act in 1981. President Reagan, himself a student of Kemp's supply-side economics, went on to introduce his own legislation the next year. Though neither would advance far in the United States during the decade, they did in China.

The 3rd Plenary Session of the 11th Communist Party of China

Central Committee met in December of 1978 and marked the ascent to power of Deng Xiaoping. Though a five-year Soviet style plan had been adopted in 1976, this was scrapped in 1977 to pave way for a more Western-style approach to the development of China. A part of the "Reform and Opening Up" policy announced at the congress was the famed Four Modernizations. First proposed in 1963 by Zhou Enlai, this program called for increasing agriculture, industry, national defense, and science and technology. Yet unlike the approach of both Stalin and Mao towards development, the Four Modernizations would be achieved through a reduction in central planning:

"The meeting noted that a serious disadvantage in the economic management system in China is the excessive concentration of power, there should be leadership boldly decentralized, more management autonomy of the local industrial and agricultural enterprises under the guidance of the national unity plan; should proceed vigorously to streamline economic and administrative bodies at all levels, the majority of their terms of reference forwarded to the business professional company or a joint company; should resolutely implement economic laws, the emphasis on the role of the law of value, and pay attention to the combination of ideological and political work and economic means to fully mobilize production enthusiasm of the cadres and workers."[321]

As a prime example of this new thinking, the National People's Congress passed the "Regulation for the Special Economic Zones of Guangdong Province" in August 1980 to encourage its economic, industrial, and technological goals. Essentially tax incentive port cities, the SEZs were aimed at attracting foreign business investment into mainland China via a very Reagan-esque, free market approach. Ironically, a number of the SEZ cities were former nineteenth century treaty ports including Xiamen and Shantou. The Chinese were reopening themselves to external modernization at the same places where it had been forced upon them almost a century and a half before. By 1984, 14 additional coastal cities including Shanghai, Dalian, Qingdao, Beihai, Fuzhou, and Ningbo were granted SEZ status to further encourage overseas investment. Finally, in 1988, the largest SEZ to date was established covering the entire island of Hainan. Overall these SEZs offered special tax incentives for foreign investment and greater independence in their international trade activities.

China's SEZs, when combined with additional economic zones including Free Trade Zones, Economic and Technological Development Zones, and New and High Tech Industrial Development Zones, have proven to be very successful tools in the economic modernization of the country. The Shenzhen SEZ alone has boasted annual economic growth of 25.8% in 30 years compared to a growth of around 9.8% for the rest of China, and by 2010 its citizens had the nation's highest per capita income at about $13,600.[322]

To further cement aid from the outside world, China also sought to gain admittance to various international organizations. Since its acceptance into the UN, thanks in large part to President Nixon, as the official "China" in 1971, the PRC had sought to broaden its integration into the international community. In 1980, China was granted access to the World Bank, ironically a group that it had been a founding member of during World War II under the Nationalist government. This act opened the door to millions of dollars in loans and grants. Minister of Finance Wang Bingqian summed up his nation's view of the move, calling

China a "developing country", which would rely "mainly on our own efforts, but at the same time endeavor to develop our foreign trade, import advance technologies, make use of foreign capital, expand economic cooperation and technical exchanges with other countries, and learn from their advanced expertise in science".[323]

Additionally, in July 1986, China applied for membership in GATT (General Agreement on Tariff and Trade), a move made urgent by its recent trade liberalization. The GATT framework was established in 1947 to promote an orderly expansion of free trade. Again, the Republic of China had been one of the founding members of the group before the communist takeover of the mainland. Though the membership process would take fifteen years to conclude, it did begin the process of bringing Beijing into the world of free trade. That same year, China gained acceptance to the Asian Development Bank, a regional version of the World Bank. Each of these moves was backed by President Reagan whose own policies of free trade and anti-protectionist views were complemented by China's expansionist ambitions.[324]

Reagan's agricultural policy toward China was multifaceted. He sought to boost American exports and aid American farmers, thus relieving some of the economic distress the country had experienced since the 1970s. At the same time, the Chinese saw the American grain trade as an opportunity to free up more labor for use in its emerging factories. In addition, the continuing cotton imports from America provided the raw materials for the first basic export textile factories developed by the Chinese.[325] The agricultural trade begun by Carter and expanded upon by Reagan and Deng served as the initial stepping stone for Chinese economic modernization. This was a successful application of the basic ideas first posited by Mao in the Great Leap Forward.

President Reagan further normalized and encouraged trade

between the two nations through a series of executive and legislative actions. By easing restrictions and lowering tariffs, the president built upon the previous commercial agreements of President Carter and the U.S. Congress of the late 1970s. His actions allowed China to gain more traction in the U.S. market, furthering its development as an exporting nation. Reciprocal actions by China encouraged the two-way street approach that would lead to additional cooperation by that nation in other domains. Reagan went as far as to identify China's easing of trade restrictions as an example of the success of American economic activities at conquering totalitarian states in his 1985 State of the Union address: "America's economic success is freedom's success; it can be repeated a hundred times in a hundred different nations. Many countries in East Asia and the Pacific have few resources other than the enterprise of their own people. But through low tax rates and free markets they've soared ahead of centralized economies. And now China is opening up its economy to meet its needs."[326]

Reagan's contributions to the modernization of trade with China have been the most studied and appreciated. Besides deeper interests and intents though, they differed little from the policies of the previous administration except in scale. Yet these actions served as only the opening salvo of a much more useful barrage of actions from the Reagan and others. The normalization and liberalization of trade between the two nations, initiated by the actions of both the President and Deng, allowed for financial, military and cultural exchanges that ultimately would serve to modernize China.

Reagan and the New Silver Trade
As mentioned previously, the most important American export to China during the Reagan administration would prove to be

capital. Deng Xiaoping himself called for "billions of dollars" in foreign funds to aid in the modernization of China, during his 1979 trip to America.[327] This would parallel the American economy's own rise following the War of 1812 which was largely due to an influx of foreign capital, combined with the re-chartering of the United States Bank that allowed for the effective dissemination of these funds to entrepreneurs. As John Copper pointed out in a briefing book presented to Reagan on his first trip to Beijing, China lacked both of these vital elements.[328] Thus, Reagan and the Chinese government pushed a similar strategy for the development of the nation, one centered on both increasing foreign aid and encouraging private investment.

Between 1979 and 1985, China would receive $20.3 billion in foreign loans from the United States and various international organizations. These would be used for both the construction of infrastructure as well as raw material importation, two vital components of modernization. During the same time period an additional $16.2 billion was provided by other Western nations and Japan in the form of loans and investments. Perhaps the best measure of the sheer amount of capital that began to flow into China is the fact that by 1986, only $4.6 billion of the total amount of foreign aid received had been spent by Beijing.[329] This figure represents less than 15% of the total available capital within China during that time. Yet, while government loans from both the United States and the Western world were important for the development of China, they came with certain restrictions. While repayment of the loan was less stringent than with a traditional bank loan, it did allow for future foreign governmental interference much as with the various loans of the late nineteenth and early twentieth centuries. Thus, the Chinese leadership also sought NGO and NPO loans as well as private investments.[330]

The next realm from which China profited was foreign direct

investment (FDI) by both individuals and businesses. Throughout the 1980s, American businesses invested more than $400 million in the PRC.[331] China seemed a unique opportunity to American investors, with almost unlimited potential and the need to build up quickly and on a massive scale. Yet two fears loomed in the minds of foreign investors — infrastructure and security. China's backward infrastructure could significantly hamper efforts to transport goods and materials into or out of the country, a weakness which could effectively offset potential profits. Thus one of the largest realms initially focused upon by both the World Bank and FDI was China's transportation network.[332] By far the largest share of Wold Bank loans, at 29%, was dedicated to projects aimed at improving transportation. These investments subsequently paid major dividends for the People's Republic of China in its own efforts to modernize. Once again, this development parallels America's case, where internal improvements consumed the majority of national and state budgets from 1818-1860, but would ultimately produce spectacular results for the modernization of the nation. Foreign nations and corporations, by investing in infrastructure for the Chinese, saved China a vast fortune, as well as much human capital.

The second fear of outside investors regarding China was caused by the nation's past disregard for the sanctity of contracts. Investors needed assurances that investments were worth the risk and that Cold War politics would not cost them principle or profit. To help push investment, the Reagan administration used the U.S. Export-Import Bank to provide credits to American businesses and increase trade with and investment in China.

This Executive Branch body was chartered in February of 1934 during the Great Depression by Executive Order 6581. Roosevelt's aim was twofold, firstly to serve as the government's agent in trading with the U.S.S.R., and secondly to provide loans to fund exports to businesses deemed unimportant or risky by regular lenders. The bank was initially funded by $11 million in capital stock mostly set aside from appropriations for the NIRA. A month after its establishment, a second Export-Import Bank was founded to provide similar funding for the country of Cuba. By July, this second Bank saw its purview expanded to include all nations of the world except the Soviet Union. Finally in 1935, both banks were combined into one entity. Roosevelt's aim was to bolster weak American production by using the thriving Soviet economy. During the Cold War, the Ex/Im Bank became a useful tool for pushing worldwide development and the modernization of American allies as well.[334] Reagan hoped to employ the loan capability and export credit insurance available through the Export-Import Bank to achieve a similar result as Roosevelt, *vis-à-vis* China.

Upon entering office, Reagan's Office of Monetary Budget Director David Stockman had initially criticized the Export-Import Bank for serving a small group of major manufacturers. By 1981, two-thirds of its direct loans benefited such groups as Boeing, Lockheed, General Electric, Westinghouse, McDonnell Douglas, and Western Electric. Stockman thus proposed that $752 million be cut from the bank's budget, in line with the free trade principles championed by Reagan during the election. "Supporters of the subsidies made a practical argument: the U.S. companies, big as they were, needed the financial subsidies to stay even against government-subsidized competition from Europe and Japan."[335]

After much resistance the White House began to backtrack from Stockman's threats. In fact, by November of 1981, the administration was pledging to continue working towards the extension of $2 billion of credit below market rate to China that had been promised by Vice President Mondale in 1979. Secretary of the Treasury Donald T. Regan announced during talks with the Chinese that with regards to loans to China, "we keep advancing the ball. There have been no spectacular plays, but a lot of solid things have been happening. This is a long term relationship."[336] Yet at the same time, Regan and others in the administration conceded that China was unlikely to rush towards accepting the loans at the-then current 11.75% interest rate. In effect, though Mondale had made tremendous promises to the Chinese, they were largely moot as long as the American economy remained mired in stagflation.

To further augment its support for the Export-Import Bank the White House helped to push through the Export Trading Act of 1982, which allowed for domestic banks to invest capital in export trading companies. Likewise, Senator Chafee (R-RI) introduced a bill into the Senate Banking Committee to clarify provisions of the Foreign Corrupt Practices Act of 1977, which opponents argued was burdening American businesses to the point of costing them in terms of exports to foreign countries. Finally, as was previously mentioned, Reagan helped to negotiate a treaty with the Chinese aimed at eliminating double taxation for American companies investing abroad. Talks on this issue began in 1982, with steady progress being made including a preliminary agreement signed by Reagan during his trip to China in 1984, until the final protocol entered into force on January 1, 1987. Reagan's efforts resulted in the first complete income tax treaty to ever be signed with the PRC.

In one of its first moves, in 1982 the Export-Import Bank granted a $68 million loan to aid in the construction of a steel plant. By the time of Reagan's trip to China in 1984, the US Ex/Im Bank had already granted US$100 million in credit for exports to the PRC.[337] Thanks largely to his use of the Bank, investment would triple in China by the end of Reagan's presidency.[338] In effect, President Reagan was using the United States to safeguard and encourage individual investments in the modernization of China, a modern version of the Depression era Glass-Steagall Act.

Yet many politicians at the time who were concerned about drawing closer to China attempted to stifle the president's use of the Bank. In his signing statement for the re-chartering of the Export-Import Bank in 1986, Reagan personally took umbrage towards certain amendments drafted into the Bank's charter aimed at restricting the Bank's actions in China. He wrote,

"Although I have signed this bill, I must express some reservations about several of its provisions. I am disappointed that the bill sets severe restrictions on the new authority for the interest rate matching program (I-Match) I proposed in the budgets for both fiscal years 1986 and 1987. Section 8 of H.R. 5548 redefines eligibility standards for Export-Import Bank programs to exclude specified Marxist-Leninist countries, expanding the current statutory definition of Communist countries that are ineligible to participate in the Bank's programs. I note that some of the countries deemed ineligible under the new definition have been making substantial progress in redirecting their economic and political systems towards Western models. Since my administration agrees that access of Communist states to Ex-Im Bank programs should continue to be treated with special care, I am directing the Secretary of State to review the new list expeditiously and to advise me which, if any, of those countries should not be treated as Marxist-Leninist for purposes of this legislation".[339]

With the signing of House Resolution 5548 by President

Reagan in 1986, access by American investors to the Export-Import Bank became severely curtailed. Fortunately for the aims of both Reagan and China, foreign direct investment by companies had become common practice. In addition, investment in the mainland could be effectively routed through firms in Hong Kong, thus bypassing HR 5548. Overall FDI continued to rise unabated following the passing of the new legislation.

By 1986, there were over 6,200 foreign funded business in China, 2,741 of which were joint ventures. Seventy percent of these were in the realm of engaged in manufacturing, and the remainder were in the service industries. Interestingly, though, the majority of these joint ventures involved Hong Kong businesses or individuals. American joint ventures tended to be in high profit/high technology domains such as offshore drilling. This move was heartily approved by Reagan, who was busy encouraging oil production abroad in order to economically weaken the USSR. As a senior adviser to the president stated prior to Reagan's trip to China in 1984, "We are on the eve of a whole new phase in our economic, commercial, and trade relations with China... and the reason for this can be summed up in four words... oil, hydropower, coal, and nuclear power."[340]

The vast majority of FDI remained in the manufacturing sector, due to the need for foreign-funded heavy machinery, and the profit inherent in the sector. This pattern would not change much throughout the 1990s. Real estate development would, however eventually increase to account for a sizeable portion of foreign direct investment in China.

The flow of capital into China had some unintended consequences. As more and more money entered the Chinese market, it produced a glut of foreign reserves. For the first time since the Japanese invasion in 1937, the population of China were in a position to purchase and demand more consumer goods. This expenditure led to a growing trade deficit for the Chinese, which still in a mercantilist mindset, quickly began to implement trade restrictions to ensure a positive trade balance. A second and perhaps more feared consequence resulting from the purchase of Western-style consumer goods was a demand for more. During the 1980s and 1990s, demand for Western goods and culture skyrocketed and Chinese youths of the post-Cultural Revolution era became less interested in Mao's *Little Red Book* and *zhongshan* suits, and leapt at such cultural icons as Michael Jackson and Levi's jeans. In 1987, Michael Jackson made his first and only trip to the People's Republic of China. While performing in Hong Kong, Jackson took a forty-minute trip to mainland China to visit the village of Yongmo. Even in this backward farming community many of the young people knew who he was. Reagan's economic policies allowed for the arrival of this culture in China, and though it is impossible to say whether he was attempting to do so intentionally, it did bear many of the same hallmarks as similar strategies employed by the U.S. in Eastern Europe a few years earlier.[343]

Overall, Reagan's policies that allowed for the release of foreign capital into China were a catalyst for the eventual successful economic modernization of the nation. This development was itself largely brought about by his skillful use of the Export-Import Bank. As with all cases of modernization, the ability to improve upon the industrial base, infrastructure, and health and human services is dependent upon the amount of capital in the system. With liberalized trade laws and available funding, China now simply required the technology to produce advanced equipment both for its own consumption as well as for trade. Perhaps the surest example of the success of Reagan and Deng in pushing the nation forward was China's establishment of its own Export-Import Bank in 1994. In under two decades

Beijing had gone from a nation being modernized to a nation seeking to modernize and invest in others.

Reagan and Technology Transfers

The U.S. State Department recognized in a report issued in 1984 that the acquisition of Western technology was "essential" for China's modernization.[344] While China's need for technology may have been undeniable, the issue of whether or not the U.S. should provide that technology was much more open to debate. "China may be a constructive trading and strategic partner, or it may choose a more divergent path. US decisions on technology transfers will be an important determinant of which path is followed and the implications for the world."[345] Yet at the same time aiding in the development of China could lead to increased global competition or even outright regional domination. The fates of Taiwan, Japan, the Philippines, and South Korea, should too much technology be sent to China, was surely on the minds of many Cold War warriors in America, not the least of whom was Ronald Reagan.

From the beginning of China's economic modernization program in the late 1970s, the advancement of technology emerged as one of the nation's main goals. This aim was given a prominent place in both Deng's Four Modernizations and China's Seventh Five-Year Plan. The latter began in 1986 and set the acquisition of technology as one of its highest aims, "To further open up to the outside world, combining domestic economic growth with expanding external economic and technologic exchanges."[346]

This goal became even more of a necessity as the nation sought to increase its industrial output by immense margins throughout the 1980s. China's staid production methods proved unable to meet requirements. In many ways, it was this lack of modern, outside technology that doomed Mao's backyard steel foundries of the Great Leap Forward and various previous attempts at modernization. China was too far behind the modern world in many advanced forms of technology, it could not hope to catch up by following the same path as other nations. Such things as satellites, computers, and aircraft needed to be acquired, not developed. How far would America go in aiding this endeavor?

Reagan's liberalized trade rules discussed previously allowed for the export of formerly restricted technology to China. The restrictions had largely been in place since the Export Control Act of 1949, which was used to restrict trade with communist nations. In China's case, this became applicable following its entry into the Korean War. The 1969 Export Administrative Act modified these restrictions, allowing for the government to approve the sale of items with no military potential. Reagan further expanded upon this in order to increase the flow of technological goods to China. America's role in technology transfers was thus twofold, supplying much-needed technology by allowing private industries to do so as well as by direct transfer from the American government.

Some examples of American companies involved in the former include GE, American Motors, McDonnell Douglas, and IBM. These companies rushed into the China market in the 1980s, eagerly pursuing the one billion potential customers that lay just over the Pacific Ocean. The "so-called communist country," as Reagan called it during his 1984 visit was ripe for investment and sales. These joint ventures allowed China to gain access to a variety of modern production technology. Yet not all of these joint ventures proved to be successful for American companies, with AMC perhaps representing the paradigm of this failure.[347]

AMC entered the Chinese market in 1983, greeted with, "red carpets and exotic, sweet, flowery scents."[348] The struggling

American car company, most famous for the Jeep, joined with Beijing Automotive Works to form Beijing Jeep. AMC would own a 31% share of the venture while at the same time contributing $16 million in both capital and technology. Among the goals of the venture was to modernize China's only front-wheel-drive vehicle, the BJ 212, a car based on a 30-year-old Soviet design. While the original outlook of the project was promising, the expected sales did not materialize. The average Chinese consumer at that time had not built up the needed savings to purchase such products. However, while AC did not initially benefit overall from the exchange, the Chinese did. Besides the various jobs associated with the projects, the Chinese acquired massive amounts of American machinery, technology and know-how at little to no cost; technology that would later be used to further the economic and technological modernization of the nation.

An example of a successful linkup between American and Chinese businesses involved McDonnell Douglas and Shanghai Aviation Industrial Corporation. McDonnell Douglas had been active as a minor supplier to China since 1972, in which year the Department of Commerce approved a temporary export license for the company to ship a $21 million aircraft to China as a demonstration model. SAIC began to supply parts in return by 1979, following a visit by Deng to a McDonnell Douglas plant in Seattle. In 1980, China began to produce components for the DC-9, McDonnell Douglas's small-to-medium range carrier that had been in production since the mid-1960s.

Beijing began to purchase planes in earnest as the 1980s progressed, buying ten Boeing 737-200s in 1982, two Super 80's from McDonnell Douglas in 1983, and four MD-11s in 1986. The first two sales alone brought $200 million into the American economy. More importantly they allowed China, a nation roughly the size of the United States to improve its transportation infrastructure, a sorely needed criterion for modernization, and one that had been sought-after since the time of Zeng Guofan a century before. China's purchase of a promotional set of DC-9 Super 80s in 1982 eventually led to the signing of a co-production agreement between McDonnell Douglas and SAIC in 1984 which allowed for both companies to begin producing MD-80s in China. The American aviation giant agreed to provide parts, subassembly, training, technology assistance, and production aid towards the endeavor.

This deal expanded in 1985 to include the joint production of 35 MD-82 twin jets for use by Chinese state airlines. Cooperation would continue into the 1990s, eventually resulting in the co-production of such other aircraft as the MD-90. The endeavor was viewed as successful enough by the White House, that during George P. Shultz's trip to China in March 1987, the Secretary of State made a point to tour a McDonnell Douglass aircraft factory in the country.

The Reagan White House served to actively encourage this trade. In July 1984, Olin L. Wethington, the Deputy Under-Secretary of Commerce, told American aerospace leaders that China wanted to buy advanced jetliners, small and medium distance carriers, commuter planes, aviation equipment, and to enter into co-production and assembly agreements. He estimated that these deals could result in "billions in this decade".[349]

For its part, the White House was willing to match low interest credit and loans to make American businesses more competitive with European ones. This statement came at the same time that Craig L. Fuller, who was Reagan's Director of Cabinet Administration, was heading a 17-member delegation to China. This exchange, which was arranged during Reagan's trip to China in 1983, reached agreement for industrial and technological cooperation in aerospace. Included in the deal was the hosting of an American aircraft exhibition in two years, various technology seminars, and a trade mission. The Fuller Mission also discussed possible civilian, helicopter, broadcast satellite, air-traffic control system, and advanced avionics sales. The White House was actively laying the groundwork for increased deals between America and Chinese businesses.

In a similar fashion, General Electric signed a number of deals with China throughout the 1980s to both sell advanced technology and jointly produce goods on the mainland. GE had a long history in China dating back to the production of light bulbs in 1910. One of the first modern episodes involved the sale of 220 diesel-electric C36-7 locomotives in November 1983. The deal was valued at $220 million and the first 24 units rolled off the line in Erie, Pennsylvania in July, 1984. GE became more involved with Beijing in June 1985, when the company agreed to train Chinese executives in management while at the same time helping to co-design and co-manufacture steam turbine engines with a Sichuan factory.

Cooperation between the two continued with another transfer signed in December 1986. In this agreement, the Chinese government pledged to buy five jet engines from GE for use in its aircraft. These engines included those used in 747 as well as 767 aircraft.[350] Finally in 1985, the company became part of a 50/50 joint venture with a French company to produce engines for Chinese 737s. Thus, much like with McDonnell Douglas, GE, while seeking a smaller segment of the Chinese economy than did AMC, experienced some success. China itself acquired from the deal the technical know-how to begin to upgrade its aged air and rail fleets.

In 1979, following Energy Secretary James R. Schlesinger's trip to China, President Carter signed the Science and Technology

Protocol with the PRC. This document laid out the process by which later technology transfers would take place. Some of the domains included under it were space technology, high energy physics technology, meteorological equipment, marine technology, medical equipment, and seismological technology. Yet this agreement was flawed by its failure to deliver vital modern equipment, such as computers to the Chinese.

During Haig's visit to China in 1981, the communists presented him with a wish list of 65 additional technologies that they wished to acquire from the Unites States. A few weeks after the Secretary's 15 day trip, the NSC announced that the Reagan administration had made, "a decision in principle to be more flexible", in terms of technology transfers to the nation.[351]

Following calls by former President Nixon in June 1983 for the White House to expand the sale of goods and technologies even further, Secretary of Commerce Baldrige announced that the Reagan administration was willing to ease even more restrictions.[352] This was followed in September with a similar announcement by Weinberger with regard to the sale of weapons as well. By November, China had been moved under a series of new regulations to the same level as a NATO or non-aligned country for the purposes of equipment sales, thus no longer requiring items to be approved by the administration on a case-by-case basis. In 1984, during his trip to the Pacific Rim, President Reagan signed a new accord on industrial and technological co-operation. Besides continuing the process of allowing business transfers begun under Carter, the Reagan-Zhao agreement set up the permanent China-US Joint Commission on Commerce and Trade. This body would meet on an ad hoc basis to discuss further technology and trade agreements between the two nations, answering directly to the Executive Branch. Reagan's actions were in keeping with the traditional Republican view of true free trade.

President Reagan was subsequently responsible for not only extending these transfers, but increasing the spheres which they covered as well. His administration added building technology, nuclear technology, equipment for hydro-electric and controlled magnetic fusion research, biomedical equipment, surveying equipment, LANDSAT technology, and the granting of access to the Chinese of CDC equipment.

Reagan's technology transfers even affected one of China's current wonders of modernization, the Three Gorges Dam on the middle reaches of the Yangtze River. The president learned of the project during his 1984 trip to China and assigned his former national security advisor William Clark to serve as a liaison to work wsith the Chinese on the project. Clark briefed various members of private industry on the matter and formed the "US Three Gorges Working Group" to investigate investment opportunities for the United States in the dam project. Private groups and businesses such as Merrill Lynch and the Morgan Bank pledged $3 millionin funds, while Reagan made available the Department of the Interior and the U.S. Army Corps of Engineers as advisors. While in the end the proposed joint US-PRC venture failed to raise enough capital (an estimated $8 billion was required) or enough interest on the part of the Chinese, it did show the lengths to which the Reagan administration would go to help modernize China. The president who had vigorously argued against the TVA of President Roosevelt was now participating in his own privately-funded version of it half way around the world.

Perhaps Reagan's two greatest contributions in this area were in the realms of nuclear and military technology sharing, the latter of which will be dealt with in a subsequent section. As for nuclear technology, the decision to grant the Chinese access to American equipment and research was, and remains a contentious issue. This is clearly highlighted by the various reactions to the Chinese theft of US nuclear weapons secrets from Los Alamos in the 1980s and 1990s.

The beginnings of the program stretch back to 1978, when Deng Xiaoping announced that China would build enough nuclear plants to supply 5% of its electrical needs by the year 2000. With the cost estimated at US$10-20 billion, this proclamation spurred much interest in the American nuclear construction industry. Negotiations began with the United States in 1981 to provide the necessary technology to build the plants. As many in Washington were concerned about possible Chinese nuclear proliferation to Pakistan, China agreed to join the IAEA in 1984.

In April 1984, Reagan initialed a nuclear cooperation agreement with China while in Beijing, stating that the move "will open broad opportunities for joint work in development of the energy base which China needs for her modernization." But problems remained as the Chinese refused to comply with the US Atomic Energy Act, which would have required them to notify Washington before reprocessing or selling any acquired nuclear materials. Senator John Glenn moved to block funding for nuclear exchanges until China could prove its peaceful use and intents, by attaching an amendment to the 1986 continuing appropriations resolution (H.J. Res. 465). Though the motion passed in a voice vote, it eventually died in committee. Reagan, sensing resistance in Congress, acted decisively and postponed the agreement for a year to provide China time to agree to some sort of pledge.[353]

Party Secretary Li Peng finally agreed in January 1985 to a pledge of non-proliferation to non-nuclear states. Therefore, in July 1985, during Chinese President Li Xiannian's visit to Washington, President Reagan finally submitted the agreement to Congress and in December 1985, Senate Joint Resolution 238 became Public Law 99-183. The sale of nuclear technology and material to a communist, nuclear-armed country that only a decade before had been a staunch American opponent remains a milestone in the process of relationship building by President Reagan and further demonstrates his free market approach to dealing with nations of the world.

A related field that was visited by the two nations was space technology and exploration. The Chinese space industry had begun in earnest following the Korean War, and was closely tied to its development of nuclear weapons. Yet for a variety of reasons, mostly due to the collapse of Sino-Soviet cooperation, the industry stagnated in the 1960s. China would not launch a satellite into space until 1970, and very little else had been accomplished by 1980.

By 1981, Japan had emerged as the sole alternative for investment by the American space technology industry. Reagan sought to broaden this by aiding China in the development of its space program. The president announced this during his trip to Beijing in 1984. Following his return home, China announced it was studying a joint space venture with Chinese astronauts traveling aboard American shuttles. Cooperation extended to the extent that by 1986, following the *Challenger* disaster and the failure of various West European rocket launches, China sought to build its own space center in Hawaii. Their partner in this was to be Howard Hughes' former company. At the same time China signed an agreement with Terasaton June 15 to purchase two defunct satellites removed from faulty orbits and re-launch them in 1987 and 1988.

Technology had become by the 1990s the largest category of U.S. exports to China. At the same time and due in large part to this development, the total number of Chinese exports produced by machinery increased, thus boosting exports in general. China also began to sell its own machinery and technology abroad, especially to other underdeveloped nations. Thanks to the importation of these newest technologies, made possible by the capital reserves sent to China, it was able to industrialize on both a speedy and safe path. This approach differed considerably from the haphazard and dangerous methods by which the U.S.S.R. had previously tried to do so, and Mao had attempted. Yet the holy grail of technology that the Chinese Communist Party strived to obtain, and which had driven its initial wanderings into both the Soviet and American camps was the acquisition of military equipment. Such equipment was a trade item and tool of modernization heavily opposed by both the Taiwan lobby and the early candidate Ronald Reagan himself.[354] Would the neo-liberal approach to trading with China initiated by Reagan carry over into this sphere as well?

Reagan and the Military Modernization of China

In large part, the main impetus behind China's desire to modernize as a whole lay in its fear of attack by the Soviet Union. As Carter faltered, and as Reagan abandoned tri-polarity and reaffirmed his commitment to both Japan and Taiwan, Beijing began to fear that it may have to stand alone against the U.S.S.R. in the event of a future war.[355] Though the Chinese military outnumbered the Soviets in the sheer number of men it could field, it was quite weak in terms of the quality of its equipment.[356] Thus, technology transfers between the United States and China soon extended from the world of industry to that of the military as well.

Military aid from the United States to China was a delicate affair for President Reagan. Having campaigned against the perceived abandonment of Taiwan by the Carter administration, and as a staunch anti-communist, the president could not be seen as too eager to supply the PRC with the latest weaponry. Likewise, many still doubted that China could be used as a ally against the Soviet empire. Prof. Hungdah Chiu of the University of Maryland perhaps best summed up the central issues of Sino-American détente and alliance during his participation in a Congressional hearing on the original Shanghai Communique in 1983. "To say a country as big and as populous as China, with five thousand years of history and experience of 'managing barbarian affairs,' can be played as a card is... naïve." China had a long history of "playing the barbarians against each other to attain national security."[357] The division in American political thought around the question of militarily aiding China was played out on a smaller scale as well within Reagan's executive department.

Reagan's cabinet was balanced between the pro-China lobby of Secretary of State Alexander Haig and the more moderate wing of Secretary of Defense Caspar Weinberger, George P. Schultz, and Paul Wolfowitz. A product of the Nixon administration and Kissinger school of realist thought, Haig sought to push Reagan to build upon the US-China alliance.[358]

The result of this effort would be the Shanghai Communiqué of August 1982. While vague at best in terms of aid or trade, the Communiqué did pledge the United States to gradually reduce its arms shipments to Taiwan, although Reagan and others took the view that it still gave him space to continue to supply Taiwan for a number of years. In a worst-case scenario, he could argue that the Communiqué was null and void as it had not been approved by the Senate and in fact violated the pre-existing Taiwan Relations Act of 1979, which as an act of Congress would constitutionally supersede any agreement the President made with China. Reagan continued to straddle the Haig-Weinberger divide throughout the early 1980s.

As with trade, the president's initial actions in this arena involved the easing of pre-existing restrictions. This relaxation began following Secretary of State Haig's trip to China in 1981. The White House announced in June of that year that it was ending the 31-year-old arms embargo that had existed between the two countries since the Korean War. Reagan played down the deal, stating that it was simply, "a normal part of the process" towards improving relations.[359]

Secretary Haig likewise sought to calm fears or hopes of an alliance between the two by emphasizing that, "Reagan intends to treat China as a friendly nation with whom the United States is *non-aligned* but with whom it shares many interests."[360] This put China squarely in the same camp as Yugoslavia in terms of receiving American arms. The White House promised that each weapons system would be individually approved and it would probably take China years to build up its force to anything approaching a modern military. As well, it was pointed out that the previous administration had begun the process back in 1979 when it worked to retrofit China's Harbin Z-5s with Pratt and Whitney PT6T-6s. The next year, Carter's Secretary of Defense, Harold Brown visited China in January and promised the sale of various non-lethal weapons, though at the time Beijing made no orders. In addition, as China had recently slashed its military budget, Haig announced that the $2 billion in credit promised by the Carter administration would be applied to the sale of weapons and equipment to China. This move by the Reagan White House was largely seen as a reaction to the Soviet occupation of Afghanistan. Though it would not prompt the opening up of an eastern front in the Cold War, it would at least serve to continue to tie down the 45 Soviet divisions stationed along the Chinese-Mongolian border. Finally, it was hoped that this move by Reagan could drive Taiwan to purchase more weapons from the United

States, adding to sales that already reached $700 million a year. In effect America would create an additional arms race in East Asia, hurting the Soviets and boosting the American economy.[361]

This new policy began with a revision to the Export Administration Act of 1979. Reagan pushed to remove restrictions on trading munitions with the PRC., a move that was quickly and predictably denounced by the U.S.S.R. A few weeks later, on July 8, 1981 the president signed NSC-NSDD 5, the Conventional Arms Transfer Policy. This directive laid out the procedure for approving technology transfers between the US and other countries.

This was followed by the China specific NSC-NSDD 11, "Munitions/Technology Transfer to the People's Republic of China," which laid out the principles by which weapons could be sold to China:

US munitions/technology transfers to China should minimize the national security risks in special mission areas of nuclear weapons or their delivery systems, anti-submarine warfare capabilities, electronic warfare capabilities, or intelligence gathering capabilities.

US munitions/technology transfers should not contribute significantly to improvements in Chinese offensive and power projection capabilities.

For requests which would enhance China's conventional defensive capabilities, the U.S. will be willing to consider the transfer of weapons, components, technical assistance, and weapons technology (including some coproduction/ licensed) production where sensitive technologies are not involved.

For requests which fall into less clearly defensive categories, the U.S. will look first to the selective transfer of components and technical assistance rather than the transfer of complete weapon systems or their production technology.

U.S. classified military information will be disclosed in accordance with the criteria and procedures established by the National Disclosure Policy.

These trade moves were soon followed in 1982 by NSC-NSDD 70. This presidential directive extended to the world of ballistic missile technologies the same concepts that had been applied to conventional weapons. Once again, President Reagan reserved for himself the power to extend high-level technological grants to nations such as China. Finally, as mentioned in the previous section, by December 1982, the president even announced that the United States would begin aiding the nuclear energy development of China.[362]

Further policy changes soon followed. In September 1983, Secretary of State Weinberger paid a visit to China and announced what became known as the Three Pillars Policy. The United States and China would 1) Exchange High Level Visits, 2) Undertake Functional Level Exchanges, and 3) Have Military Technology cooperation.[363] The third of these policies had been under consideration since Reagan's first announcement in 1981 and would continue to expand as his administration wore on. Shortly after Weinberger's return to the United States, China was moved to category V of the export commodity control list. This change essentially placed it on par with other American allies, and though each export would still need to be approved on a case-by-case basis, it did provide for the first time actual weapons exports to China.

Weinberger's retinue in Beijing included such other lukewarm Chinese alliance individuals as Assistant Secretary of State for East Asian Affairs Paul Wolfowitz, Assistant Secretary of

Defense for Security Policy Richard Armitage, Dr. Fred Ikle, and General Colin Powell. During his exchange with his opposite number in Beijing, Zhang Aiping, China sought to acquire as much American military hardware as possible. Weinberger resisted, and instead insisted upon following the previously laid out process of approving military technology transfers on a case-by-case basis. China would essentially become militarily supplied by the United States, but not in the haphazard hardware dumping fashion of the late Sino-Soviet period. Weinberger and Zhang would eventually agree to sales of Hawk air defense missiles, TOW missiles, improved artillery, various other military technologies, and even discussed the possibility of acquiring a license to produce TOW missiles in China. All in all, by the end of the negotiations, over 32 specific applications for technology transfers were approved.[365]

Foreign military sales began soon after the adoption of the 1984 budget, with Reagan informing Congress that arming China would, "strengthen the security of the United States and promote world peace." In 1985, it was reported that China had an interest in purchasing anti-submarine warfare gear, submarine detection devices, torpedoes, and ship defense weapons.[367] These deals would finally be signed in 1987, when the United States undertook four large military technology sales to the PRC. One involved a $22 million large-caliber artillery plant modernization program, an $8 million Mk46 Mod 2 Torpedo sale, a $62 million AN/TPQ-37 artillery locator radar sale, and $500 million for an F-8 avionics modernization program. Finally, in August 1985, GE won a contract to supply five gas turbine engines to the PLA Navy. Reagan's contribution to the modernization of the Chinese military was to supply difficult-to-reproduce advanced technology in the two spheres that Beijing was the weakest—communications and defense.

The second of the Three Pillars, functional-level exchanges, also began to materialize following Weinberger's trip to Beijing. Zhang Aiping proceeded on a tour of American weapons factories and military bases in June 1984. He was followed by Secretary of the Navy John Lehman who visited China that August. Four months later, a delegation of Chinese officials visited American naval bases. General John Vessey Jr., Chairman of the Joint Chiefs of Staff, became the highest ranking US officer to visit the communist nation during the early months of 1985. In 1986, the US Navy conducted a port call to Qingdao. This was the first such event since the Navy departed from that same city in 1949. Likewise, the US Air Force dispatched the Thunderbirds demonstration team to Beijing in 1987 in a show of friendship. In response the PRC sent Yang Shangkun to the United States in May 1987. The permanent Vice-Chairman of the Central Military Commission, Yang was at the time described as "instrumental in furthering military-to-military contacts."[368] He was certainly an influential figure within the Chinese government and served as the direct liaison between Deng and the PLA.

A further example of cooperation between the two nations during the 1980s joint biological weapons researc. Though China had famously accused the United States of employing biological weapons during the Korea War, by the late 1980s they were actively working with them to develop defenses against biological attack from the Soviets. Hubei Province Medical University and the U.S. Department of Defense worked jointly to investigate the effects of disease agents upon 200 hospitalized volunteers. The victims, suffering from hemorrhagic fevers with renal syndrome were given varieties of medicines to test possible treatments and their effectiveness. The program began in 1987 under a Chinese initiative and mirrored similar American partnerships in Argentina and Bolivia under the Reagan administration.

Reagan-Deng Foreign Policy Cooperation
Under Reagan, US-Chinese cooperation took a larger step forward. As part of the Reagan administration's policy of actively confronting the Soviet Union, the president ramped up Carter's Operation Cyclone, the aiding of the Afghan mujahedeen during the Soviet-Afghan War. One of the initial problems in the operation, the means by which to supply the Afghanis, was solved using Chinese assistance. American planners in effect re-opened portions of the Silk Road, the trade routes by which the region had been supplied for two thousand and more years.

Weapons, food, and material began to flow to the mujahedeen on the backs of Chinese mules.[369] By 1983, the CIA was purchasing both infantry weapons and light anti-aircraft weapons from China. Over 10,000 tons of equipment was clandestinely purchased and shipped to Pakistan for subsequent distribution to the mujahedeen.[370] China even began to donate weapons directly to the Pakistanis themselves.[371] By 1987, this weapons trade had grown to 65,000 tons and netted the Chinese an estimated $100 million a year.[372] China was subsequently used by various splinter members of the Pentagon to lobby Reagan for the Stinger missiles which became synonymous with the conflict.[373]

The Afghanistan episode was soon followed by China's involvement in what became known as the Iran-Contra Scandal. Reagan sought to supply the Contras in Nicaragua with shoulder-launched missiles similar to the successful Stingers sent to Afghanistan. But following the passage of the Boland Amendment in 1984, the US government was forbidden from supplying further aid to the Contras. Colonel Oliver North then proposed to President Reagan the idea of acquiring Chinese produced SA-7 missiles. Following a variety of clandestine meetings, these were shipped from China, through Guatemala and Honduras, to the Contras. Chinese acquiescence was linked to further grants of nuclear technology to the PRC.[374] The China Card was being played as it had been during the 1970s, but the nation was also emerging on its own as a world player.

Arms sales to China were far from being an obvious domain for America to become involved in. As Beijing feared ties between Washington and Taipei, it had begun to seek military hardware deals with various European nations. The British offered Harrier jets and Sea Dart SAMs, Germany hoped to sell Leopard tanks and Milan ATMs, Italy wished to sell its frigates, and France sought buyers for its Mirage 2000 fighters. All came close to finalizing sales with China during that nation's row with Washington over arms sales to Taiwan from 1981-1983, yet all the European sales would eventually fail to materialize for a variety of reasons. The most important of these was simply China's lack of capital.[375] It has been estimated that to fully modernize its four million-plus military, China would have had to spend at least $40-50 billion.[376] Japan and Taiwan were clearly better choices politically, strategically, and economically for American arms sales. In addition, China itself was merely seeking sample weapons to reverse engineer and reproduce. No arms manufacturer and few countries would ever agree to this arrangement. The U.S.S.R. had practiced this style of dogmatic weapon sales for a generation, selling arms at below market prices or even giving them for free as a means to augment its reach and standing in parts of the world. Reagan's moves toward arms transfers to China clearly broke the traditional relationship of the United States as a free market arms salesman to the world, and instead placed it within the U.S.S.R.'s former role as a military mentor. Yet it should be noted that the United States still made a profit off of all sales, and only approached the dogmatic style of Soviet arms sales in opening access to *types* of weapons.

The modernization of the PLA fulfilled Nixon's original goal of pushing the containment of the USSR back from Da Nang to the Mongolian border. Finally, it satisfied China's goals of security and economic independence. Reagan was elected on a platform of dissatisfaction with Carter's various foreign policy blunders. He had promised to confront communism and did so in the shape of the Soviet Union. Yet at the same time, he had continued the correction of the myopic view that the American government had possessed for the better part of 40 years of a monolithic communist foe bent on world domination. Economically, politically and socially, for both the United States and China, military cooperation with the PRC. was in the best interests of both nations at the time. Reagan went far beyond what many would have expected of his administration in his decision to arm China, but in terms of the Cold War, it proved to be the right thing to do. The level of trust established by this move did much to strengthen additional economic and cultural ties between the two nations.

Reagan and Chinese Students
Perhaps one of the most successful cultural exchanges between the two countries lay in the domain of education. A trickle of Chinese students had been flowing into the US since the late 1970s; likewise, a small number of American scholars had been admitted into China during the same period. Reagan's cultural exchange protocol of 1984, however, opened up the floodgates to Chinese students who wished to pursue higher education in America. While the overall number of Chinese studying abroad increased between 1980 and 1988, it did so at a much greater rate in the US. China, for its part, would spend an estimated US$75 million on student exchanges with the US from 1983-1985 alone.[377]

Fear of Chinese students becoming over-acculturated with American ideas or simply wishing to stay in the United States eventually led Premier Li Peng to issue new regulations on exit visas. In November 1987, Li signed into law a document outlining the exact number of years a Chinese student could stay in America. Reactions from Chinese students abroad were very negative. A massive letter-writing campaign between these students and the Chinese government ensued. Dissent, the cornerstone of American political activity, seems to have been one of our stronger lessons to these visiting academics.[379]

America's acceptance of Chinese scholars proved to be one of its most useful gifts to Beijing during the Reagan administration. Though often overlooked compared to the more important economic and military cooperation initiated between the two nations during the decade, the returning scholars would largely be the ones to spearhead the subsequent modernization of their own nation. As the president of the Chinese Academy of Sciences stated in 1987, "the main scientific and technological force" of the Academy must be aimed at "the main battlefield of serving economic construction."[380] In fact, recognition of the value of these scholars, combined with their high attrition rate to foreign nations and companies, has led the PRC to spend 350 million RMB since 1990 to provide science and technology startup grants to any that agree to return to the mainland.[381]

To illustrate the value of these returning scholars to China, one need only examine the most recent listing of the wealthiest people in the country. The richest person was current head of one of China's most successful real estate development companies, Yang Huiyan, a graduate of Ohio State University. Many other returning students now occupy high positions in the Chinese Academy of Sciences, Chinese Academy of Engineering, universities and government research programs. In addition, many of the most profitable and successful multinational corporations in China are headed by these foreign-trained students.[382] Once again, following the American model of development, the growth of China has been borne upon the backs of those trained in already developed nations.

Machiavelli once famously stated regarding the treatment of enemies that they, "ought either to be well treated or crushed, because they can avenge themselves of lighter injuries, of more serious ones they cannot." China was one such enemy which had been repeatedly isolated and targeted by America since 1949. Yet the actions undertaken by President Reagan in the 1980s marked a clear departure from this trajectory and a move towards a more positive, "Machiavellian" treatment of Beijing. In essence, President Reagan followed a free market policy of Taoist passivity, or laissez-faire economics, toward China. While his administration helped to finance China's development and provided a legislative framework for Sino-American relations to progress, he did not attempt to direct China's course in the same way that the U.S.S.R., or others had before. China was almost entirely responsible for the process itself. The Reagan administration proved to be ideologically color-blind in its dealings with its former enemy. The economic and geopolitical backlash from Tiananmen that largely isolated China provided the final impetus for Beijing to use its newly-found resources to better itself. Whether these improvements were due to fear of either outside aggression or domestic unrest is immaterial. China *could* modernize thanks to President Reagan, and now China *would* modernize.

Ronald Reagan represented a milestone in American history. As president he brought to fruition nearly a half century of American efforts to bring down the U.S.S.R. and totalitarianism in Eastern Europe. During the same period, China began its meteoric rise to the heights it has achieved today. Yet Reagan's role in the process, and impact upon its direction has been often overlooked. Through his various economic and social policies towards the People's Republic of China, and his laissez-faire approach toward the process of modernization itself, President Reagan and his administration proved invaluable to the economic and technological development of modern China.

8

REPUBLICANS IN THE SHADOW OF TIANANMEN

SINO-AMERICAN RELATIONS FROM 1989-2009

WHEN REAGAN LEFT office in 1989, the world was on the verge of unprecedented changes that would have seemed impossible back in 1980. The once-feared Soviet Union was on the edge of collapse, ending almost a half century of Cold War. Likewise, China seemed to be on the edge of a political and social revolution following its economic and technological modernization, aided by almost a decade of Republican policies. Yet the fall of the Berlin Wall was not replicated on the other side of the globe in Beijing, instead similar protests there resulted in the tragic June 4 confrontation, in and around Tiananmen Square.

Tiananmen serves as a key marker in the story of China's modernization. Reagan's policies and aid to Beijing in a way provided the conditions that led to the tragedy.[383] Classical liberal thought hinged upon the notion that the growth of economic freedom would be followed by political freedom as well. Following the storm of weeks of protests followed by the bloody crackdown, American and world aid, investment and trade were largely withdrawn and China was forced to face the choice of either falling behind again or else continuing modernization on its own.

George H. W. Bush had more previous experience than

most Republican presidents when it came to China. While serving as Nixon's ambassador to the United Nations from 1971 to 1973 he was frequently mentioned by the president as a possible contender to visit China in the run-up to Nixon's own trip. Following Ford's assumption of the presidency, Bush was appointed chief of the US Liaison Office in Beijing, which served as the informal embassy. His time in that position was dominated by the presence in the White House of Henry Kissinger, but he did acquire much practical knowledge of China and its people.

Once in office, Bush planned his first major trip abroad as a grand tour of East Asia in February 1989, attending the funeral of Hirohito in Japan, spending three days in China, and landing briefly in South Korea before returning home. The President continued the Reagan approach of following an Open Door policy, downplaying any strategic message with the trip:

"I don't know what signal it sends in that regard. But let me just remind you that I'm the one who does not believe in 'playing the Soviet card' or 'playing the China card.' We have a strong bilateral relationship with the People›s Republic of China. I have a personal acquaintance with the leaders with whom I will be meeting there, including Deng Xiaoping, and being that close -- it just seemed like an appropriate visit, but not to signal a playing of the card to go one up on Mr. Gorbachev. There's nothing of that nature in this visit. That is a strong, important strategic and commercial and cultural relationship that we have with the Chinese -- the largest number of people in the world, in that country. And so, the visit stands on its own and does not have any signaling that should be detrimental to anybody else's interest."[384]

Instead, Bush said he simply wished to expand upon all of the various exchanges begun under Reagan, informing a Xinhua news reporter on February 16, 1989, that he sought to increase economic, cultural, scientific, technological, and military connections between both countries.

The protests that erupted in Tiananmen Square in April 1989 must have been viewed with some excitement by the Bush White House. It came only two months after his trip there in which he had spoken of "a new breeze blowing in the world today... a worldwide movement toward greater freedom, freedom of human creativity and freedom of economic opportunity...China was one of the first nations to feel this new breeze, and like a tree in a winter wind, you›ve learned to bend and adapt to new ways and new ideas and reform", the president must have surely seen parallels with what was transpiring in Eastern Europe.[385]

Yet as June unfolded and the Chinese government moved to end the standoff by force, much of the world reacted with horror. Bush for his part issued a public statement denouncing the use of violence and urging China to "return to the path of political and economic reform and conditions of stability so that this relationship, so important to both our peoples, can continue its growth."[386]

The Bush administration initially attempted to carry on business as usual to a degree with the Chinese, dispatching Brent Scowcroft, his national security advisor, to Beijing only a month after the massacre. The president even went so far as to approve the sale of three communication satellites to China in December 1989. For its part, Beijing continued to cooperate with Washington in intelligence gathering from missile and nuclear monitoring sites along the Soviet border. A State Department memo issued at the time describes President Bush as "sharing the same broad view as the masses," yet at the same time realizing that the relationship between the United States and the PRC. was the "important factor."[387]

During the protests themselves, the President resisted proclaiming his full support for the movement, fearing that doing so would, "stir up a military confrontation".[388]

Bush feared that returning China to isolationism would do little to help either nation or the trend of democratization that seemed to be developing there.

But President Bush also wrote to the Chinese leaders, explaining that Congress was a co-equal branch of the United States government, and would demand a reaction against the People's Republic. This was especially true as the Democratic Party at the time held a clear majority in both houses of Congress. Indeed, reactions did quickly follow. Japan, the United States and other nations froze assets, cancelled military sales and withdrew advisors. The European Union and the United States even placed an arms embargo on China that was still in place twenty years later.

Various forms of aid, trade, and exchanges by the United States were likewise cut off with the passage of Public Law 101-246, the so-called "Tiananmen Square Legislation" in February 1990. The act not only praised the response of President Bush to the crisis, but also sought to internationalize the response and hinged continued economic and military dealings with China on its efforts to reform its practices. As a means of punishing Beijing, Congress recommended that Bush should put a halt to further Export-Import Bank loans, end the sharing of nuclear and space technology, and oppose China's acceptance into various world trade bodies.

After 1989, the United States limited foreign aid to China to specific localities and causes, including Tibet and Yunnan and such issues as HIV/AIDS prevention and treatment, and natural disaster recovery. These restrictions stayed in place until 2002. OPIC (Overseas Private Investment Corporation) and USTDA (US Trade and Development Agency), both of which functioned within the Import-Export Bank to finance private investment in China, likewise were withdrawn from mainland China until after 2002. Finally, the United States used its leverage in the World Bank and IMF to turn down Chinese applications for loans and assistance, which would have totaled $2.2 billion in 2005 alone.[389] American investment in China for a time fell.

Under the Arms Control Act, Congress restricted the access of China to American weaponry and dual use military technology. Likewise, the United States announced that it would restrict the import of ammunition from China into America. This was caused by a combination of those who feared a militarized China as well as those who despised the actions of Beijing against its own people. As was previously mentioned, the European Union passed similar sanctions.

China was dropped from duty-free status following the June 4 crackdown, a move which was aimed at hampering trade. Its pending applications in the WTO and IMF were also delayed for over a decade. At the same time, restrictions were placed on various dual-use items and chemicals by the Department of Commerce's Bureau of Industry and Security. Even computer sales to China became restricted, based on the processing power and possible dual use of the equipment.[390] Additionally, items related to space exploration and nuclear energy would have to be approved for trade on a case-by-case basis.

Yet Bush worked to continue both diplomatic and trade relations with the country. This is perhaps best exemplified by the trip of national security advisor Brent Scowcroft to Beijing in July, only a month after the bloody invasion of the center of the city by Chinese troops and tanks. Kept secret at the time, details of the meeting only emerged in December. Democrats were quick to pounce on it, with Democrat George J. Mitchell, the Senate majority leader calling it, "another midnight mission, barely a month after the brutal killing of pro-democracy student demonstrators," while Lee Hamilton of Indiana opined that, "they apparently were doing what they told us they were not doing."[391] Information about the trip emerged just as Bush had officially dispatched a second mission by Scowcroft and Lawrence Eagleburger to China. Clearly, Bush thought that if freedom was to develop in China it would do so organically, and that removing the economic basis for it would not expedite its development but merely continue the repression of the government. Former President Nixon, likewise stressed that while "punitive policies would be politically popular and emotionally satisfying for the great majority of the American people", they would have almost no impact on the myopic, hardline Chinese administration.[392]

As a further sign of this view, in March 1992 Bush refused to sign the United States-China Act of 1991 which sought to place restrictions on the latter nation's status as a Most Favored Nation for terms of trade. Bush staunchly opposed this, arguing that, "The end result will not be progress on human rights, arms control or trade. Anyone familiar with recent Chinese history can attest that the most brutal and protracted periods of repression took place precisely when China turned inward, against the world."[393] Instead, he insisted, "We are making a difference in China by remaining engaged." The President continued to use his office to waive all restrictions on trade with China for the remainder of his administration, vetoing a similar measure in September 1992. The issue was even brought up during the presidential debates that year, with Bill Clinton accusing Bush of "coddling tyrants".

George W. Bush

The eight years of Democratic rule between the administrations of the two Bushes saw both a growing and increasingly strong China and, "anemic formulations" regarding Sino-American relations on the part of the Clinton White House.[394] Clinton vacillated between strong responses and Open Door trade deals, with a Chinese campaign finance scandal clouding many of his interactions with Beijing. In fact, the issue of modernizing China had so largely been pushed from the public sphere of discussion that apart from a brief mention with regards to the Kyoto Treaty, the nation was not even brought up during the 2000 election debates.

President Bush, while continuing the New Open Door Policy of cooperation and free exchange with China, also had to contend with its rising power and influence on the world stage that precipitated a number of incidents. A statement by Colin Powell following his selection as Secretary of State, connected Bush's view of China to those of his predecessors. "We will work with those nations in the world that are transforming themselves, nations such as China and Russia. We will work with them not as potential enemies, and not as adversaries, but not yet as strategic partners, but as nations that are seeking their way."[395]

During his first year in office, the growing influence of China was almost immediately made apparent when reports surfaced that it was building anti-aircraft missile sites in Iraq. The President queried Beijing regarding this move and was soon after able to defuse the situation. By far the most serious case, though, came in April 2001 when a Navy EP-3E surveillance plane collided with a Chinese fighter jet over the South China Sea. Though flying in international air space, American military planes had begun to be challenged by the increasingly modernized Chinese air force. The Chinese fighter crashed, killing its pilot, and US plane was forced to make an emergency landing on Hainan Island where the crew were detained for 10 days before being released. The crew were in no way mistreated, but the incident, including a demand from Washington for an apology, showed a similar though augmented level of confrontation to that which Reagan had experienced upon first becoming president.

But neither the Hainan Island Incident nor the subsequent September 11 attacks deterred Bush's trip to China in October of that year to attend the APEC Summit in Shanghai nor a subsequent tour of East Asia the following February. Bush pushed hard, like his Republican predecessors, for increased exchanges with China. Among his achievements were supporting China's accession to the WTO and the permanent granting of MFN status shortly afterwards. The modernization of China is made most thoroughly evident by the fact that much of the talk between Bush and Jiang Zemin during the former's visit touched on such "First World" issues as greenhouse gas emission, the environment and human rights.

Likewise, China early on expressed its support for America in its global war against Islamic terrorism. Jiang Zemin stated during Bush's visit in October 2001 that, "we are opposed to terrorism of all forms. And what we have done in the past has shown this attitude of ours very clearly. We hope that antiterrorism efforts can have clearly defined targets. And efforts should hit accurately and also avoid innocent casualties. And what is more, the role of the United Nations should be brought into full play."[396] This is not surprising considering Beijing's own problem against Uighur separatists in Xinjiang for decades. In a similar vein, China also aided Bush in his efforts to maintain a nuclear-free Korean peninsula.

Overall, the eight-year administration of George W. Bush saw the culmination of the Open Door Policy that had restarted under Nixon. By the 2000s, free trade had largely become a reality between the two countries, with far fewer barriers remaining between them than at any time since the opening of trade in the 18th century. Likewise, the modernization of China continued apace economically, technologically, and socially, with only political advancement trailing behind. Finally, China was beginning to assert itself beyond its borders, a trend that would accelerate during the administrations of Hu Jintao and Barack Obama with confrontational results.

POSTSCRIPT

CHINA INC. VS TRUMP INC.

REPUBLICANS AND CHINA IN 2016

THE NOMINATION of Donald Trump to head the Republican ticket in 2016 presented an interesting break in the narrative of Sino-American relations of almost the same magnitude as Reagan's victory in 1980. Having switched his party allegiance several times from 1987 to 2012, and with no previous political role, it was difficult to gauge his initial views on the traditional Republican attitude towards China. Clouding this identification still further was his record as a businessman, which would tend to suggest he would be supportive of a traditional Open Door Policy policy.

Yet a study of Trump's speeches and pronouncements on China reveal a nuanced view much in keeping with early Federalists and with Reagan. As early as the announcement of his candidacy in June 2015, Trump focused heavily on the trade imbalance between the United States and China, but not from a position of nativism or xenophobia as was often stated by his opponents. Trump was quick to point out that, "I love China... But their leaders are much smarter than our leaders, and we can't sustain ourself with that."[397] This is strikingly similar to Reagan's own pronouncements regarding China in 1980. The imbalance of trade between the two nations, which grew from almost nothing in 1985 to $343 billion by 2015 became a cornerstone of his populist campaign. His opponents and the media tended to focus on Trump's exaggeration of the number, which he often stated as ranging from $300 billion to $500 billion, rather than on the economic issue that it represented.

On November 10, 2015, Trump issued a major policy announcement detailing how he would reform Sino-American relations in terms of trade. Interestingly, the vast majority of his proposals dealt not with reforming China but with American practices. He argued much of the same laissez-faire economic policies that dominated Republican thought for two centuries. The problem, as Trump saw it, was not the economic growth and development of China, but the recent economic contraction of America which he saw as stemming from governmental policies and actions. Likewise, in a similar way to Reagan, Trump promised to take a hardline against Beijing when necessary.

He recognized his party's role and responsibility for the economic state of China. "We've rebuilt China," Trump opined in an April 2016 interview. Yet this truism also had a deeper implication. The candidate was also presenting a harsh critique of American foreign policy towards China during the previous eight years. The Obama administration, despite its famed "Pivot to Asia", had been largely passive when dealing with Beijing. Trump highlighted China's practically uncontested construction and fortification of islands in the South China Sea as a prime example of this.

Overall, Trump's stated position on China was little different than Reagan's over 36 years before. He vowed to take a hard line to oppose the growing overseas influence of China, yet was not opposed to the Chinese helping to solve problems in America's interests in countries in which Beijing already had significant influence, particularly North Korea. Trade would be continued and expanded on a free market basis, but America needed to be truly capitalistic itself in order to successfully compete, he said. Finally, the modernization of China was to serve a practical purpose of slowly achieving the political modernization of the country, a development that was not to be pushed artificially but allowed to happen organically.

Since the latter days of Mao in the 1970s, China had made use of the divide-and-rule traditions once practiced in imperial times with regard to those beyond its borders. Beijing clearly understood the American political system, and just as North Vietnam did in 1968 and 1972, it took certain measures to take advantage of the democratic process. The transition from one president to another would often be used by China as a time to expand its power and test the resolve of the United States.

The challenges made to Reagan following his inauguration have already been discussed. As seen, his forceful replies to these challenges helped to contain China's expansive tendencies for a decade and paved the way for groundbreaking exchanges between the two. Likewise, the Chinese harassment of American surveillance planes in the region in 2001 led to the Hainan Island Crisis that greeted the new Bush White House. Then in March of 2009, the USNS Impeccable was harassed by numerous Chinese ships and planes as it conducted operations in the South China Sea.

Interestingly, though, Trump broke with the trend of initial Chinese provocation and launched his own shot across the bow in December 2016. A new China Lobby, using Bob Dole as its proxy, organized a phone call between president-elect Trump and the president of the Republic of China government on Taiwan, Tsai Ing-wen. It was the first communication between occupants of the two posts since at least 1979, and was strategically undertaken before the new president was officially inaugurated in order to lessen blowback from Beijing. An article in Foreign Policy in

November, 2016, by Alexander Gray and Peter Navarro attacked the Obama administration's perceived final abandonment of Taiwan, recommending that the new Trump administration work towards bolstering the defenses of this "beacon of democracy".[398]

In response, Beijing sought to both test Trump and express its anger towards the enervated Obama administration. Several weeks later, the Chinese navy seized an underwater drone being operated by the USNS Bowditch in the South China Sea. The ship had previously been harassed by Chinese vessels in 2001 in the same area, shortly after Bush was inaugurated. While the Obama White House chose to follow its standard diplomatic path of complaint, president-elect Trump bitterly denounced the seizure as "unprecedented".

Overall, initial statements and moves by Donald Trump seemed to suggest that he would take a hardline towards Chinese aggression while remaining open to cooperation with them on key issues. This was further reinforced by his appointment of Terry Branstad as the new ambassador to China, a man who has over thirty years of contact and experience with the Chinese leader, Xi Jinping. At the same time, the new president indicated he would direct his economic anger largely at the American system in an effort to make it truly competitive in a free market competition against Beijing.

CONCLUSION

RELATIONSHIPS BETWEEN NATIONS are never static. Intervening events, changes in leadership and shifting economic conditions make interactions between countries mercurial at best. Yet at the same time, for various reasons, some nations have often historically help long-term, consistent outlooks towards certain other nations. Examples include the Anglo-Portuguese alliance which persisted for over six centuries as well as the animosity that has existed between China and Vietnam for close to two thousand years. While these views may usually be driven by geography, religion, strategy or economics, occasionally it is purely ideologically-based.

The Republican Party in its various incarnations throughout the past two centuries and more has played the dominant role in American politics in both opening of trade and relations with China as well as helping to modernize that nation. From the early days of the Federalist Party's intent to use Canton as both a marketplace for American merchandize as well as a source of exotic goods, to President Reagan's efforts to drastically modernize the country, the party has not only stood at the forefront of Sino-American relations, in sharp contrast to the Democratic Party.

This divergence of views arose from a number of factors inherent to both political parties. The Federalist/Whig/Republican focus on trade certainly was a primary motivator for closer connections with China. The profit to be garnered from such a distant trade network presented a tempting marketplace for New England traders. Thus the opening of relations with China started as being largely a regional issue, with the party simply following the economic demands of its base. Jefferson and his party's initial focus on the agrarian South left them unconcerned with China.

The desire of classical conservatives to maintain a policy of non-interventionism in the world was best served by working to deny European powers territorial possessions and influence in China. Likewise, a powerful and independent China was seen at the turn of the twentieth century as a possible counterweight to Japan and in the 1970s to the USSR. This created the counterintuitive need for America to actively involve itself in China to avoid confrontations with other, more powerful nations.

A Republican world view built around the concept of natural rights and the free market would have no racial or ethnic hostility towards empowering China. In fact, in an attempt to further separate themselves from Europe and develop an "American" culture, various members of the Founding and later generations looked to China and other non-traditional nations for political, artistic, literary, cultural, and social ideas.

The Democratic Party's focus on racial politics from its initial concerns over slavery and the expulsion of Native Americans, to its later apprehension over the movement of the Chinese into California, and onward to its modern internment of the Japanese in WWII and programs for Affirmative Action, have made it particularly susceptible to view foreign policy through a lens of race rather than economic or strategic concerns. Regardless of whether these efforts are couched in the notion of opposing one group or aiding in the rise of another, they invariably produce hostility towards a select segment of the national and international population.

Early Democrats feared losing agricultural jobs to China while later manifestations of the party feared both an influx of cheap, Chinese workers and the direct loss of manufacturing jobs to China itself. Therefore China was seen as more of a market competitor than England which tended to be a buyer of American raw materials.

A focus by the Left on Western values, culture and democracy as the key to world peace as personified by the internationalism of Wilson, placed Europe at the forefront of American interests and affairs. This is clearly shown by both our Europe first strategy in WWII as well our early focus on that continent's security rather than the situation in East Asia at the start of the Cold War.

While the goal of the Republican Party to open trade with China was largely accomplished in the nineteenth century unilaterally by the American side, the larger hope of modernizing China as well as the push to restore trade relations after the communist takeover in 1949 required a bilateral approach. Early attempts by Burlingame and other Republicans in the latter nineteenth century to modernize China largely failed in the face of opposition from the Qing government. The conservative clique under Cixi, which dominated court politics in the later decades of the century, worked against the various modernizing moves of both the United States as well as individuals within its own government. Likewise, attempts by the Republicans in the 1920s to assist in the modernization of China, though meeting with a likeminded confederate in the person of Chiang Kai-shek, found the latter leader to be too constrained fighting warlords, communists, and later the Japanese to fully follow through. Finally, moves by Nixon and Ford to bring China into the twentieth century occurred too close to the Cultural Revolution and the decline of Mao. Only the rise of Deng Xiaoping brought to the fore in China a leader who was willing to fully commit his country to modernization outside the ideological constraints of Marxist economics.

The modernization of China can best be compared to that of Japan a century before. The rapid economic, political, social, and technological development of Japan following the Meiji Restoration was viewed as unprecedented at the time. Japan emerged from over two centuries of near isolation and rapidly grew to parallel the Western world. This was accomplished by largely following a policy in which the government was willing to both work with international partners as well as radically change nearly every element of Japanese society. Perhaps the best example of this was the fact that the government seriously considered adopting both English as the official language of the empire as well as Christianity as the official religion. But China's slavish adherence to traditional norms in the nineteenth century as well as the tenets of Marx and Mao after 1949 limited its ability to modernize. Deng's willingness to work with Reagan and take such drastic measures as the establishment of the Special Economic Zones was necessary to achieve the same degree of modernization as had Japan. It took almost two hundred years for the combination of these two men to arise in order to enable the final modernization of China.

The success of Chinese modernization and the commitment of its leaders is perhaps best exemplified by its "Going Out" Policy launched in 1999. The then Chinese leader Jiang Zemin, largely continuing the policies of Deng, pushed the policy which encouraged Chinese businesses to invest abroad. The fact that only a generation after it had begun to modernize, China was now expanding economically overseas was a mark of considerable and unprecedented achievement. Active overseas investment and movement of capital abroad were not unknown in Chinese history, as the nation had had trading arrangements in place with many parts of Southeast Asia at least in the Ming Dynasty period of the fifteenth and sixteenth centuries.

Since the presidency of Bill Clinton, the Democratic Party has moved towards incorporating parts of the Republican policy towards China. While hints of this were evident in the actions of Jimmy Carter, his moves were more of a misreading of Nixon's strategy rather than pure aping or acceptance. Yet while both Clinton and Obama continued economic interactions with Beijing and agreed to numerous technology transfers, they failed to maintain the strong commitment to containing Chinese expansion. Indeed, during the latter's term in office, China began to militarize territory in the South China Sea, a move which directly threatened stability and trade in the region. All of this occurred despite Obama's much-vaunted Pivot to Asia which actually produced more results in Southeast Asia than with China.[399]

In the end, Republican interests in China arose not out of pure altruism towards the latter nation, but built upon a concern for American improvement at home and secure expansion abroad. This statement describes well the message of Donald Trump during his election campaign in 2016. As a candidate, the businessman frequently cited unfair practices by China as a component of the anemic American economic recovery. Likewise, he saw the burdensome regulations and taxes put forward by the federal government as unfairly aiding that nation as well. In so doing, he was not abandoning the centuries old party view towards China of trade and modernization, but merely asserting that it existed primarily for the benefit of America.

Overall, the connection between the Republican Party and China arose *organically* out of the hopes and needs of both. In this, it followed one of the dearest principles of conservatism, that change should occur naturally and not out of sudden planning. From the 1790s to 2016, Sino-American relations vis-à-vis the Republican Party in its various forms has consistently sought to modernize the former and economically and strategically benefit the latter. Claims of a historical "special relationship" with the United Kingdom put forth at various times since WWII, pale in terms of the age of cooperation between the United States and China. America in general, and the Republican Party in particular, has served as the Prometheus of Chinese modernization and development, the bringer of knowledge and technology to an otherwise chaotic world.

Some may criticize or question the actions of Burlingame, Reagan, and others in seeking to strengthen and modernize China. Their argument would revolve around questioning the wisdom of building up a potential rival to the United States. Yet this argument actually conflates two positions, the first economic and the second strategic. The economic buildup of China has been a long-term process that has overall financially benefited both American businesses and consumers along the way. China's emerging market domination rests in areas of production that are no longer prevalent in the United States, in fact the two countries economically balance each other out in terms of production, with China focusing on building basic products while America produces food, resources, or more advanced technologies. This would be similar to England's contributions to the economic growth of the United States during the 1820s and 1830s, which, rather than create an economic rival instead produced an economic partner. Trade is global and no one nation can or should seek to dominate it. Competition benefits more individuals than does isolated production. In addition, China's growing economic power is in part due to the United States' enervation of its own industries and free market opportunities.

Money and production flow to the path of least resistance. Finally, China's continued growth is hardly an assured prospect and in fact has shown many signs of weakening in recent years.

China certainly poses a potential security threat to the United States, but based upon its history would be more of a regional rather than a global player. This is why numerous previous presidents have been sure to contain Beijing's territorial and power ambitions while still openly cooperating with them economically, truly a carrot and the stick approach. Appeasement of China since the 1960s has tended to appear more as a product of Democratic action, or lack thereof, rather than Republican. This can clearly be seen in the actions of Carter, Clinton, and Obama, especially the latter's inaction towards China's buildup in the South China Sea. Yet overall, how is the buildup of China by Washington different than America's approach to almost any other nation? After WWII American helped to build up the strength of Japan, Italy, Germany, and Thailand, nations that were bitter enemies only a decade before. While our goals may align with those nations now, the future is always uncertain. Starting so far behind America in terms of power and military capability, China will only grow to be an equal in terms of power if the United States allows itself to stagnate. Rome became great due to its century long war with Carthage, America came to dominate the world during its Cold War with the USSR, perhaps China will serve to reinvigorate the United States militarily, economically, and socially. Finally, China's overall goal historically has been regional stability rather than imperialism or conquest. Due to this it actually could prove to be a valuable partner to America in the area.

Laozi once opined that, "those who have knowledge, don't predict. Those that predict, don't have knowledge." It's always difficult to portend what path the future will take with things as complicated and as intricate as foreign affairs. Despite the rapid economic and military growth of China, will the Republican Party continue along its two-century old path of actively trading with and aiding the nation's development? Or, will the perceived economic and strategic threat posed by the awakening East Asian giant alter this?

America has openly traded with and equipped other powerful nations for decades, including the United Kingdom, Germany, Japan, South Korea, and India. No nation is inherently evil and there is nothing within the historical or cultural makeup of China that makes it intrinsically opposed to the United States. In addition, could the original goal of those free traders still be realized? That the free exchange of Western goods and ideas will eventually transform China into a free and open country? Again, there is nothing genetically preventing this in the region as has been seen in Taiwan, South Korea, and Japan. While some may scoff and point to the solid 60 year grip of the CCP on Chinese life or the supposed failure of the embargo in Cuba, we must begin to think of foreign affairs not in the immediate Western sense, but in the long term Chinese mindset. At some point in the future the CCP will fall, either violently or peacefully, no dynasty lasts forever. The question becomes, could the open trade and interaction policy of the Republican Party help to catalyze this? Already the China of Xi is not that of Mao. Nor is China's advance occurring within a vacuum. While its acquisition of its first aircraft carrier in 2012, the *Liaoning*, was greeted with celebration in Beijing and fear in other nations, the ship is severely limited in its capabilities and half the weight of the older American *Nimitz* class. Meanwhile, Washington has already launched the first ship of its new *Gerald R. Ford* class supercarrier. One can predict that China's march forward will be paralleled by America's own continued military and economic advancement and may in fact help to encourage it. Hannibal ad portas.

Prometheus brought civilization to the Greeks, introducing them to the tools and habits of the gods. Many opposed his efforts, none less than Zeus who condemned him to an eternity chained to a rock for his actions. The titan saw the eventual overthrow of the king of the gods as the gifts he gave would eventually raise others to a similar height of power. The opening and advancement of China by the Republican Party, has and will continue to benefit the vast majority of people on the planet. The Promethean belief in the free trade of goods and ideas between people, while opposed by many, has always been the direction of modernization and advancement in the world.

BIBLIOGRAPHY

Ali, A. Mahmud. *US-China Cold War Collaboration*. New York: Routledge, 2005.

Beale, Howard. *Theodore Roosevelt and the Rise of America*. Baltimore: The Johns Hopkins University Press, 1984.

Benton, Thomas Hart. *Speech of John Floyd in Thirty Years View: A History of the Working of the American Government for Thirty Years from 1820-1850*. New York: Appleton and Company, 1883.

Boggs, Hale and Ford Gerald. "Impressions of the New China". Washington: US Government Printing Office, 1972.

Brazinksy, Gregg Andrew. "From Pupil to Model: South Korea and American Development Policy during the Early Park Chung Hee Era". *Diplomatic History* (2005): 83-115.

Brzezinski, Z. *The Geostrategic Triad: Living with Europe, China, and Russia*. Washington DC: CSIS, 2000.

Bundy, William. *A Tangled Web: The Making of Foreign Policy in the Nixon Presidency*. New York: Hill and Wang, 1998.

Burr, William ed. *The Kissinger Transcripts: The Top Secret Talks with Moscow and Beijing* New York: The New Press, 1995.

Burton, Bruce. "Contending Explanations of the 1979 Sino-Vietnamese War." *International Journal* 34, 4 (Autumn 1979): 699-722 .

Cohen, Warren. *America's Response to China*. New York: Columbia University Press, 2010.

Copper, John F. "The Lessons of Playing Tough With China," *The*

Heritage Foundation. Aug. 23, 1983.

Copper, John. *President Reagan's Trip to the PRC.* Washington DC: Heritage Foundation, 1984.

Coxe, Trench. *A View of the United States of America, in a Series of Papers, Written at Various Times, between the Years 1787 and 1794,* Vol. 28. Philadelphia, 1794.

Dayal-Gulati, Anuradha and Husain, Aasim M. "Centripetal Forces in China's Economic Takeoff," *IMF Staff Papers* 49, 3 (2002)

Deans, Bob. *The River Where American Began: A Journey Along the James.* New York: Rowman & Littlefield Publishers, Inc, 2007.

Dinh, Viet D. "How We Won Vietnam," *Policy Review-Hoover Institute.* 104 (Dec. 2000)

Dolin, Eric Jay. *When America First Met China: An Exotic History of Tea, Drugs, and Money in the Age of Sail.* New York: Liveright, 2013.

Downs, Jacques M. *The Golden Ghetto: The American Commercial Community at Canton and the Shaping of American China Policy.* Hong Kong; HK Press, 2014.

Edwards, Lee. *Goldwater: The Man Who Made a Revolution.* Washington DC: Regnery, 2015.

Elleman, Bruce A. *Wilson and China: A Revised History of the Shandong Question.* London: M.E. Sharpe, 2002.

English, William Hayden. *Conquest of the Country Northwest of the River Ohio, 1778–1783, and Life of Gen. George Rogers Clark,* Vol. 1. Indianapolis: Bowen-Merrill, 1896.

Felt, Joseph B. *The Annals of Salem,* Vol. 2. Salem: W. & S.B. Ives, 1845.

Freedman, Paul. "Spices and Late Medieval European Ideas of Scarcity and Value," *Speculum* 80, 4 (Oct. 2005): 1209-1227.

Garrison, Jean A. "Framing Foreign Policy Alternatives in the Inner Circle: President Carter, His Advisors, and the Struggle for the Arms Control Agenda." *Political Psychology* (Dec. 2001): 775-807.

Gittings, John. *China Through the Sliding Door*. London: Simon & Schuster/Touchstone, 1999.

Gordon, Bernard K. "The United States and Asia in 1982: A Year of Tenterhooks," *Asian Survey*, 23, 1 (Jan. 1983): 1-10.

Gray, Alexander and Navarro, Peter. "Donald Trump's Peace through Strength Vision for the Asia-Pacific", *Foreign Policy* (Nov. 7, 2016).

Green, Mike. "The Legacy of Obama's 'Pivot' to Asia," *Foreign Policy* (Sept. 3, 2016).

Greider, William. "The Education of David Stockman". *The Atlantic* (Dec. 1981).

Hopkins, James F. *The Papers of Henry Clay: Secretary of State 1826*, Vol. 5. Lexington: University Press of Kentucky, 1973.

Huang, Jikun et al. *China's Great Transformation*. Cambridge: Cambridge University Press, 2008.

Jacobson, Harold Karen. *China's Participation in the IMF, the World Bank, and GATT, Towards a Global Consensus*. Ann Arbor: University of Michigan Press, 1990.

Jia, Ruixue. "Weather Shocks, Sweet Potatoes, and Peasant Revolts in Historical China", *The Economic Journal* 124, 575 (2014): 92-94.

Jiang, Arnold Xiangze. *The United States and China*. Chicago: University of Chicago Press, 1988.

Kenny, Henry. "Underlying Patterns of American Arms Sales to China". World Military Expenditures and Arms Transfers, 1986. US Arms Control and Disarmament Agency (April 1987).

King, Rufus. *The Life and Correspondences of Rufus King*, Vol. 5. New York: Putnam and Sons, 1898.

Komine, Yukinori. *Secrecy in US Foreign Policy: Nixon, Kissinger, and the Rapprochement with China*. Farnham: Ashgate, 2013.

Labree, Benjamin. *The Boston Tea Party*. New York: Oxford UP, 1964 .

Langley, Harold D. "Gordon Nye and the Formosa Annexation Scheme", *Pacific Historical Review* 34 (1965): 398-406.

Lum, Thomas. "China's Trade with the US and the World," Congressional Research Service (2007).

Macmillan, Margaret. *Nixon in China*. New York: Penguin, 2006.

Mann, Charles C. *1493: Uncovering the New World Columbus Created*. New York: Vintage, 2011.

Mann, James. *Beijing Jeep: The Short, Unhappy Romance of American Business in China*. New York: Touchstone Books, 1990.

Mann, James. "One Company's China Debacle." *Fortune* (Nov. 6, 1989).

Mann, James. *About Face*. New York: Alfred Knopf, 1999.

Mao, Joyce. *Asia First: China and the Making of Modern American Conservatism*. Chicago: University of Chicago Press, 2015.

McClure, J.B. *Anecdotes of Abraham Lincoln and Lincoln's stories: including early life stories, professional life stories, White House stories, war stories, miscellaneous stories*. Chicago: Rhodes & McClure, 1879.

Mudge, Jean McClure. *Chinese Export Porcelain for the American Trade 1785-1835*. Wilmington: University of Delaware Press, 1981.

Rennack, Dianne. "China: Economic Sanctions," Congressional Research Service Report for Congress (Feb. 1, 2006).

Ross, Robert S. *Negotiating Compromise: The United States and China, 1969-1989*. Stanford: Stanford University Press, 1995.

Rowe, David Nelson. *The Carter China Policy: Results and Prospects*. New York: D.N. Rowe, 1980.

Schlesinger, Arthur M. Jr. "The New Isolationism" *The Atlantic* (May 1952).

DAVID PETRIELLO

Shaw, Tony. "The Politics of Cold War Culture". *The Journal of Cold War Studies* 3, 3 (Fall 2001): 59-76.

Siomn, John Y. *The Papers of Ulysses S. Grant, Oct. 1, 1878-Sept 30, 1880*. Carbondale: SIU Press, 2008.

Solot, Ilan B. "The Chinese Agricultural Policy Trilemma," *Perspectives* 7, 1 (March 2006): 36-46.

Sutter, Robert G. "Increased US Military Sales to China: Arguments and Alternatives". Washington DC: Congressional Research Services, 1981.

Spero, Joan and Hart, Jeffrey. *The Politics of International Economic Relations*. Boston: Wadsworth, 2003.

Stapleton, Edward J. *Some Official Correspondences of George Canning*, Vol. 2. London: Longmans and Green, 1887.

Takai, Ronald. *Strangers from a Different Shore*. New York: Little, Brown and Company, 1998.

Tsai, Shih Shan Henry. *Maritime Taiwan: Historical Encounters with the East and West*. New York: Routledge, 2014.

Tucker, Nancy Bernkopf. *Straittalk: United States-Taiwan Relations and the Crisis with China*. Boston: Harvard University Press, 2011.

Woon. Eden Y. "Chinese Arms Sales and US-China Military Cooperation" *Asian Survey* 29, 6 (June 1989): 601-618.

Wunderlin, Clarence. *The Papers of Robert A. Taft, 1939-1944*. Kent: Kent State Press, 2003.

Yang, Yongzheng and Zhong, Chuanshui. "China's Textiles and Clothing Exports in a Changing World Economy." *The Developing Economies*. 36, 1 (March 1998).

Yousaf, M. and M. Adkin, *The Bear Trap*. Cambridge: Pen and Sword Books Ltd., 2002.

Yule, Henry. *Cathay and the Way Hither*. London: Hakluyt Society, 1866.

Zhao, Dingxin. *The Power of Tiananmen: State-Society Relations* and the 1989 Beijing Student Movement. Chicago: University of Chicago Press, 2004.

Zhao, Ziyang. Prisoner of the State: The Secret Journal of Premier Zhao Ziyang. New York: Simon and Schuster, 2009.

The Cambridge History of China: Volume 8, Part 2. New York: Cambridge University Press, 1998.

Letters of the Missionary Jesuits, Vol. X. London: Royal Society of London, 1753.

Reception and Entertainment of the Chinese Embassy. Boston: Alfred Mudge and Sons, 1868.

"US Congress, Office of Technology Assessment, Technology Transfer to China". OTA-ISC-340. Washington DC, US Government Printing Office, (July 1987).

ENDNOTES

1   Henry Yule, *Cathay and the Way Hither* (London: Hakluyt Society, 1866), xxxvi

2   Pliny the Elder, *Natural History*, Book XII, Chapter 84

3   Seneca the Elder, *Excerpta Controversiae*, 2.7

4   Odoric of Pordenone, "The Eastern Part of the World Described", as quoted in Yule, 114 and 120

5   Paul Freedman, "Spices and Late Medieval European Ideas of Scarcity and Value," *Speculum*, Vol. 80, No. 4 (Oct. 2005): 1209-1227.

6   John E. Wills, "Relations with Maritime Europe, 1514-1662," in *The Cambridge History of China: Volume 8, Part 2* (New York: Cambridge University Press, 1998), 336.

7   Nina Siegal, "How China Conquered the Dutch", *NY Times* (Oct. 13, 2015)

8   Bob Deans, *The River Where American Began: A Journey Along the James* (New York: Rowman & Littlefield Publishers, Inc, 2007), 94

9   Ruixue Jia, "Weather Shocks, Sweet Potatoes, and Peasant Revolts in Historical China", *The Economic Journal*, Vol. 124, Issue 575 (2014): 92

10   Charles C. Mann, *1493: Uncovering the New World Columbus Created* (New York: Vintage, 2011)

11   William Garden Blaikie, *The Catholic Presbyterian, Vol. 8* (Baltimore: J. Nisbet Company, 1882), 325

12   Father Jartoux, "The Description of a Tartarian Plant, Call'd
     Gin-Seng; with an Account of its Virtues. In a Letter from
     Father Jartoux, to the Procurator General of the Missions of
     India and China," (April 12, 1711), *Letters of the Missionary
     Jesuits*, Vol. X (London: Royal Society of London, 1753), 238

13   Ibid., 241

14   *The Pennsylvania Gazette* (July 27, 1738)

15   Benjamin Labree, *The Boston Tea Party* (New York: Oxford
     UP, 1964), 7

16   "Seaport of Amoy in China Furnished Tea for Boston Tea
     Party," *Schenectady Gazette* (May 11, 1928)

17   George Rogers Clark to Patrick Henry (Feb. 3, 1779) in Wil-
     liam Hayden English, *Conquest of the Country Northwest
     of the River Ohio, 1778–1783, and Life of Gen. George Rogers
     Clark*, Vol. 1 (Indianapolis: Bowen-Merrill, 1896), 262-263

18   "The Committee for Foreign Affairs to the American Com-
     missioners", Letter (Dec. 2, 1777)

19   de la Corbiere to Benjamin Franklin, Letter (Nov. 2, 1778)

20   George Washington, "Farewell Address" (Sept. 17, 1796)

21   Ezra Stiles to Benjamin Franklin, Letter (Feb. 26, 1766)

22   Benjamin Franklin to John Bartram, Letter (Jan. 11, 1770)

23   Benjamin Franklin to Court de Gébelin, Letter (May 7, 1781)
     and *The Interest of Great Britain Considered, With Regard to her
     Colonies, And the Acquisitions of Canada and Guadaloupe. To
     which are added, Observations concerning the Increase of Man-
     kind, Peopling of Countries, &c.* London: (London: T. Becket,
     1760)

24   Benjamin Franklin to Thomas Percival, Letter (October 15,
     1773)

25   Benjamin Franklin to Cadwalader Evans, Letter (Sept. 7,
     1769) from Samuel Hazard, ed., *Hazard's Register of Pennsyl-
     vania*, XVI, no. 5 (August 1, 1835), 66-7

26 "The Colonist's Advocate: X" in *The Public Advertiser* (Feb. 19, 1770)

27 *Journal of Benjamin Franklin* (Jan. 2, 1782)

28 John Adams (July 16, 1783) in *Observations Extracted from the Private Papers of Congress, 14 April 1783 to 22 July 1783*

29 John Adams to Robert Livingston, Letter (July 16, 1783)

30 "III-A-2. Account of Items in the Estate Used by Martha Custis, 1759", *Washington Papers*

31 Thomas Jefferson to Rayneval, Letter (March 3, 1786)

32 Benjamin Franklin to Benjamin Vaughn, Unpublished Letter (July 26, 1784)

33 Benjamin Franklin to the Managers of the Philadelphia Silk Filature, Letter (July 29, 1772) in *The Pennsylvania Gazette*

34 John Thaxter to John Adams, Letter (Jan. 19, 1784)

35 Joseph B. Felt, *The Annals of Salem, Vol. 2* (Salem: W. & S.B. Ives, 1845), 285

36 *Journal of George Washington* (Sept. 1784)

37 Neil Jamieson to Thomas Jefferson, Letter (July 12, 1784)

38 Robert Morris, *Papers of Robert Morris 1781-84* Vol. 5 (Pittsburgh: University of Pittsburgh Press, 1980), 66

39 Ibid., 65

40 Richard Henry Lee to John Adams, Letter (May 28, 1785)

41 William Grayson to James Madison, Letter (May 28, 1785)

42 John Adams to Richard Henry Lee, Letter (Sept. 7, 1785)

43 Thomas Jefferson to Comte de Vergennes, Letter (Oct. 21, 1785)

44 John Adams to John Jay, Letter (Nov. 5, 1785)

45 Richard Henry Lee to James Madison, Letter (May 30, 1785)

46 Abigail Adams to Cotton Tufts, Letter (Sept. 16, 1785)

47 Benjamin Franklin to Benjamin Vaughn, Unpublished Letter (July 26, 1784)

48 George Washington to Tench Tilghman, Letter (Aug. 17, 1785) and George Washington to John Barry, Letter (June 30, 1789)

49 Thomas Randall to Alexander Hamilton, Letter (Aug. 14, 1791)

50 John Adams to John Jay, Letter (Nov. 11, 1785)

51 Randall Letter

52 "Import Duties" (April 18, 1789) in *The Papers of James Madison*, vol. 12, ed. Charles F. Hobson and Robert A. Rutland (Charlottesville: University Press of Virginia, 1979), 88

53 John Adams to Richard Henry Lee, Letter (Sept. 7, 1785)

54 John Adams to Richard Cranch, Letter (Dec. 12, 1785)

55 John Adams to John Jay, Letter (Nov. 11, 1785)

56 James Monroe to Thomas Jefferson, Letter (June 16, 1785)

57 Thomas Jefferson to G.K. van Hogendorp, Letter (Oct. 13, 1785)

58 Rufus King, *The Life and Correspondences of Rufus King*, Vol. 5 (New York: Putnam and Sons, 1898), 562

59 Thomas Jefferson to John Jay, Letter (July 14, 1786)

60 Thomas Randall to Alexander Hamilton, Letter (Aug. 14, 1791)

61 Tench Coxe, *A View of the United States of America, in a Series of Papers, Written at Various Times, between the Years 1787 and 1794, Vol. 28* (Philadelphia, 1794), 309–10

62 John Adams to Alexander Bryan Johnson, Letter (March 1, 1823)

63 Tench Coxe to Thomas Jefferson, Letter (Feb. 22, 1802)

64 Ibid.

65 Tench Coxe to Thomas Jefferson, Letter (March 1, 1802)

66 Thomas Jefferson to George Rogers Clark, Letter (Dec. 4, 1783)

67 Ibid.

68 Merriweather Lewis to Thomas Jefferson, Letter (Sept. 23, 1806)
69 Thomas Jefferson to John Jacob Astor, Letter (April 13, 1808)
70 James Madison to Edward Carrington, Letter (April 19, 1807)
71 Isaac Chauncey to James Madison, Letter (June 9, 1807)
72 Eric Jay Dolin, *When America First Met China: An Exotic History of Tea, Drugs, and Money in the Age of Sail* (New York: Liveright,2013), 123-125
73 Robert Smith to Thomas Jefferson, Letter (Aug. 29, 1807)
74 Thomas Jefferson to Albert Gallatin, Letter (July 25, 1808)
75 John Jacob Astor to Albert Gallatin, Letter (Feb. 14, 1813)
76 Washing to James Madison, Letter (Oct. 9, 1813)
77 China American Merchants to James Madison, Letter (Jan. 22, 1816)
78 Philip Ammidon, who served as supercargo aboard the ship, had previously petitioned Pres. Madison in 1813 to made consul at Macao.
79 Data from US Congress, *American State Papers*, Vols. I and II
80 Data from Douglas Irwin and Peter Termin, "The Antebellum Tariff on Cotton Textiles Revisited", 794
81 J. B. McClure, *Anecdotes of Abraham Lincoln and Lincoln's stories: including early life stories, professional life stories, White House stories, war stories, miscellaneous stories* (Chicago: Rhodes & McClure, 1879), 22-23
82 Jean McClure Mudge, *Chinese Export Porcelain for the American Trade 1785-1835* (Wilmington: University of Delaware Press, 1981), 39
83 John Quincy Adams, "First Annual Message" (Dec. 6, 1825)
84 Speech of John Floyd in Thomas Hart Benton, *Speech of John Floyd in Thirty Years View: A History of the Working of the American Government for Thirty Years from 1820-1850* (New

York: Appleton and Company, 1883), 13

85   George Canning to Lord Liverpool, Letter (July 7, 1826) in *Some Official Correspondences of George Canning*, Vol. 2 (London: Longmans and Green, 1887), 73-74.

86   "Memorandum of Merchandise & Specie Exported to Canton by Thomas H. Smith in Season of 1825" in James F. Hopkins, *The Papers of Henry Clay: Secretary of State 1826*, Vol. 5 (Lexington: University Press of Kentucky, 1973), 192.

87   Andrew Jackson, "Third Annual Message" (Dec. 6, 1831)

88   John Shillaber to Andrew Jackson, Letter (Dec. 3, 1831)

89   "Memorial of R.B. Forbes and others, American citizens, merchants in Canton" House doc 40, 26th Congress, 1st Session

90   John Shillaber to Andrew Jackson, Letter (April 20, 1834)

91   John Shillaber to Edward Livingston, Letter (Sept. 25, 1834)

92   John Quincy Adams to James Brook, Letter (Jan. 20, 1842)

93   Daniel Webster to Peter Parker, Letter (1842) included in Jacques M. Downs, *The Golden Ghetto: The American Commercial Community at Canton and the Shaping of American China Policy* (Hong Kong; HK Press, 2014), 263

94   John Tyler, Special Message to Congress (Dec. 30, 1842)

95   Daniel Webster to Thomas Curtis, Letter (March 12, 1843)

96   Daniel Webster to Caleb Cushing, Letter (May 8, 1843)

97   Treaty of Wangxia, Article XXXIII

98   Ibid., Article III

99   Ibid., Article IV

100 John Tyler, "Special Message to Congress" (Dec. 30, 1842)

101 James K. Polk, "Third Annual Message to Congress" (Dec. 7, 1847)

102 Millard Fillmore, "Third Annual Message to Congress" (Dec. 6, 1853)

103 Ibid.

104 Matthew Perry, *Narrative of the Expedition of the American Squadron to the China Seas and Japan* (1856)

105 Harold D. Langley, "Gordon Nye and the Formosa Annexation Scheme", *Pacific Historical Review*, 34 (1965): 401

106 See Shih Shan Henry Tsai, *Maritime Taiwan: Historical Encounters with the East and West* (New York: Routledge, 2014), 115-118

107 The most recent ships that were seized or sunk included the *Iskanderia* and *Lucky Star*, both lost off of Taiwan.

108 "Anson Burlingame's Speech", *Reception and Entertainment of the Chinese Embassy* (Boston: Alfred Mudge and Sons, 1868), 24

109 Ibid., 27

110 Ibid., 6

111 Ibid., 19

112 Ibid., 20

113 Prince Gong to S. Wells Williams, Letter (July 8, 1865)

114 Yung Wing, as a former resident of the North, even offered to volunteer in the Union Army, but was graciously refused by the US government.

115 Ulysses S. Grant, "First Annual Message to Congress" (Dec. 1869)

116 Ibid.

117 Ulysses S. Grant, "Second Annual Message to Congress" (Dec. 1870)

118 Ibid.

119 Ibid.

120 Ibid.

121 Ulysses S. Grant, "Fifth Annual Message to Congress" (Dec. 1873)

122 Ulysses S. Grant, "Sixth Annual Message to Congress" (Dec. 1874)

123 Ibid.

124 John Y. Simon, *The Papers of Ulysses S. Grant, Oct. 1, 1878-Sept 30, 1880* (Carbondale: SIU Press, 2008), 86

125 Ibid., 83

126 Ibid., 81

127 Ibid., 84

128 Ibid., 82

129 Ibid.

130 Ibid., 84

131 Ulysses S. Grant to Edward F. Beale, Letter (June 7, 1879)

132 Simon, 84

133 *Nashville Union and American* (Oct. 26, 1871)

134 "From Sand Lot to Palace," *The Anaconda Standard* (Oct. 4, 1899), 6

135 Ronald Takai, *Strangers from a Different Shore* (New York: Little, Brown and Company, 1998)

136 Rutherford B. Hayes, "Veto Message" (March 1, 1879)

137 Ibid.

138 Rutherford B. Hayes, "Third Annual Message to Congress" (Dec. 1, 1879)

139 *Helena Weekly Herald* (Dec. 2, 1880)

140 Ibid.

141 James A. Garfield, "Letter Accepting the Presidential Nomination" (July 12, 1880)

142 *Stark County Democrat* (March 10, 1881)

143 "The Great Demonstration", *The Sacramento Daily Record-Union* (March 6, 1882), 2

144 Ibid.

145 "Latest Telegrams: Forty Seventh Congress," *The Salt Lake Herald* (March 2, 1882), 1

146 Ibid.

147 Ibid.

148 Chester A. Arthur, "Veto Message" (April 4, 1882)

149 Ibid.

150 Ibid.

151 *New Ulm Weekly Review* (April 12, 1882)

152 Chester A. Arthur, "Veto Message" (April 4, 1882)

153 Chester A. Arthur, "Third Annual Message to Congress" (Dec. 4, 1883)

154 "Republican Party Platform of 1884" (June 3, 1884)

155 Benjamin Harrison, "Letter Accepting the Presidential Nomination" (Sept. 11, 1888)

156 William McKinley, "Third Annual Message to Congress" (Dec. 5, 1899)

157 William McKinley, "Letter Accepting the Republican Presidential Nomination" (July 12, 1900)

158 William McKinley, "Proclamation Number 452"

159 William McKinley, "Second Annual Message to Congress" (Dec. 5, 1898)

160 McKinley, "Third Annual Message"

161 "Conger to go to China: Effort to end boycott", *NY Times* (Aug. 18, 1905)

162 William McKinley, "Fourth Annual Message to Congress" (Dec. 3, 1900)

163 McKinley, "Fourth Annual Message"

164 Howard Beale, *Theodore Roosevelt and the Rise of America* (Baltimore: The Johns Hopkins University Press, 1984), 229-232

165 Theodore Roosevelt, "First Annual Message to Congress" (Dec. 3, 1901)

166 "Conger to Go to China: Effort to End Boycott", *NY Times* (Aug. 18, 1905)

167 Roosevelt, "First Annual Message"

168 Ibid.

169 Theodore Roosevelt, "Third Annual Message to Congress" (Dec. 7, 1903)
170 Theodore Roosevelt, "Seventh Annual Message to Congress" (Dec. 3, 1907)
171 Chester A. Arthur, "Fourth Annual Message to Congress" (Dec. 10, 1884)
172 Theodore Roosevelt, "Fifth Annual Message to Congress" (Dec. 5, 1905)
173 Ibid.
174 Ibid.
175 Theodore Roosevelt. "Message to Congress" (April, 14, 1908)
176 Theodore Roosevelt, "Eighth Annual Message to Congress" (Dec. 8, 1908)
177 Ibid.
178 William H. Taft, "First Annual Message to Congress" (Dec. 7, 1909)
179 William H. Taft, "Second Annual Message to Congress" (Dec. 6, 1910)
180 Ibid.
181 Ibid.
182 "Nation, State, City Welcome Royal Visitor," *The San Francisco Call* (April 23, 1910)
183 Ibid.
184 Taft, "Second Message"
185 William H. Taft, "Third Annual Message to Congress" (Dec. 5, 1911)
186 William H. Taft, "Fourth Annual Message to Congress" (Dec. 3, 1912)
187 Ibid.
188 Ibid.
189 "Statement of the American Government in Regard to Sup-

port Requested by the American Group" (March 18, 1913)

190 Bruce A. Elleman, *Wilson and China: A Revised History of the Shandong Question* (London: M.E. Sharpe, 2002), 36

191 "Three Presidents Ask for Aid to China", *The Pioneer Express* (April 12, 1921)

192 "Chinese Seek Ideas Here", *The Evening World* (June 24, 1921), 6. As coal does not normall exist around Shanghai, the official may have meant Shandong Province here, unless he was simply attempting to spark American interest.

193 Arnold Xiangze Jiang, *The United States and China* (Chicago: University of Chicago Press, 1988), 79

194 Calvin Coolidge, "Address at the Dinner of the United Press at New York City" (April 25, 1927)

195 Calvin Coolidge, "Address Before the Forty-Second International Convention of the Young Men's Christian Associations of the United States and Canada, Washington, D.C." (Oct. 24, 1925)

196 Calvin Coolidge, "Fourth Annual Message to Congress", (Dec. 7, 1926)

197 Ibid.

198 Calvin Coolidge, "Sixth Annual Message to Congress" (Dec. 4, 1928)

199 Herbert Hoover, "Message to Congress on US Foreign Relations", (Dec. 10, 1931)

200 Ibid.

201 Robert A. Taft to Vincent Starzinger, Letter (March 29, 1940) in *The Papers of Robert A. Taft*, 1939-1944, Vol. II (Kent: Kent State Press, 2003), 127

202 Robert A. Taft, "Statement on the Stabilization Fund" (Dec. 5, 1940)

203 *The Papers of Robert A. Taft*, 437

204 *The Papers of Robert A. Taft*, Vol. III, 407

205 Ibid., 408
206 "Capitol Report", Number 60, Featuring Senator Robert A. Taft (June 29, 1950)
207 Ibid.
208 Ibid.
209 Arthur M. Schlesinger, Jr. "The New Isolationism" *The Atlantic* (May 1952)
210 Robert A. Taft, "United States Foreign Policy: Forget United Nations in Korea and Far East" (May 26, 1953)
211 Joyce Mao, *Asia First: China and the making of modern American conservatism* (Chicago: University of Chicago Press, 2015)
212 "Republican Party Platform of 1952"
213 Dwight D. Eisenhower, "First Annual Message to Congress" (Feb. 2, 1953)
214 Ibid.
215 Dwight D. Eisenhower, "News Conference" (Aug. 17, 1954)
216 Dwight D. Eisenhower, "Statement by the President Recorded Before Leaving for the Far East" (June 12, 1960)
217 Dwight D. Eisenhower, "Remarks Upon Arrival at Sungshan Airport, Taipei" (June 18, 1960)
218 Dwight D. Eisenhower, "Address at a Mass Rally in Taipei" (June 18, 1960)
219 Ibid.
220 Ibid.
221 Richard Nixon, "First Annual Report to the Congress on United States Foreign Policy for the 1970s" (Feb. 18, 1970)
222 Lee Edwards, *Goldwater: The Man Who Made a Revolution* (Washington DC: Regnery, 2015)
223 Yukinori Komine, *Secrey in US Foreign Policy: Nixon, Kissinger, and the Rapprochement with China* (Farnham: Ashgate, 2013),18

224 Ibid., fn
225 Richard Nixon, "The President's News Conference" (Jan. 27, 1969)
226 Ibid. (March 4, 1969)
227 Richard Nixon, "Informal Remarks in Guam with Newsmen" (July 25, 1969)
228 Richard Nixon, "Address Before the 24th Session of the General Assembly of the United Nations" (September 18, 1969)
229 Richard Nixon, "First Annual Report to Congress on United States Foreign Policy for the 1970s" (Feb. 18, 1970)
230 Ibid.
231 Richard Nixon, "Second Annual Report to Congress on United States Foreign Policy for the 1970s" (Feb. 25, 1971)
232 Ibid.
233 Nixon, "First Annual Report"
234 Nixon, "Second Annual Report"
235 Viet D. Dinh, "How We Won Vietnam," *Policy Review-Hoover Institute* No. 104 (Dec. 2000).
236 William Bundy, *A Tangled Web: The Making of Foreign Policy in the Nixon Presidency* (New York: Hill and Wang, 1998), 104.
237 See Margaret Macmillan's, *Nixon in China,* "The Dobrynin-Kissinger Transcripts" National Security Archives Briefing Book No. 233 (2007), and Warren Cohen, *America's Response to China,* for a discussion of the various benefits to be accrued by the US in "opening up" China. In addition see the Nixon Tapes, April 14, 1971 for a conversation between Nixon and Kissinger on this issue.
238 "TELCON: The President/ Mr. Kissinger" (April 27, 1971)
239 "Message from Premier Chou En Lai" (April 21, 1971)
240 "Memorandum for Henry Kissinger of Meeting with Chou En-lai" (July 29, 1971)

241 Quoted in David Stokes, "Buckley, Nixon, and Mao," (Feb. 29, 2008)
242 Richard Nixon, "Special Message to the Congress on Science and Technology" (March 16, 1972)
243 Data Source: George D. Holland, "China-US Trade Issue Brief Number IB75085" (Library of Congress: 1981) http://china.usc.edu/App_Images//crs-us-china-trade-1981.pdf. Accessed Dec. 6, 2009.
244 Data Source: *A History of American Agriculture* http://www.agclassroom.org/gan/timeline/ag_trade.htm. Accessed Jan. 6, 2010.
245 George D. Holliday, "China-US Trade". Issue Brief Number IB75085. Congressional Research Service (Nov. 19, 1981) http://china.usc.edu/App_Images//crs-us-china-trade-1981.pdf. Accessed Dec. 6, 2009.
246 Richard Nixon, "Talk with White House Staff" (July 19, 1971)
247 Boggs and Ford, "Impressions of the New China", (Washington: US Government Printing Office, 1972), 8
248 See Anuradha Dayal-Gulati and Aasim M. Husain, "Centripetal Forces in China's Economic Takeoff," *IMF Staff Papers* Vol. 49, No. 3 (2002) for a discussion of the importance of FDI to regional economic development.
249 William Burr, ed., *The Kissinger Transcripts: The Top Secret Talks with Moscow and Beijing* (New York: The New Press, 1995), 204-205.
250 Ibid, 50 and 204.
251 See William Bundy, *Tangled Web* for an analysis of Nixon's China Policy.
252 Gerald Ford to Richard Nixon, Letter (July 20, 1972)
253 Gerald Ford, "Address to 29th Session of General Assembly of United Nations" (Sept. 18, 1974)

254 Gerald Ford, "Presidential News Conference" (Oct. 29, 1974)

255 Gerald Ford, "Address at the University of Hawaii" (Dec. 7, 1975)

256 See David Nelson Rowe, *The Carter China Policy: Results and Prospects.* (New York: D.N. Rowe, 1980) Jean A. Garrison, "Framing Foreign Policy Alternatives in the Inner Circle: President Carter, His Advisors, and the Struggle for the Arms Control Agenda." *Political* Psychology (Dec. 2001), pp775-807, and Z. Brzezinski, *The Geostrategic Triad: Living with Europe, China, and Russia* (Washington DC: CSIS, 2000) for a discussion of tri-polarity.

257 See Sen. Jacob Javits "Congress and Foreign Relations: The Taiwan Relations Act" *Foreign Affairs* Vol. 60, No. 1 (Fall 1981) for a discussion of the background and legality of Carter's recognition of China and the Taiwan Relations Act.

258 Stephen Yates, "The Taiwan Relations Act After 20 Years: Keys to Past and Future Success", *Heritage Foundation* (April 16, 1999)

259 US Department of Transportation, "Top 25 U.S. International Merchandise Trade Partners by Value: 1970 – 2001". *US International Trade and Freight Transportation* Trends (2003) http://www.bts.gov/publications/us_international_trade_and_freight_transportation_trends/2003/html/table_05.html Accessed on Jan. 10, 2010.

260 Data Source: George D. Holland. "China-US Trade Issue Brief Number IB75085" (Library of Congress: 1981) http://china.usc.edu/App_Images//crs-us-china-trade-1981.pdf. Accessed on Jan. 1, 2010.

261 Source: *China Statistical Yearbook*, various issues

262 Ibid.

263 Sen. Thad Cochran, *Delegation Mission to the PRC* (Washing-

ton DC: US Government Printing Office, 1983), 3.

264 See Bruce Burton, "Contending Explanations of the 1979 Sino-Vietnamese War." *International Journal*, Vol. 34, No. 4 (Autumn 1979): 699-722 for a discussion of the various outlooks upon the war's result.

265 Robert S. Ross, *Negotiating Compromise: The United States and China, 1969-1989* (Stanford: Stanford University Press, 1995), 171.

266 Deng had to be given sanctuary in 1976 by Gen. Xu Shiyu after he was purged following the Tiananmen Incident in April of that year, for being "an unrepentant capital roader".

267 Huang, Jikun et al., "Agriculture in China's Development: Past Disappointments, Recent Successes, and Future Challenges", *China's Great Transformation* (Cambridge: Cambridge University Press, 2008), 478.

268 See Zhao Ziyang, *Prisoner of the State: The Secret Journal of Premier Zhao Ziyang* (New York: Simon and Schuster, 2009) for further discussion of his theories and reforms.

269 "Preamble" 1982 Constitution of the People's Republic of China

270 Chapter 1, Article 18 of the 1982 Constitution of the People's Republic of China

271 Ronald Reagan, "The New Republican Party". (Feb. 6, 1977).

272 Ronald Reagan, "Fourth CPAC Speech" (1977)

273 Ross, 169.

274 Yang Yongzheng and Zhong Chuanshui."China's Textiles and Clothing Exports in a Changing World Economy."*The Developing Economies* XXXVI-1 (March 1998), 5.

275 John F. Copper, "The Lessons of Playing Tough With China," *The Heritage Foundation* (Aug. 23, 1983), 2.

276 Ibid., 3.

277 Sources: Cochrane and Copper

278 Copper, 2.

279 The China Desk at the State Department feared straining the ties between the nation that had developed since the administration of Nixon. In fact in the previous year only 8 out of 102 Chinese asylum requests were granted by the State Dept. "After Hardball, Resuming Tennis." *New York Times* (April 10, 1983).

280 "Hu Na Defection: Play it Cool," *The Milwaukee Journal* (April 11, 1983), 10.

281 "China Drops Joint Concerts With Americans," *Philadelphia Inquirer* (April 9, 1983), A05.

282 Robert A. Manning, "Reagan's Chance Hit," *Foreign Policy* No. 54 (Spring 1984), 94.

283 Copper, "The Lessons of Playing Tough With China," 3.

284 Pan Am had ended this route in 1978 in the hopes of gaining access to the China market, which it did three years later.

285 Michael Weisskopf, "China Restricts Pan Am Routes as Reprisal for Taiwan Service," *The Modesto Bee*. (June 17, 1983) A-12.

286 "China Sore Over Taiwan Arms Sale."*New Straits Times*. (Feb. 27, 1983), 15.

287 Ross, 181.

288 "Goldwater Warns of Taiwan Situation." *Kingman Daily Mirror* (June 2, 1982).

289 Copper, "The Lessons of Playing Tough with China," 6.

290 Ibid.

291 Smith Hempstone, "Concessions to Peking Unwise" *The Southeast Missourian* (Feb. 10, 1983), 3.

292 "Soviet Missiles in Syria Sobering."*The Modesto Bee*.(March 1, 1983), A-7.

293 "Address of President Ronald Reagan before the Korean

National Assembly," 12 November 1983, Oberdorfer Papers, Box 1, National Security Archives, George Washington University, Washington, D.C.

294　See Gregg Andrew Brazinksy's "From Pupil to Model: South Korea and American Development Policy during the Early Park Chung Hee Era", *Diplomatic History* (2005): 83-115 for a discussion of South Korean modernization.

295　Reagan, Radio Address to the Nation on the President's Trip to Japan and the Republic of Korea (Nov. 12, 1983).

296　"Officials: Trade Talk Progressing." Palm Beach Post (Jan. 13, 1984)

297　"China Willing to Buy US Weapons: Zhao." Ottawa Citizen (Jan. 16, 1984)

298　Ronald Reagan, "Radio Address to the Nation on the Trip to China". (4/28/84)

299　Nancy Bernkopf Tucker. *Straittalk: United States-Taiwan Relations and the Crisis with China* (Boston: Harvard University Press, 2011), 161.

300　John Gittings. *China Through the Sliding Door*. (London: Simon & Schuster/Touchstone, 1999).

301　US Congress, Office of Technology Assessment, *Technology Transfer to China*. OTA-ISC-340 (Washington DC, US Government Printing Office, July 1987), pp. 98-100

302　Ronald Reagan, "Remarks at the Shanghai Foxboro Company, Ltd., In Shanghai, China". (April 30, 1984).

303　Ronald Reagan, "A Strategy for Peace in the 80's" (Oct. 19, 1980).

304　John Copper, *President Reagan's Trip to the PRC* (Washington DC: Heritage Foundation, 1984), 32.

305　Bernard K. Gordon, "The United States and Asia in 1982: A Year of Tenterhooks," *Asian Survey*, Vol. 23, No.1 (Jan. 1983), 1-10.

306 See Director General Li-yen Yin's Letter to Pres. Reagan, "Pinpointing the Past Wrongs of US Policies and the Wise Future Course the US Should Take" (March 21, 1981) for a critical analysis of Sino-American relations from 1971-1981.
307 Cochran, 2.
308 "Reagan Said Likely to Kill Grain Embargo" *The Leader-Post* (Nov. 6, 1980)
309 *Asian Survey*, Vol. 24, No. 1, A Survey of Asia in 1983: Part I (Jan., 1984), 17-27
310 "Senate Panel Overrides a Ban on Food Assistance to China," *The New York Times* (May 6, 1982).
311 "State Department Seeks Friendly Status for China." *Lakeland Ledger* (May 4, 1982).
312 Cochran, 2.
313 Ibid 5.
314 Ronald Reagan, "Remarks at the Annual Convention of the National Corn Growers Association in Des MoinesIowa" (Aug. 2, 1982).
315 Colin A. Carter and Li Xianghong, *Economic Reform and the Changing Pattern of China's Agricultural Trade*, (July 1999). http://aic.ucdavis.edu/oa/iartccarter.pdf p.9
316 Copper (1984), 8.
317 Source: Thomas Lum, "China's Trade with the US and the World". *Congressional Research Service* (2007)http://www.fas.org/sgp/crs/row/RL31403.pdf Accessed Dec. 8, 2009.
318 Source: Thomas Lum, "China's Trade with the US and the World," *Congressional Research Service* (2007) http://www.fas.org/sgp/crs/row/RL31403.pdf. Accessed Dec. 8, 2009
319 Jack Anderson. "U.S. on Defensive Over High-Tech Sales to China." *The Pittsburgh Press* (Aug. 15, 1983).
320 Don Hirasuna and Joel Michael. "Enterprise Zones: A Review of the Economic Theory and Empirical Evidence."

Minnesota House of Representatives Research Dept. (Jan. 2005).

321 "The Third Plenary Meeting Communiqué of the Eleventh Central Committee of the Communist Party of China" (Dec. 22, 1978).

322 Chen Hong. "President Hails Shenzhen SEZ a world 'miracle'". *China Daily* (Sept. 7, 2010)

323 "China, Citing Gains, Joins World Bank", *Sarasota Herald-Tribune* (Oct. 2, 1980)

324 Harold Karen Jacobson, *China's Participation in the IMF, the World Bank, and GATT, Towards a Global Consensus* (Ann Arbor: University of Michigan Press, 1990), 20. Bernard Gwertzman. "U.S. Backs Bank Seat for China."*NY Times* (March 22, 1983).

325 Ilan B. Solot, "The Chinese Agricultural Policy Trilemma," *Perspectives* Vol.7, No. 1 (March 2006), 36-46.

326 Ronald Reagan, "State of the Union 1985" (1985).

327 Fox Butterfield, "Teng: China Needs Dollars", *Star-News* (Feb. 3, 1979)

328 Copper (1984), 17.

329 "China Trade Policies in the 1980's," *Library of Congress Country Studies* (July 1987) http://www.photius.com/countries/china/economy/china_economy_trade_policy_in_the_~934.html. Accessed Nov. 15, 2009.

330 Hon. David Kilgour, "Zhao Ziyang: A Major Opportunity Lost for China" (Sept. 28, 2009) http://www.david-kilgour.com/2009/Sep_25_2009_02.php. Accessed Feb. 22, 2010.

331 K.C. Fung, "Foreign Direct Investment in China: Policy, Trend, and Impact," (June 2002) http://www.hiebs.hku.hk/working_paper_updates/pdf/wp1049.pdf. Accessed Feb. 2, 2010.

332 Photis Panayides et al. *Foreign Direct Investment in China: The*

Case of Shipping and Logistics Corporations. www.eclac.cl/ Transporte/perfil/iame_papers/.../Panayides_et_al.doc,

333 Source: *China Foreign Economic Statistical Yearbook,* various issues

334 This became specifically stated in HR 2957 (Aug. 3, 1983)

335 "The Education of David Stockman". *The Atlantic* (Dec. 1981).

336 "Reagan Backs Pledge by Carter to Aid China", *The Telegraph* (Nov. 19, 1981)

337 Copper (1984), 35.

338 Joan Spero and Jeffrey Hart, *The Politics of International Economic Relations* (Boston: Wadsworth, 2003), 411.

339 Ronald Reagan, "Statement on Signing the Export-Import Bank Act Amendments of 1986" (October 15, 1986).

340 "China Trade: Prodding the Sleeping Giant". *Boston Globe* (April 22, 1984)

341 Source: Foreign Investment Department of the Ministry of Commerce of China (2007).

342 Source: K.C. Fung, "Foreign Direct Investment in China: Policy, Trend, and Impact" (June 2002)

343 Tony Shaw. "The Politics of Cold War Culture". *The Journal of Cold War Studies* Vol. 3, No. 3 (Fall 2001) pp59-76.

344 Jay Taylor, "China's View of the US and USSR" (3/27/1984): 2.

345 US Congress, Office of Technology Assessment, "Technology Transfer to China," OTA-ISC-340 (Washington DC: US Government Printing Office, July 1987), 1.

346 Letian Pan, ed. "7th Five Year Plan" (1985) http://www.gov. cn/english/2006-04/05/content_245695.htm. Accessed Nov. 5, 2009.

347 See Jim Mann, *Beijing Jeep: The Short, Unhappy Romance of American Business in China.* (New York: Touchstone Books, 1990)

348 Jim Mann, "One Company's China Debacle", *Fortune* (Nov. 6, 1989).

349 Michael Parks. "US Aviation Industry Eyes Billions in Chinese Market", *The Telegraph* (July 31, 1984)

350 "Company News: GE-China Deal," *The New York Times* (Dec 10, 1986)

351 "US to Let China Buy More Technology", *Milwaukee Journal* (June 6, 1981).

352 "Nixon Pushes Reagan to Sell Technology", *Milwaukee Journal* (June 2, 1983)

353 William C. Triplett II, "Reagan's Experience on China," *Washington Post* (March 18, 1998).

354 Ronald Reagan, "The American Citizen Views the Republic of China: Taiwan vs. The People's Republic of China" (July 1, 1978) and Ronald Reagan, "Letter to Dr. and Mrs. C. F. Koo" (Jan. 15, 1979) PPP Box 22 Folder RR Chron January 79.

355 Ross, 171: As highlighted in Ross's review of contemporary Chinese sources, the Chinese did not only fear standing alone against Russia in the event of a cross border war, but began to see themselves as the sole force confronting "Soviet hegemony."

356 Robert G. Sutter, *Increased US Military Sales to China: Arguments and Alternatives*, (Washington DC: Congressional Research Services, 1981)

357 "Hearing Before the Subcommittee on Asian and Pacific Affairs of the Committee on Foreign Affairs House of Representatives" 98th Congress (Feb. 28, 1983), 29-30.

358 A. Mahmud Ali, *US-China Cold War Collaboration* (New York: Routledge, 2005), 151.

359 "US to Sell Weapons to China", *The Rock Hill Herald* (June 17,1981).

360 Ibid.

361 "US Weapons for China", *The Montreal Gazette* (June 18, 1981).

362 NSC-NSDD 76 Ronald Reagan

363 Eden Y. Woon. "Chinese Arms Sales and US-China Military Cooperation" *Asian Survey* Vol. 29, No 6 (June 1989): 601-618.

364 Source: Henry Kenny. "Underlying Patterns of American Arms Sales to China". *World Military Expenditures and Arms Transfers, 1986* US Arms Control and Disarmament Agency (April 1987).

365 Mann, 140.

366 Source: Henry Kenny. "Underlying Patterns of American Arms Sales to China". *World Military Expenditures and Arms Transfers, 1986*US Arms Control and Disarmament Agency (April 1987).

367 "China Likely to Buy US War Gear", *Anchorage Daily News* (January 13, 1985).

368 http://www.gwu.edu/~nsarchiv/NSAEBB/NSAEBB114/chipak-16.pdf

369 James Mann, *About Face.*(New York: Alfred Knopf, 1999), 136.

370 Reyko Huang, *Lessons from History: US Policy Towards Afghanistan 1979-2001.*Center for Defense Information. (Oct. 5, 2001). http://www.cdi.org/terrorism/afghanistan-history-pr.cfm

371 Steve Coll. "Anatomy of a Victory: The CIA's Covert Afghan War" *The Washington Post* (July 19, 1992).

372 M. Yousaf and M. Adkin, *The Bear Trap* (Cambridge: Pen and Sword Books Ltd., 2002), 83-84.

373 Mann, 139. Specifically Paul Wolfowitz.

374 See the Walsh Report, especially Chapters 2 and 17.

375 Gwynne Dyer, "It's No Sale For West Armament Dealers in China", *Ottawa Citizen.* (Sept. 22, 1983) p 8.

376 Copper(1984), 8.

377 Leo Orleans. *Chinese Students in America: Policies, Issues, and Numbers* (Washington: Office of International Affairs: National Academic Press, 1988)

378 Data Source: Leo Orleans

379 Ibid.

380 Zhou Guangshao as quoted in Orleans, 116.

381 "Work Related to Students and Scholars Studying Abroad", Ministry of Education of the People's Republic of China. http://www.moe.edu.cn/english/international_2.htm

382 "China Beckons Overseas Students Home", *Forbes* (July 2, 2009) http://www.forbes.com/2009/07/01/china-economy-innovation-business-oxford-analytica.html

383 See Dingxin Zhao, *The Power of Tiananmen: State-Society Relations and the 1989 Beijing Student Movement* (Chicago: University of Chicago Press, 2004) for an analysis of the links of modernization to the Tiananmen Movement.

384 George H. W. Bush, "President's News Conference" (Jan. 27, 1989)

385 George H. W. Bush, "Interview with Chinese Television Journalists in Beijing" (Feb. 26, 1989)

386 George H. W. Bush, "Statement on the Chinese Government's Suppression of Student Demonstrations" (June 13, 1989)

387 State Department Document, NSAEEB 16 (June 29, 1989), accessed via http://www.gwu.edu/~nsarchiv/NSAEBB/NSAEBB16/documents/#30-35

388 Walter R. Mears. "Bush Stays Steady Course on China." *Rome News-Tribune* (July 6, 1989)

389 Dianne Rennack, "China: Economic Sanctions," *Congressio-*

nal Research Service Report for Congress (Feb. 1, 2006).

390 See Title 15 CFR Part 740.7

391 Maureen Dowd, "2 U.S. Officials Went to Beijing Secretly in July," *NY Times* (Dec. 19, 1989)

392 Ibid.

393 George H. W. Bush, "Message to the House of Representatives Returning Without Approval the United States-China Act of 1991" (March 2, 1992)

394 "Newt Gingrich on China", *NY Times* (April 1, 1997)

395 George W. Bush, "The President-Elect's News Conference Announcing the Nomination of Colin L. Powell as Secretary of State" (Dec. 16, 2000)

396 "The President's News Conference With President Jiang Zemin of China in Shanghai, China" (Oct. 19, 2001)

397 Donald Trump, "Remarks Announcing Candidacy for President in New York City" (June 16, 2015)

398 Alexander Gray and Peter Navarro, "Donald Trump's Peace Through Strength Vision for the Asia-Pacific", *Foreign Policy* (Nov. 7, 2016)

399 Mike Green, "The Legacy of Obama's 'Pivot' to Asia," *Foreign Policy* (Sept. 3, 2016)

ABOUT THE AUTHOR

David Petriello teaches at Caldwell University in New Jersey. He received his doctorate from St. John's University, specializing in East Asian history and the impact of disease upon history. He has written several books, most notably *Bacteria and Bayonets* and *A Pestilence on Pennsylvania Avenue*. The author lives in New Jersey, and apart from teaching, he frequently appears in print and on podcasts as a commentator on Sino-American relations and other topics.